"Linje Manyozo is back in academia after years in development practice, and with his most important book to date. This is a very well-written, strong critique of development theory and practice. It is a thorough deconstruction of the spectacle of development, and a solid suggestion for a reconstruction of deliberative development. Provocative in his style, thoughtful in essence and novel in his perspectives, Manyozo's voice is fundamental."

– Thomas Tufte, School of Media, Communication and Sociology, University of Leicester, UK

"Linje Manyozo brings to the fore refreshing analysis of one of the silent issues in the development lexicon. *Communicating Development with Communities* is a truly timely contribution to fundamental principles of development practice. This is a call for the balance of power and respect for those on the 'receiving' end of development."

– Jonathan Makuwira, Department of Development Studies, Nelson Mandela Metropolitan University, South Africa

"Linje Manyozo is one of the most exciting scholars writing in the field of media, communication and development today. He combines academic rigour and insights, his experience of working as a communication for development practitioner, and his own personal trajectory, to provide a searing contemporary critique of the field and its problems and possibilities. This book is a wonderfully colourful account of the importance of speaking, listening and deliberative development."

– Jo Tacchi, Institute for Media and Creative Industries, Loughborough University in London, UK

"Linje Manyozo has a very special talent. He achieves an insightful blending of the personal and the political, drawing upon a wide range of critical traditions in academic research and upon his own life experience. Alternative development pathways may be borne through speaking development with and alongside communities. For him, this is the route through which the subaltern perspective can be acquired and in a way that informs action. Manyozo's proposals for theory and practice offer a pathway for a journey which, through experimentation, can create opportunities for deliberative development at the community level."

– Robin Mansell, Department of Media and Communications, London School of Economics and Political Science, UK

I0888240

COMMUNICATING DEVELOPMENT WITH COMMUNITIES

Development theory and practice are often taught in a manner that strips them of their historical context and obscures alternative intellectual assumptions and critical frameworks. This prevents students from acquiring a holistic understanding of the world and consequently, when it comes to development practice, most lack the skills to live and engage with people. It has become crucial to properly consider what it means to conceive and implement participatory development out in the field and not just in the boardroom.

Building on the work of Robert Chambers and Arturo Escobar, *Communicating Development with Communities* is an empirically grounded critical reflection on how the development industry defines, imagines and constructs development at the implementation level. Unpacking the dominant syntax in the theory and practice of development, the book advocates a move towards relational and indigenous models of living that celebrate local ontologies, spirituality, economies of solidarity and community-ness. It investigates how subaltern voices are produced and appropriated, and how well-meaning experts can easily become oppressors. The book propounds a pedagogy of listening as a pathway that offers a space for interest groups to collaboratively curate meaningful development with and alongside communities.

This is a valuable resource for academics and practitioners in the fields of Development Studies, Communication for Development, Communication for Social Change, Social Anthropology, Economic Development and Public Policy.

Foreword by Robin Mansell.

Linje Manyozo is a Senior Lecturer in Communication for Development, School of Media and Communication, RMIT University, Australia. He is also an Honorary Research Associate of the Department of Development Studies, Nelson Mandela Metropolitan University, South Africa.

RETHINKING DEVELOPMENT

Rethinking Development offers accessible and thought-provoking overviews of contemporary topics in international development and aid. Providing original empirical and analytical insights, the books in this series push thinking in new directions by challenging current conceptualizations and developing new ones.

This is a dynamic and inspiring series for all those engaged with today's debates surrounding development issues, whether they be students, scholars, policy makers and practitioners internationally. These interdisciplinary books provide an invaluable resource for discussion in advanced undergraduate and postgraduate courses in development studies as well as in anthropology, economics, politics, geography, media studies and sociology.

Celebrity Advocacy and International Development
Daniel Brockington

International Aid and the Making of a Better World
Reflexive practice
Rosalind Eyben

New Media and International Development
Representation and affect in microfinance
Anke Schwittay

Art, Culture and International Development
Humanizing social transformation
John Clammer

Celebrity Humanitarianism and North-South Relations
Politics, place and power
Edited by Lisa-Ann Richey

Education, Learning and the Transformation of Development
Edited by Amy Skinner, Matt Baillie Smith, Eleanor Brown and Tobias Troll

Learning and Volunteering Abroad for Development
Unpacking Host Organisation and Volunteer Rationales
Rebecca Tiessen

Communicating Development with Communities
Linje Manyozo

COMMUNICATING DEVELOPMENT WITH COMMUNITIES

Linje Manyozo

Routledge
Taylor & Francis Group
LONDON AND NEW YORK

First published 2017
by Routledge
2 Park Square, Milton Park, Abingdon, Oxon OX14 4RN

and by Routledge
711 Third Avenue, New York, NY 10017

Routledge is an imprint of the Taylor & Francis Group, an informa business

British Library Cataloguing-in-Publication Data
A catalogue record for this book is available from the British Library

Library of Congress Cataloging-in-Publication Data
Names: Manyozo, Linje, 1975- author.
Title: Communicating development with communities / Linje Manyozo.
Description: Abingdon, Oxon ; New York, NY : Routledge, 2017. | Series: Rethinking development
Identifiers: LCCN 2016056821| ISBN 978-1-138-74599-5 (hb) | ISBN 978-1-138-74604-6 (pb) | ISBN 978-1-315-18052-6 (ebk)
Subjects: LCSH: Communication in economic development. | Mass media—Economic aspects—Developing countries. | Economic development—Social aspects. | Economic development—Citizen participation.
Classification: LCC HD76 .M383 2017 | DDC 307.1/4014—dc23
LC record available at https://lccn.loc.gov/2016056821

ISBN: 978-1-138-74599-5 (hbk)
ISBN: 978-1-138-74604-6 (pbk)
ISBN: 978-1-315-18052-6 (ebk)

Typeset in Bembo
by FiSH Books Ltd, Enfield

CONTENTS

ACKNOWLEDGEMENTS

I would like to thank the good people who read and provided feedback to the whole and parts of the manuscript: Thomas Tufte, Shakuntala Banaji, Gayatri Spivak, Jo Tacchi, Jonathan Makuwira, and, significantly, Robin Mansell who has been a mentor, a mother and a friend. I also acknowledge the extended family at the Wurundjeri Tribe Land Compensation and Cultural Heritage Council in Melbourne for their lessons in the power of cooperative development, despite the immensity of the socio-political struggles they have to constantly contend with in order to achieve justice and dignity for Aboriginal Australians. I acknowledge the copy editing skills of Klare Lanson add Simon Barraclough. The support of Martyn Hook, Carey Walden, Judy Lawry and my son, Biny'amin Manyozo has allowed me to settle in a new professional environment. I sincerely acknowledge the influence of three wise women—my mum, grandmother and great-grandmother for shaping my thinking to look at the world from the perspective of women. This book is a celebration of this *Weltaunschauung*.

FOREWORD

This book is an account of Linje Manyozo's struggle with dominating knowledge systems and practices, especially as they operate in the field of media and communications. It is at one and the same time a deconstruction of the dominant paradigm in the development communication field and, crucially, a proposal for the theory and practice of a deliberative development in and with communities. A deliberative development framework acknowledges that asymmetrical power relations are never resolved fully. Conflictual relationships have to be worked through if the oppressed, whomever and wherever they are, are to make a positive difference in their own lives, a difference that they can claim as their own pathway to something we call 'development.' This is a passionate and, at the same time, a scholarly book. It is also a hopeful account. Notwithstanding the myriad of ways in which the oppressor—even the oppressor with the best of apparent intentions—represses, wreaks harm and damage in communities in the global south, this book explains why the potential exists to create spaces within which there can be a celebration of the agency of oppressed groups.

Linje Manyozo has a very special talent. This is to achieve an insightful blending of the personal and the political, drawing upon a wide range of critical traditions in academic research and upon his own life experience. The dominant paradigm of communication and/for development is characterized as a spectacle of development rooted in 'bullshit' conceptions of development. Throughout the post-war period, however, alternatives have been articulated. Sometimes these are characterized as participatory communication or as communication for social change approaches, often with an emphasis on the role of the media and various information and communication technologies, but these approaches themselves become complicit in oppression. Training programmes produce local and external 'experts' who find themselves working on communication and/for development initiatives, but they cannot engage with communities, or they do so without the ability to listen and to value community insights and practices. This book addresses crucial questions: What does a praxis of deliberative development entail and how is it experienced? Is it possible for educators to work in solidarity with oppressed and marginalized groups, despite the domineering pressure created by the spectacle of development?

A pedagogy of 'listening through communicating' and 'speaking development alongside communities' is carefully explained in this book. Listening is critical because *all* those who find themselves engaged with a process of communicating about development, of necessity need to rethink their understanding of, and position in, the world. This is not something that happens once or in a particular media or digital technology project for development. It is instead a continuous process of learning to acknowledge the voices of the subaltern, of actually living with the people, of encountering change in all of its complexity, and of fostering an art of listening. Paolo Freire's (Shor and Freire 1987, 98) comment that "dialogue is a moment where humans meet to reflect on their reality as they make and remake it," is the tradition that Linje Manyozo builds upon. He argues that, in this way, it becomes possible to transform the reality of lived experience. The experience of listening and speaking opens the possibility for unexpected meanings and actions to emerge, especially through the encounter of the self with others. The struggle for educators is to find ways of creating a critical pedagogy that can be institutionalized within degree programmes and through the practices of agencies operating in the global south, but also in the global north, where a pedagogy that enables action against oppression is also needed.

I am very honoured to be invited to write the foreword for this book. I am a white Western woman who lives, was trained, and conducts most of my research, in the global north although I have worked in collaboration with academic colleagues, policy makers and non-governmental organizations who live and work in the global south. My own work does not meet Linje Manyozo's criteria for a dialogical approach to development. Reading this book caused me to reflect on what might have enabled me to develop a critical stance towards what Linje Manyozo calls the development industry and why it was possible for he and I to have many productive conversations during his time as a faculty member in my department. This is not fully explained by the fact that the reader will notice that he generously cites an early paper that I wrote while I was a doctoral student. In that paper I criticized the prevailing paradigm in the development communication field and argued that, despite a turn to participatory models of engagement, the basic assumptions of the traditional model remained deeply entrenched and unchallenged. A close reading of that paper will reveal that I did not offer solutions and would not claim to have done so since.

There are two main reasons that I think we were able to listen and speak to each other in a way that sustained a meaningful dialogue. The first is that we both understand that it is essential to acknowledge that "without context, words and actions have no meaning at all" (Bateson 1979). A continuous engagement with the contexts in which our lives are lived, with the challenges, the disappointments, and the rewards is, I suggest, a preliminary step towards an effective critique of universal or hegemonic theories and practices of development. In the dominant paradigm of the spectacle of development, context is lost in the name of simplicity and in the race to engage in problem solving where the problems are typically specified by those who are behaving as the oppressor. The second reason is that we bring a commitment to historicizing contemporary struggles. In so doing, we are both committed to the view that sources of knowledge arising from intuition, and which are acquired through practice and personal experience, are vital to transformative action. In an edited collection of papers, Marglin writes about "the decolonization of the mind" (Marglin and Marglin 1990). He highlights the importance of this kind of knowledge or *techne* as contrasted with *episteme* or logical deductions from universal principles, which are associated with scientific knowledge. It is the latter which is so frequently accorded an imperial position in guiding development communication initiatives. And it is the singular reliance on *episteme* without respect for *techne* that leads to the replication of the dominant paradigm of development.

Yet historically, and in contemporary times, resistance to the dominant paradigm is present and articulated in multiple contexts. This often leads to an insistence on 'another' approach to development. The Dag Hammarskjöld Foundation's influential report on development and international cooperation in the 1970s, for example, emphasized not just the production of new technologies but the direction or pathway of innovation. In this report it was observed that "the capacity of technology to transform the nature, orientation and purpose of development is such that the question of who controls technology is central to who controls development" (Dag Hammarskjöld Foundation 1975/2006, 93). The report called for "another development" that would be informed by a needs-based approach and contribute to self-reliance—one that would not be locked into trajectories of technological, cultural, social and economic change that have been, and continue to be, dominant. As Linje Manyozo emphasizes in this book, there are multiple pathways towards change that could be consistent with enabling people to improve their conditions, individually and collectively. Persistent asymmetrical power relations suppress certain voices and privilege others and they privilege certain institutions and practices over others. These relations punish, exclude and disable human beings and it is for this reason that the project of resistance requires constant renewal through dialogue.

In contemporary times with the renewal of the Sustainable Development Goals and in the face of vivid evidence of poverty and conflict as well as the challenges of global warming, it is more important than ever to interrogate what kind of knowledge counts. The notion that digital technologies—broadband infrastructures, social media such as Facebook, digital platforms designed to mediate in conflict or crisis situations, or multiple forms of electronic commerce, can simply lift people out of poverty is discredited in the critical academic literature, but its remnants circulate and inform far too many initiatives launched by the development industry. Even when they are labelled "participatory," Linje

Manyozo's strong and convincing message is that the consequence is harm and oppression *unless* the main emphasis is on valuing difference, context and local aspiration. As he insists, if there is no insight into the "hidden injuries" (Escobar 1999) resulting from the privileging of *episteme* over other kinds of knowledge, then counter-discourses and practices will also languish.

Alternative development pathways may be borne through speaking development with and alongside communities. In Linje Manyozo's words, this is

> fundamental to deliberative development, which opens up pathways for imagining possibilities of social change, whose seeds will be sown when oppressed individuals and groups learn to accept that their current situation is unacceptable; that positive change itself, even the very idea of it, is revolutionary and confrontational in nature.

For him, this is the route through which the subaltern perspective can be acquired, and in a way that informs action. Linje Manyozo's proposals for theory and practice do not obviate the need for struggle, but they do offer a pathway for a journey which, through experimentation, can create opportunities for deliberative development at the community level.

Professor Robin Mansell
Department of Media and Communications
London School of Economics and Political Science

References

Bateson, Gregory. 1979. *Mind and Nature: A Necessary Unity*. New York: Bantam Books.

Dag Hammarskjöld Foundation. 1975/2006. What Now? The 1975 Dag Hammarskjöld Report on Development and International Cooperation. Prepared on the occasion of the Seventh Special Session of the United Nations General Assembly, September 1–12, Motala: Dag Hammarskjöld Foundation Fifth Printing. Accessed November 20 2016. www.daghammarskjold.se/wp-content/uploads/2016/07/What-Now-1975.pdf.

Escobar, Arturo. 1999. "Gender, place and networks: A political ecology of cyberculture." In Wendy Harcourt (ed.), *Women@Internet: Creating New Cultures in Cyberspace* (pp. 31–54). London: Zed Books.

Marglin, Federique and Stephen Marglin (eds). 1990. *Dominating Knowledge: Development, Culture, and Resistance*. Oxford: Clarendon Press.

Shor, Ira and Paulo Freire. 1987. *A Pedagogy for Liberation: Dialogues on Transforming Education*. Granby, MA: Bergin and Garvey.

PART I
Deconstruction

On 25 June 1832, Delacroix disembarks in Algiers for a short stopover. … This Orient, so near and of his own time, offers itself to him as a total and excessive novelty. … Delacroix spends only three days in Algiers. … For the first time, he penetrates into a world that is off-limits: that of the Algerian women … What his eyes saw was the permanent spectacle of an exteriority made up entirely of pomp, noise, cavalcades, and rapid motion.

Assia Djebar 1992, Women of Algiers in their Apartment, *133*

1

SPECTACLE OF DEVELOPMENT

Setting the context

The primary aim of this book is to examine the challenges and opportunities of curating and experimenting with more cooperative, horizontal and participatory forms of deliberative development in and with communities. It does this, first and foremost, in the first two chapters, by unmasking and unpacking what Robin Mansell (1982) depicted as the dominant paradigm of development which this book defines as the spectacle of development. Second, the book argues that despite the pervasiveness of problematic approaches and methodologies, especially in donor-driven models of development, there are liminal spaces that celebrate the agency of oppressed groups and thus allow for genuine exploration of, and experimentation with, deliberative development alongside communities. The third aim is to emphasize that the role of humanist educators—who exercise what the pioneer of liberation theology Gustavo Gutiérrez (1988) defines as the "preferential option for the poor"—is significant. These educators exercise solidarity with marginalized groups by carving out spaces within spectacles of development, within which they lay solid foundations for sustainable development interventions.

It is significant that this chapter, and indeed the book, opens with an observation by Assia Djebar (1992) regarding the 1832 arrival of the French orientalist painter, Eugene Delacroix, in Algeria. This is critical for the analysis that is undertaken in this book. The famous painting by Delacroix, *Women of Algiers in their Apartment*, can be considered the beginning of organized forms of orientalism in the south (Said 1978). This painting constructed a very orientalist, flat, static and problematic representation of the 'four' women Delacroix encountered in an Algiers harem that had nothing to do with historical realities (Djebar 1992). Much scholarship seems to observe or suggest that there are three women in the painting. Yet one notices that, apart from the three light-skinned women sitting down, there is also a black female servant standing and showing her backside. Over the years analytical focus has been on 'three women.' By editing out a female black servant from discussions of representations in this photo, it could be argued that class and race are critical considerations when it comes to representation of otherness and difference. In this book I will insist on counting the servant in, because she is a woman too and she is still in that painting.

Years after his painting, Delacroix would keep 'remembering again' and changing the angling and colouring in the original painting. Problematic representation is an understatement, considering he did not talk to the women; rather, he just observed them for a few hours and three days later he left the country to work on the painting back home in France. In effect, this famous painting actually launched the spectacle of development in practice in which exogenous development institutions' concern was not with how 'the others' experienced reality, but rather with the way these external agents imagined and conceived what would become dehistoricized and fictionalized events.

This book comprises two parts. The first part exposes the spectacle of development and the institutions that govern its systems and language of oppression. This part is itself a continuation of a conversation with Mansell (1982, 42) who, in response to claims of a new development paradigm in the late 1970s, argued that the dominant paradigm of development had not passed away but had just undergone a "superficial revisionism." While Mansell had exposed the similarities between the modernist development paradigm and the 'new' participatory paradigms to support her claim, this part of the book, comprising two chapters, seeks to profile the network of actors and discourses that oil the engine of that dominant paradigm. The second part of the book examines the opportunities that, despite the financial, logistical and technical challenges, still offer spaces for negotiation between outsiders and insiders to co-curate and experiment with deliberative development in the community.

The first part comprises two chapters and is itself a deconstructionist project that aims to discursively undermine the machinery of the development industry, which engages in what Escobar (1995) defines as the construction of the 'politics of the truth,' or a spectacle of development, to borrow from Stuart Hall's (1997) and Assia Djebar's (1992) notions of a spectacle of representation. Whereas Hall, Djebar and Said were concerned specifically with interrogating the politics of constructing and exchanging orientalist, colonial and stereotypical representations of other people, places and issues, in this book 'spectacle' refers to a regime and repertoire of attitudes and behaviours by the key actors in the development industry. These actors comprise donor agencies, corporate institutions, governments and even civil society organizations. The root causes of their behaviour span total ignorance, misinformation and outright arrogance as well as a frequent disregard for the real interests of beneficiary groups and their representatives and institutional structures.

Having undermined the dominant syntax and approaches to the development spectacles, what does the future hold for development? Do we abandon everything? Is there anything we can do to recover the praxis of deliberative development? To answer these questions, the second part is a reconstructionist or recovery project, comprising four chapters. It is primarily about the four points of negotiation that shape the theory and practice of deliberative development. This kind of development is cooperative, participatory, horizontal but also conflictual, yet one that emphasizes the collaboration of various stakeholders, notwithstanding the diversity in their classes, identities and interests.

This second part aims to achieve three things. First, it demonstrates the contradictions and difficulties of working with and alongside communities to conceive deliberative development. Even though as a black person I have emotional and social capital in Southern Africa, there were moments when I behaved as and was treated as an outsider in some of the places I worked. This shows that the politics of class and belonging is very complex and goes beyond identity, education and place of origin. Second, it explains that liberatory educators who are westerners, outsiders, and who are not from oppressed groups, can very much offer critical opportunities that enable communities to speak and unspeak realistic development interventions, so long as they acquire the subaltern perspective. In this case, a westerner or an outsider does not have to become an oppressed person in order to appreciate alternative development discourses. Through research, education and living with marginalized groups, they can acquire subaltern perspectives that allow them to rethink dominant development syntax with and alongside oppressed classes. Third, the aim in this part is to show that in development theory and practice, two contending elements are increasingly becoming antagonistic against each other. On one hand, there is the need to generate evidence and use that as a platform for development programming—known as investment thinking (UNAIDS 2012). On the other hand, there is this demand for more participatory, action-oriented and more democratic forms of learning and experimenting with deliberative development. In this book, all these positions come together in the pedagogy of listening.

This book is therefore an interrogation of the culture, the traditions, and practices of speaking development with and alongside communities. It is significant that the book's title is *Communicating Development with Communities*, since this is intended to signpost that my discussion is about the sharing of power and *speaking* development with local people. Not making. Not planning. Just *speaking* and, as will become clear, *listening* as well. This choice is deliberate. *Speaking* is a critical concept that implies a number of reflexive actions and behaviours that amount to a praxis. This *speaking* combines elements of becoming as understood by Deleuze and Guattari (1987), Freire (1970, 1996a, 1996b) and Gutiérrez (1988). It also integrates elements of 'mediation' as expounded by Sonia Livingstone (2009). But it is also rooted in the participatory process of consciousness building, a fundamental building block of class formation. For Edward Palmer Thompson (1963), class is an active process of becoming and not necessarily a social category that exists out there. As used in this book, it refers to historical processes in which social groups are engaged in daily struggles to define and curate their place in the world. These groups could be oppressed or oppressors or somewhere in between, since there are moments when one is neither oppressed nor an oppressor.

Thus, as Thompson (1963) explains, class happens. This book likewise argues that class is not a static and frozen structure that exists out there. I consider class as a constant negotiation of individual and collective identities that enables people with similar interests and experiences to curate relationships and networks with people and institutions. In this book the discussion examines how class identities are formed in and through deliberative development interventions. In this case, *Communicating Development with Communities* refers to nodal points that are themselves the methodological and communicative spaces that empower non-persons (Gutiérrez's and Freire's oppressed people) to contest the formulation and implementation of development policies. These are spaces in which the catalysing educator, the field worker or the radical humanist educator, engages in communicative action with people, mediated by enablers and undermined by the constraints of logistical and financial resources, all the while aiming to generate evidence and theory, and manage socio-political expectations. In this sense then, deliberative development is a site of conflict that facilitates individuals to become a class within a social rhizome. Deleuze and Guattari (1987) describe how a wasp becomes a component in an orchid's reproductive scheme that enables both of them to form a rhizome. This becomes more than a relationship of dependence, rather, it becomes a consciousness of the importance of the symbiotic roles various stakeholders have to play out in the course of development practice.

This book therefore explores the conceptions, values, attitudes and consciousness that so often govern the design and implementation of development interventions by people and institutions. Thus, in considering the *speaking* of development at the community level, the book examines the culture of development by oftentimes-antagonistic groups, as they negotiate and leverage power before and during the act of speaking interventions. My notion of speaking also includes elements of subjectivity and agency drawn from Bourdieu's (1983) symbolic power and an element of reflexivity derived from Jay Ruby's (2000) work in social anthropology. *Speaking* refers to a deliberate and fraternal process of building class consciousness in which subaltern groups are understood to become, thereby enabling these groups to collectively contest the production and exchange of power asymmetries.

What *Communicating Development with Communities* examines then are the five critical communicative spaces that can allow for the method-driven and theory-informed praxis of negotiated or deliberative development that has listening and experimentation at the centre of its practice. The successful design and execution of such interventions depends very much on understanding these five spaces, namely (a), the language of oppression (b) capturing subaltern voices, (c) living with the people, (d) encountering poverty, and (e) the pedagogy of listening. Yet to deconstruct these communicative spaces one needs to undertake a critical audit of development in practice, and that is what this book—especially the first two chapters—attempt to do. The discussion aims to emasculate the modernist ethos that characterizes much of development practice by exposing the spectacle of long-standing traditions, features, values and strategies that perpetuate, obscure and justify marginalization, dependence, and disempowerment.

In critical analytical traditions, the notion of spectacle is often used to describe problematic representations that employ stereotypes, are condescending, objectify the other, are vulgar and derogatory, and which undermine the identity and humanity of other people, history and cultures (Djebar 1992; Hall 1997). In this context, scholars such as Stuart Hall (1997), Ruby (2000), Tomaselli (2006) and others have undertaken semiotic analyses of popular art representations of marginalized social groups, demonstrating how symbolic power figures large in the construction of orientalist discursive repertoires. As borrowed and applied to development, the spectacle of development is framed here to describe various forms of deliberate and well-orchestrated class and capitalist disregard for fairness and the appropriate context in the design and implementation of policies by governments, corporations and other institutions. This strategic dishonesty and obfuscation of development narratives through the use of coopted methodologies, irrelevant theories and strategies, could constitute what the Princeton Professor Emeritus in Philosophy, Harry Frankfurt (1988), conceptualized as "bullshit." The bullshit of development then comprises the fundamental building block of a colourful, theatrical and vain spectacle of development. Each of these components is vulgar and inconsequential for the lives of the majority of targeted beneficiaries.

Dominant scholarly work and narrative conceptualize development as an aspirational idea—problematic as it is—with its narrow, frequently economically deterministic and technology-driven conceptualizations within orthodox traditions (Lerner 1958; Mansell 1982; Rostow 1960; Schramm 1964). In this book, the exposition of the speaking of this development, that is, the undermining of its spectacle, will be achieved in two ways. Firstly, I critically converse with two of the leading thinkers in development today: Arturo Escobar (1995) and Robert Chambers (2005), both of whom have called for new and alternative ways of thinking about and doing development. Within post-development there is an attempt, as Escobar points out in a revised 2012 Preface to *Encountering Development*, to move away from centralizing development in our discursive imaginary, achieved by discarding the civilizational and globalization models of modernity. After all, as Aimé Césaire (1955) points out, western modernity and civilization are beyond repair and indefensible. Instead, it is argued that theory and practice should move towards relational and endogenous models of living that celebrate local ontologies, spirituality, environmental sustainability, economies of solidarity and community-ness. In this way, all students of society might begin to contribute to the various ontological struggles that are striving for a different way of imagining life (Escobar 1995).

In the context of this intellectual positioning, the discussion refers to Frankfurt's (1988) philosophical theory of bullshit that comprises the deliberate and sometimes, careless disregard and indifference for the truth and reality. Frankfurt argues that bullshitters are neither concerned with the truth nor falsehood, but they are interested in achieving certain objectives that are of concern to them only. As conceptualized in this book and in this chapter specifically, such bullshit is similar to the dominant paradigm of development that never passed away. As elucidated by Mansell (1982), the dominant paradigm referred to modernist development, its ideologies, practices and the capital-intensive, technologically deterministic and classic economics-informed traditions and practices that governed and continue to govern the way interventions are conceived and implemented. Thus, the dominant paradigm encompasses the whole regime of doing and speaking development theories taught in universities, the cultures of policy making, methodological approaches in evaluation, and the actual implementation on the ground. For Mansell therefore, the dominant paradigm was and remains a system of thought, itself a pathway that allows the development industry to achieve specific organizational objectives—be they ideological, political or socio-economic—which considered together constitute Escobar's notion of developmentalization. Such objectives generally are not intended to benefit oppressed and marginalized groups as is ideally articulated in policy and strategy guidelines. Frankfurt's notion is particularly relevant since there is frequently a callous and positivist attempt to persist with interventions even when they are not working, instead of rethinking the theory, methodology, and the evidence that has led to the spectacle in the first place.

The second aspect of this book is reflexively practical since it concerns constructing what Mosse (2005) and Escobar (1995) define as new ethnographies of development. There has been a clear and growing recognition of the voices of various marginalized groups the world over who are indicating their dissatisfaction with the current order of things. This encompasses situations where neoliberal financial institutions continually perpetuate what the Nigerian writer Chimamanda Ngozi Adichie (2009) conceives as "the single story" of development spectacles. This single story assumes that, unless certain transformative economic conditions, structures and behaviours are in place, the global community will have to make do with poverty, inequality and marginalization (Adichie 2009; Chambers 2005; Escobar 1995; Tufte and Mefalopulos 2009). Even if the centrality of the neoclassical economics model as a guiding model of development has produced tragic results, financial institutions, governments, and organizations continue to design and implement the same neoliberal, market-driven, economics-informed model of development, which may be coated with terms and concepts that are seemingly transformative and radical (Mansell 1982). There is an implicit assumption in all these models that, "what the West is, the East seeks to become," borrowing the statement about the intention of civilizing modernity that Daniel Lerner (1958, 38) depicted in *The Passing of Traditional Society*. It is Lerner's conceptualization that Mansell (1982) probably had in mind when she defined the dominant paradigm—the system. Escobar shows that poverty would eventually be conceptualized as the principal organizing factor of the other world, and it is through its problematization that the professionalization of development would be made possible. The consequence, however, is that an indefensible western modernity has disrupted organic societies and economies that were communal, cooperative, democratic, empathetic, and fraternal (Césaire 1955).

What Escobar (1995) seems to be calling for is a celebration of a Bakhtinian (1981) *heteroglossia* of voices, or 'multiple ontologies' of a plural universe with an emphasis on diversity, the sanctity of the environment and the celebration of life itself. The concept of ontology is vital since, as Mansell (2011) indicates, it becomes essential to understand the knowledge that really counts. Labels, concepts and models can be revised, which make it seem as if the dominant paradigm has passed (Mansell 1982). Yet, there is still a need for *pluriversal* ontologies that will constitute a new, non-civilizational, non-modernist framework for conceptualizing, defining and romancing an alternative understanding of the world. In this case, it is not just a question of revisiting the labels as Mansell (1982, 2011) contends—otherwise, we will still be experimenting with the dominant system. Therefore, methodologically, new ethnographies of development must aim to capture such decolonized multiplicities in ways that recognize the subjectivity and agency of marginalized classes in conceptualizing life. In the case of this book, the new ethnography of development becomes a facility for demonstrating agency at work, the agency of oppressors and the oppressed, and how such agency interacts with various social and organizational networks within a machine, an industry, that has come to be known as development.

Defining development: The problem of definition

It seems defining development, offering its prescriptions, and drawing parameters within which the conceptual framework is made sense of, has become a major preoccupation of a great number of scholars who are increasingly considering themselves 'development experts.' My aim is not to belabour readers with the complex jargon that seeks to outshout previous or current scholars by 'cleverly' using and arranging words with the single aim of showing that one knows better than others. Auto-ethnographically, I simply provide an operational definition, which itself is an explanation born of my experiences of growing up in and working within extreme poverty. Yet, it also has to be acknowledged that in practice—and this has been problematized well by Escobar, Césaire, Gutiérrez and others—the term 'development' is itself highly problematic since it is often used to target poor classes, with a focus on economic growth, modernity, civilization and transformation of social processes to replicate so-called developed societies, which unfortunately has "disrupted natural economies" (Césaire 1955, 7). What is crucial however is that development, even when following Escobar and Gutiérrez in rejecting this discursive concept, cannot be deconstructed without first defining and understanding oppression and liberation.

My understanding of both poverty and development are shaped by the oppressive empirical experiences of growing up in Africa, getting educated, and then working in various countries—Malawi, South Africa, Mozambique, Zambia, Australia, the United Kingdom and continental Europe. As will be demonstrated in Chapter 2, "Language of oppression," I grew up on the tea and tobacco plantations owned by British and Italian commercial farmers. My childhood was a happy one even if, by western standards, we did not have enough to sustain our livelihoods. We never at any point defined ourselves as poor. In fact, even if someone had not eaten at home, he or she would refuse to join in another family's dinners or lunches by lying and saying that they were already fed. We feared being smacked by parents, since indicating we had not eaten would make everyone think we were poor. Of course, I also remember being hungry most of the time, which made it hard for me to concentrate in school and in church.

Years later I would encounter the word 'poor' in policy documents and meetings when the concept was being employed to define a category of people like us villagers. As I navigated through my undergraduate and graduate training at various universities the world over, including stints with international development organizations, I encountered semiotic *firstness* with regard to the process of developmentalization as it manifested in the spectacles that characterized the thinking and practices of the development industries: at the level of research, teaching, policy making, implementation and even during my personal involvement in public and community health initiatives. This book therefore is not only a scholarly exercise, but also a moment of reflection on the ethnographic experiences of encountering development as a poor person, as a community development worker, as an academic, and as a policy maker. I also acknowledge the contradictions; there were moments when I simultaneously functioned as an oppressor in order to advance programme goals that were, in my understanding in the moment, liberatory. This is a duality that Freire and Gutiérrez recognize and that challenges scholars and practitioners alike to be reflexive about.

What is critical is that all this experience has allowed me to understand that development cannot be defined unless it is known. This is where the problem begins. To know a phenomenon, to understand it, and to define it, largely depends on where one is standing when the process of knowing occurs. For Freire (1970, 1996a, 1996b), to understand and deconstruct dehumanization one must primarily have lived through it, or through careful study and research. Gutiérrez (1988) describes the notion of a preferential option for the poor which is a firm commitment by any student of society expressed to and with marginalized groups. To know development, one must understand and appreciate the humiliating, marginalizing and dehumanizing life conditions, thus enabling these groups to acquire a semiotic firstness—either through living these experiences or through a careful empirical study and analysis that results in the researcher assuming a solidarity with the cause of the oppressed. Semiotic firstness therefore can either be lived, experienced, or studied, and it allows one to appreciate what Aimé Césaire (1955) calls *thingification* (the process of dehumanization) of oppressed groups. It highlights the necessity for radical and liberating development interventions.

The focus therefore is on the contexts that have an impact on the way development is designed and implemented, but the question is which development is this? Is it the bourgeoise development—imagined, conceived, dreamt and fantasized in the boardrooms of capital cities, expensive hotels, fancy workshops, seminars or conferences? Or is it the subaltern development—embracing the material and existentialist notion that most oppressed groups want to eat, touch and feel in their hearts? In my discussion, development is conceptualized as a historical process that is a compromise between, and is simultaneously compromised by, theories, context, practices, ideologies and class experiences.

To borrow Edward Palmer Thompson's (1963) concept of history from below, or Raymond Williams's (1961) structure of feeling, development can be conceived of as a historical process and occurs as such. For Hegel and Marx, history happens when men and women work together to intervene in their social conditions. As a historical process therefore, development involves conflict, or is a site of conflict. It is a conflict over resources and, of course, over power. In these critical traditions and perspectives, development is a class conflict—it is about the contestation of power between antagonistic classes over how to design and implement policies that are going to benefit the majority of the people. The fierceness of these conflicts emanates from the fact that, within the nation state, the state itself is inclined to protect the interests of the landed and feudal classes. Consequently, the involvement of either the national or supra-national state protects the capitalist interests and not subaltern groups. The bourgeois development displays attributes of land dispossession, unfair trading practices, profit-centric regulation, coordinated tax evasion, poor or low wages, and capture, or co-opting, of the state by private interests (Césaire 1955). Equally, the subaltern are forced to enter into a tenuous and conflictual relationship with the state and its capitalist partners in dealing with what one might reasonably assume are the common-sense responsibilities of the state—service delivery, housing, water, electricity and utility bills, and so forth.

This conflict is very vital in generating a consciousness that, according to Marx, Gutiérrez and Freire, leads to the creation of a new being and this, in turn, can lead to the process of liberation. When Marx observed "they cannot represent themselves, they must be represented," (1852, 62) he must have been referring to the necessity of this historical process and a process of conflict that ultimately will conscientize the oppressed classes into forging identities; becoming active participants in authoring and making their own history; and creating and forging their own aspirations. This consciousness becomes the critical tool that is employed by men and women to challenge the oppressive ruling class values that promote a twisted, biased and unequal reality in which the majority are denied the opportunity to live and enjoy freedom. In this context, freedom is not an abstract concept but, instead, very real and very material. It is itself a result of a class struggle that seeks to yield a "total and complete fulfilment of the individual in solidarity with all humankind" (Gutiérrez 1988, 71).

As such, when we define development, class perspective must be an important consideration. Perhaps to borrow again from Lerner's (1958, 38) determination that "what the west is, the east seeks to become," we can conceive of the dominant paradigm as asserting that what the bourgeoisie is, the oppressed seeks to become. For the oppressed landless and peasant classes, as a result of class struggle they will come to look forward to strong communities, improved livelihoods, satisfying spirituality, healthy lives and ecological sustainability: elements that are seemingly present in most of the experiences of the bourgeoisie and middle classes. Eventually, development therefore becomes a site of conflict over imagining, over resources and power, among coalitions of classes that drink, process and sell tea on the one hand, and a confederacy of those who grow that tea, on the other. But importantly, for Marx, Gutiérrez, Freire and Escobar, development is a conflict over representation and even over the instruments and discourses of that representation. To foster a liberating development policy, a dialogue must be reimagined and constructed. Within critical traditions, the classes that grow tea do not always have sufficient and necessary social capital or social investment with and in their communities because they are so preoccupied with trying to survive. As a result they cannot develop a critical consciousness of their own conditions which prohibits them from "entering into manifold relations with each other" (Marx 1852, 62), and this disempowers them so that they cannot represent themselves and must, therefore, "be represented by the executive power which subordinates society" (Marx 1852, 62). In the end, it is this class that processes, sells and drinks tea and this process is what Marx (1852) describes as the subordinating power that constructs the discourse of representation on behalf of the subordinate classes. The whole history of development in general is littered with unequal relationships and often ends up with bullshit approaches to interventions.

The theory of bullshit provides a scientific methodology for understanding deceptive strategies that deliberately misrepresent thoughts and feelings (Frankfurt 1988). In this view, the confederacy of the classes who drink tea (perhaps in collaboration with certain power elites among those who grow tea) engage in the production, representation, circulation and implementation of development bullshit that is framed within realities they are often ignorant about (Frankfurt 1988). For Escobar, the development industry is deliberately complicit in the creation of an epistemological phantom through constructing a regime of thought and practice that has led to the creation and maintenance of a problematic politics of truth. Within this political construct of truth, poverty is the problem and development is the solution. As such, even if interventions addressing poverty are not working, new development interventions are initiated and implemented again because in the minds of major actors within the development phantom, there has to be a development solution and nothing else.

In this case then, Frankfurt's bullshit can be seen as a building block in Escobar's politics of truth. This regime of bullshit can be understood to comprise what Escobar (1995, 45) regards as comprising a "set of techniques, strategies, and disciplinary practices that organize the generation, validation, and diffusion of development knowledge, including the academic disciplines, methods of research and teaching, criteria of expertise, and manifold professional practices." Yet there are spaces within the development bullshit regime that allow for defiance and negotiation. For instance, in the middle of a ravaging famine in 2005, the Malawi government defied the international community's advice by providing subsidized fertilizer to subsistence farmers. The Malawi government rejected the development bullshit, or the politics of truth perpetuated and propagated by the World Bank, the International Monetary Fund and other donor agencies that doubted the ability to avert hunger through increasing subsistence farmers' production of food crops. This strategy would be replicated in other countries and these development strategies were based on the realities on the ground—poor subsistence farmers cannot afford unsubsidized fertilizer, increasing pressure on diminishing land resources and perennial food insecurity. This book, therefore, argues that development is not a given, nor does it happen only through policies that follow from common sense. Rather, development is a problem that must be investigated using the social resources of both reason and experience by the very people experiencing the challenges.

The spectacle of development

The notion of the spectacle of development is partly borrowed from Stuart Hall's (1997) iconic essay, 'The spectacle of the other,' which examines the challenges of constructing representations of other people, places and issues, especially when difference is factored in. The other part of spectacle comes from Assia Djebar's (1992) analysis of the "permanent spectacle of an exteriority" as manifested in the orientalist oil painting, *Women of Algiers in their Apartment* by Delacroix. For Hall, as well as for Djebar (1992) and Said (1978), the notion of spectacle is relevant because of the unequal power relations that exist between those constructing representations and those being represented, a process which perhaps prompted Gayatri Spivak (1988) to ask the famous question, "Can the subaltern speak?" From the viewpoint of Hall, Djebar, Said and Spivak, perhaps one can argue that in dominant development theory and practice there exist various forms of bullshit, that together frame and shape the construction of these spectacles. Such development spectacles have little to do with advancing objective representations of people, places and their development challenges. So what are the attributes of these development spectacles?

The first attribute of the spectacle is the spectacle of knowledge infrastructure or what Mansell (2011) conceptualizes as the political economy of "knowledge that counts." Such knowledge is generated by and through orientalist research, financial and implementing organizations upon which the theoretical discursive imaginary of the prevailing development thinking rests. Said (1978) describes orientalism as a mode of discourse, an academic practice, and a corporate institution through which western civilization manages the production of knowledge about the south. This form of spectacle has become a desired habitat for orientalist, condescending and colonial institutions and structures and is usually sustained by a network of international development organizations. Within this spectacle of knowledge is the increased role of the civil society and beneficiaries (who are often motivated by short-term returns and petty politics, environmental fetishism and unrealistic human rights concerns). Together, all these forms, layers and categories of development practices that generate and are sustained by orientalist and colonialist discourses of difference constitute what I understand as the spectacle of development. Spectacle alludes to the production, exchange and utilization of development imaginaries that are rooted in stereotypes, a failure to acknowledge difference and a disregard of the voices of subaltern groups.

The second attribute of the development spectacle concerns the total disregard for the emotional well-being of the local people either by design or as a consequence of policies and actions bordering on the edges of professional immorality and obscenity. Immorality in development starts with the amounts of resources that are spent on consultants, international staff, insignificant studies, useless interventions or unnecessary policies and strategies that are a minor footnote or of no benefit to the communities in question, yet it is governments and citizens that seem to have no agency to interrupt and stop such immorality and corruption. Cases in point include the medical circumcision and female condom programmes that are touted as breakthroughs in HIV prevention, even when there are other more cost-effective interventions such as male condoms. Why would one go through the pain of a circumcision when it can only provide 60 per cent protection instead of using condoms that are almost 100 per cent effective? Or, why would female condoms be emphasized as contraception methods when even the industry itself recognizes that unequal power relations make it almost impossible for most women to negotiate any sexual encounters?

The third attribute of the spectacle of development bullshit involves a seemingly pleasurable experience for the major actors but not for the audiences who can only witness these development cabarets, perhaps even enjoying the experience of watching what is going on but never being able to be part of it. An informal examination of conditions of service for international staff in organizations such as the United Nations (UN) shows that salaries are not only obscene but, also, more experienced local staff can only hope to enjoy the same benefits, even if they are more qualified and knowledgeable. In fact, this seems to be a tendency in most cases where such institutions recruit international consultants who are nowhere near as knowledgeable as local experts, and who, in some cases, produce low-quality work.

The fourth characteristic of the development spectacle that is visible in development bullshit concerns the illusion of self-representation. A major argument posited by post-development thinking revolves around the unequal power relations that characterize dominant approaches towards representation. The assumption is that in allowing local institutions and citizen groups to own, for instance, the means of media production, it will enable them to generate and share much more objective, culturally rich, and ethically sensitive representations. Nevertheless, even if new and participatory technologies are enabling the production of alternative development narratives and praxes, the orthodox pattern, discourse and repertoire has remained intact. There is thus a linear and modernist repertoire in alternative spectacles of development. But within these problematic development spectacles, it is important to emphasize again that there are spaces of negotiation, spaces where humanist educators, and oppressed or oppressing groups deviate from the norm and the usual expectations and are able to experiment with interventions that speak to local needs. It should also be emphasized that it is not always the case that local people know what is best for them. And it is the role of these humanist and catalyzing educators to challenge oppressed groups to rethink their understanding of the world.

This chapter emphasizes that the prevailing spectacle of development is a huge industry that relies on a system of representation that exhibits a fascination with what can be considered as poverty-porn or the pornography of development itself. Similar to Said (1978), Escobar points out clearly that the "discovery of poverty" in the 1940s allowed for renewed colonial exploration and civilizing of the other world in more coordinated ways. In a sense, therefore, poverty became a spectacle that has allowed the pornography of development to be imagined and performed. As Escobar's *Encountering Development* (1995/2012) shows, unpacking and deconstructing this spectacle requires a combination of politically conscious intervention and scholarship that unmasks policy—and the institutional, ideological and programmatic raptures—so as to destabilize the development bullshit and its syntax. Deconstructing only one or two forms of the spectacle in this chain cannot deconstruct the whole repertoire of development pornography, what is required is a gradual rethink of development theory and practice. For Escobar, deconstruction starts with new ways of imagining the future outside the bounded *Weltanschauung* of development. The new ethnographies of development that emerge through reimagining discourses and interventions offer a methodological pathway for a form of discursive unlearning and unspeaking development theory and practice.

I argue that deconstructing development requires undermining dominant development practices from planning to monitoring and evaluation—and this encompasses the transformation of training institutions that produce a calibre of graduates who have not been exposed to alternative ways of thinking about and looking at the world. It is important to mention that, despite the preponderance of formats and strategies of development bullshit, there also exist sincere, radical and ideologically conscious efforts that spring up here and there even when they operate within established frameworks, theories and methods. As such, alternative development does not necessarily imply a revolutionary abandonment of the prevailing dominant bullshit, rather it entails radical practices that undermine the dominant system while offering marginalized groups an opportunity to scheme and experiment with their own concepts of development. Nevertheless, programmers, policy makers, government officials, donors and practitioners continue to implement policies that run contrary to the objectives of genuine empowerment and liberation. This business, this whole process, this regime of dishonesty—in which the development industry designs and implements unrealistic interventions that benefit the oppressors—is what this book understands as the spectacle of development. Yet this is not always a linear process. As post-colonial theory explicates, colonization has never been a linear process—there are moments when the oppressed have become epistemologically and materially complicit in their own oppression, by, among other strategies, contributing to the design of their own oppressive development interventions.

The vulgarity of development spectacles

As pointed out by Mbembe (2001) in 'The aesthetics of vulgarity,' the metaphor of an imaginary of obscenity or pornography is not necessarily strange in subaltern politics and practice. In fact it has a long history as a central feature of subaltern citizenship and protest against capitalist and colonial regimes of material and symbolic violence. Women within traditional African politics have a history of taking off their clothes to protest against bad governance. As recently as 2016, South African women showed their bottoms to express their displeasure at the lack of intra-party democracy within the ruling African National Congress (Moatshe 2016). Likewise, female Rhodes University students have protested topless against rising sexual harassment and violence on campus (Charter 2016). In the same vein, some female University of Witwatersrand students recently protested against tuition fees increases by taking off their bras as a way of "showing the power of a woman's body."[1] Meanwhile, naked Iranian women in Paris protested against restrictions on female freedom in Iran. This symbolic struggle seemingly emulates the nude political protest by the Egyptian blogger Aliaa Magda Elmahdy, who has posted nude pictures of herself online as a rejection of the oppressive socio-political patriarchy (Fadel Fahmy 2011). Likewise, the Swedish conceptual artist, Milo Moiré, and the American Kim Kardashian, have also posted their own nude and semi-nude pictures in a bid to align themselves with causes related to female emancipation and freedom. In this case, pornography as a concept has been used to partly describe the subaltern struggles in development processes through which marginalized groups employ art or technology to harness the semantics and semiotics of profanity as a form of protest. My discussion draws from this perspective and also from the painting, *Pornography of Power*, by the South African artist, Ayanda Mabulu (Nkuna 2016), who depicts how the ruling African National Congress (ANC) and a coalition of predatory corporate capitalists have engaged in an explicit symbolic sexual encounter with a female prisoner (Nkuna 2016). Mabulu himself has decried the raw deal that citizens are getting from elected leaders who have become increasingly more violent and ruthless post-apartheid (Nkuna 2016). In response to criticism that his paintings have gone beyond the pale in representing the issues, Mabulu observes that the real obscenity and pornography are the destitute and dehumanizing conditions that characterize the lives of the majority of black people when their leaders are stealing from public coffers.

In its vulgar form, the painting, *Pornography of Power*, therefore attempts to represent and convey the "condition of black people in its truest form" (Nkuna 2016). And this condition is a direct result of this pornography, this symbolic obscene orgy that characterizes the lives of most black politicians (Fanon's oppressive native elite) who have become the new class oppressors. Mabulu alludes to the opulence of the sumptuous lifestyles of politicians including Mandela's family;

the police massacre of 34 miners at Marikana who were protesting against low wages in 2012; and the corruption scandals implicating the ruling party in South Africa, a microcosm of much of the south. In this case, *pornography* comprises a well-thought-out, calculated and cynical spectacle of material and symbolic violence by a coalition of financial and capitalist institutions, as well as a repertoire of discursive deceptions that aims to hoodwink oppressed groups into thinking it is deemed fine to have "bastards serving these hyenas" (Nkuna 2016).

Elaborating on the possible meanings that the painting *Pornography of Power* can elicit, this chapter considers some of the major forms of exploitation that are typical of the dominant development spectacles, which as Mansell (1982) argued had not passed away. In this book I consider whether this is still the case. There are several major styles of exploitative encounter that are depicted in Mabulu's painting that can be related to this spectacle of development. In these colonial, stereotypical, heterosexual and orientalist encounters, pleasure and pain seem to be simultaneously rhizomatic and symbiotic experiences. In this relationship, the oppressor and the oppressed experience orgasmic pleasure and enjoy masochistic pain.

(1) The missionary position

The notion of 'missionary position' is derived from two sources. First, it is suggested by Christopher Hitchens's (1995) criticism of Mother Theresa for manipulating the poor and their poverty to spread the Catholic theocracy and western modernity in the south during the Cold War. Hitchens's notion of a missionary position is reminiscent of the "dominant paradigm that never passed away" and it is the political economy of development practice that produces and reproduces the dominant "knowledge that counts" (Mansell 1982, 2011). Secondly, the notion is borrowed from descriptions of heterosexual encounters as articulated in two popular western lifestyle magazines: *Cosmopolitan* and *Men's Health*, which conceive of and explore the various forms of the missionary position described as the traditional form or the magic missionary position. The emphasis is on the primacy of the patriarch and the dominant. The *Cosmopolitan* observes that the "man-on-top mode is totally intimate, allowing you and your guy constant eye contact and easy access to kissing, plus, it is relatively relaxing for you, putting him in control as you lie back and enjoy."[2] The magazine then discusses the many variations of performing the missionary position. From a woman's perspective, the basic trajectory of having this sexual encounter involves "having him enter you while you are lying on your back with your legs apart." The notion of missionary here suggests that it is not just the dominant or traditional paradigm that is passed on from generation to generation in various forms, but that it is the best way to do things, in this specific case, to think, speak and do development.

From a man's perspective, as presented in *Men's Health*, the missionary position is also known as the matrimonial or the male-dominant position.[3] As in the *Cosmopolitan* conceptualization, there is much emphasis on the advantage of having adequate "eye and body contact." For the man, this is the "most commonly used position in the world" and it allows him to "control penetration depth and speed of thrusting."[4] This issue of *Men's Health* also argues that the woman "enjoys feeling your weight on her body, and the maximum skin-to-skin contact."[5]

There are parallels with dominant approaches towards development here. The essential elements of the missionary position are the confirmation of the unequal power relations of the participants and where patriarchal institutions enjoy power, control and influence in the design and implementation of development interventions. From the perspective of the marginalized and peripheral groups and communities, it signifies enjoying the benefits of development that come from governments and donor institutions. There is sometimes a perceived lack of serious fiduciary oversight by communities who expect external funding and resources to continue sustaining interventions, after all 'this is white people's money.' What this shows is that within the dominant paradigm, even the practices and behaviours of oppressed groups do sometimes become oppressive to themselves, a phenomenon described as horizontal violence by Fanon (1961, 1965). The missionary position here also encompasses the attitudes of communities that contribute to development bullshit.

The spectacle of the missionary position thus refers to symbolically speaking a heterosexual and matrimonial perspective in which the emphasis is on the assertion of the male-dominant position; as such, it is suggestive of the development industry overriding all the other participants in determining the direction and nature of development spectacles. The sustenance of these approaches relies on strict adherence to their tried and tested methodologies, theories and manuals. The emphasis is on lessons learned from elsewhere and this learning is achieved through exposure to 'knowledge that counts' within a network of transnational consultants and experts. As Said (1978) rightly points out, orientalism is a form of colonial discourse. In this view, the international experts are there to reproduce orientalist interventions in various parts of the world.

The powerful development industry comprising the funding agencies, policy makers and the transnational bourgeois specialists can be compared to the masculine subject in the popular discourse depicted in the magazines. They have the instruments for constructing the development spectacles (the financial and logistical resources) which they use to imagine the orient—the local organizations and beneficiaries, that are also conceived as the end users. In this discursive imaginary, the missionary position provides us with insights into the structure and process of development. In fact, as represented in Mabulu's painting, both the political and the financial superstructure are in control over the chained female prisoner with whom they are having a symbolic sexual encounter, in which they are in control, which is indicative of the prevailing development discourse and practice itself. In this view, development can be considered a political economy that allows those with resources to exercise control over the direction and nature of development. Both *Cosmopolitan* and *Men's Health* accept that the man will be on top while the woman lies on her back. It is this masculine control that enables both the male and female to experience maximum orgasmic pleasure.

An excellent analogue of the missionary position is the Structural Adjustment Programmes (SAPs) that were initiated in the late 1970s and early 1980s but which are still being advanced by global financial lending institutions, even though they have been shown to hurt oppressed and marginalized communities in both the global south and the global north. As can be seen from the Greek economic meltdown in 2015, the SAPs are associated with the failure of the modernization paradigm, where the expected trickle-down effect of wealth has not taken place. Yet for international financial institutions, the Greek economic tragedy has been authored by a loose financial regulatory framework which tolerated corruption, tax evasion, illicit financial flows and a growing domestic debt. To stimulate economic growth in these economic peripheries, certain measures have been introduced that include cuts to critical public-sector spending, such as on education or health care; the removal of subsidies on crucial commodities, such as farming products; the privatization of unprofitable public companies (considered to be a burden on the state); the increasing and widening of the tax base, and other stringent measures. Yet in the aftermath of the global financial and economic crisis of 2008, western governments introduced public-sector spending cuts while bailing out the key financial institutions that had caused the crisis in the first place. Such spending cuts have resulted in worsening poverty levels, increasing unemployment, unaffordable higher education, and increased levels of social and economic *thingification*. The state is becoming privatized, as forewarned by Frantz Fanon (1961, 1965), with and by business interests determining the direction and quality of socio-economic policy. From a post-colonial perspective, one can argue that the state, to put it bluntly, was originally an invention of private capital, the feudal and landed classes, to establish a mechanism for protecting their financial interests (Fanon 1961, 1965; Mbembe 2001).

The analogy with the missionary position here suggests that it is elected governments that people put in power to improve their lives that eventually exact these spending cuts. In this case, the missionary position represents the ideological establishment of the oppressive and unequal status quo. The oppressed groups are also complicit in their own marginalization insofar as they habitually elect people and institutions that work against their class interests. Consideration of the missionary position in this way provides a framework for understanding the imperialist relations between the oppressors and oppressed within the development context. While there might be consultation (in the same way that the lifestyle magazines describe a process of complicity that involves relatively constant eye and body contact), in the dominant development discourse, theory and practice, the oppressed are given a raw deal over and over again by the very institutions and practices within the prevailing political economy of development itself.

From the perspective of post-colonial theory, the infrastructure of development can be conceived of as being penetrative and violent, notwithstanding the extent to which the oppressed become, for Achille Mbembe (in Mbembe and Esprit 2008, interview), 'consciously complicit' in their own subjugation. This is well exemplified by poor communities experiencing poor service delivery in much of the south and where they openly express their disappointment with the ruling parties but nevertheless vote for them again and again.[6] Thus, the missionary position signifies maintaining the status quo, no matter how unbearably oppressive it may be even for the oppressed and subaltern groups, and this is the key message in Mabulu's representation of the *Pornography of Power.*

(2) Collaborative development

In development thinking and practice, there has been criticism of the dominant approaches and methodologies that are intrusive, very colonial and linear. Though anthropologists have invested time and resources to construct truthful and objective representations, their outputs and products are contested for promoting what have been considered to be problematic significatory phaneroscopes and frameworks. This is the context in which an anthropological tradition of cooperative representation emerged (Ruby 1991). A good example of collaborative representation of and in development can be seen in 'photo elicitation', as it provides a space for neutralizing the tension between presence and representation by enabling the post-colonial subjects to participate in the construction of their own representations. Photo elicitation is a transformative praxis that allows the integration of subaltern voices in the narrative, supplementing such representations. It does this by detaching texts from being personal experiences, so that they become a collaborative experience.

As a form of participatory action research, photo elicitation places a text into a research interview by enabling the photo to become a subject of discussion (Harper 2002). Photographic images evoke deeper elements of human consciousness, enabling informants to structure and restructure their memory (Harper 2002). Many think that photographs elicit better quality information than other methods because they enable the informant to have a point of reference (Collier and Collier 2000; El Guindi 2004; Harper 2002). They can act as communication bridges between researchers and subjects as they function as starting and reference points for discussions (Collier and Collier 2000). They are expected to open up discussions by enabling hosts and informants to take the lead in enquiry largely because they are not the point and subject of interrogation (Collier and Collier 2000).

Central to photo elicitation is qualitative observation, as in the *Semiotics of the Encounter* Project that has since transformed into the *Rethinking Indigeneities* Project (Tomaselli 2006). These projects involved studying representations of indigenous ≠Khomani San communities of the Southern Kalahari (Tomaselli 2006). The experiences and observations took place at various levels. The first level was camera observation, in which a researcher chooses and classifies what parts of interactions are important for consideration. The second was the non-mediatized observation, the eye observation, whereby a researcher, without being distracted by a camera or recorder, enters into a new space with people: a space which is a product of negotiations of different circuits of cultures and which enables them to share fears, joys and hopes. This kind of collaboration allows for the integration of reflexivity within the process of constructing development imaginaries and interventions. There are many examples of the cooperation of development in practice which have seen the construction of schools, hospitals and other social services. Yet the unequal power relations cannot be masked entirely, since both the structure and the process of the development intervention itself generally favour the external agents who possess the education and resources. In other words, even using this collaborative development approach, the template of development spectacles still frames the encounters and the outputs no matter how cooperative and consultative the process might be.

(3) The communities in control/on-top approach

In the aforementioned lifestyle magazines, the cowgirl or lusty leapfrog is considered a 'women-on-top' position. Within global politics and in post-development settings, the woman's being on top of things, or women's involvement in and being in control of development interventions, has been heralded as a radical approach that demonstrates civility and modernity, in contrast to the traditional missionary position (Djebar 1992; Mohanty 2003; Spivak 1988). There is thus a move towards empowering marginalized groups, especially women (who are often at the bottom of the social and class totem pole). In the introduction to *Communities in Control: Real People, Real Power*, the UK Government (2008, 1) expresses its desire to "pass power into the hands of local communities," which will renew local government and democracy by enabling the shifting of "power, influence and responsibility away from existing centres of power into the hands of communities and individual citizens." The essence of this approach to creating spectacles is that it is communities and community groups that are seemingly very much in control of things. Does this allow for a genuine expression of aspirations and the design of realistic and effective development interventions? Not quite. Even when they are represented, the fact that oppressed groups have been subjected to oppression for so long means that they begin to view reality based on the oppressors' sensibilities (Fanon 1965; Freire 1970; hooks 1994; Said 1978). In the end, even when oppressed groups have the instruments to exercise power, they tend to reproduce the same dominant relations. And it is for this reason that Freire emphasizes the need to liberate both the oppressor and the oppressed.

In the third chapter, I examine the gender-informed women in development perspective as a form of the communities in control approach. Responding to pressure from global and social movements, most western development institutions would, from the 1980s, begin to emphasize the inclusion of gender and alternative perspectives in development. The woman—as an oppressed social category—was often represented as the missing link in development theory and practice. Thus emerged the Women In Development Movement which apparently would give rise to a theoretically fluid 'paradigm shift' in development (Mohanty 2003; Spivak 1988). Postgraduate degrees would be established to train a cadre of professional gender-sensitive policy makers who would champion the mainstreaming of gender in development. A new generation of gender theories was generated as a critical tool for studying development. In the social sciences, a shift towards women's history emerged. Attempts were made to generate women's history with the assumption that women experience history differently from other social groups. In practice, new social mobilization and other action research methodologies emerged that placed women at the centre of social change—women as role models, women as characters who had defied tradition and oppressive structures and risen to become role models in their communities. The United Nations Development Fund for Women (UNIFEM) and then UN Women would be established to coordinate socio-economic interventions for gender equality and women's empowerment. This would lead to the universalization and globalization of struggles for women's empowerment and equality as celebrated through the high profile 1995 Beijing Platform. Years later, both analyses of the Millennium Development Goals (MDGs) and Sustainable Development Goals (SDGs) have acknowledged the challenges of meeting these gender goals.

A major criticism of the participatory approaches to development is the persistence of unequal and uneven distributions of power at the local level and among dominant and marginalized groups (Escobar 1995; Makuwira 2014). The most vocal critics are those representing various social movements. For gender activists, for example, it is often assumed that women are a marginalized social category, the missing link in development thinking. After all, they grow most of the world's food, they work the land, drive the factory engines, and are key players in the informal economy—the engine that drives the economies of the south. Yet, in Mabulu's painting, the woman being located in the centre does not necessarily imply she is at the centre of the process. She is actually depicted at the periphery with her hands tied, demonstrating that this is the role that has been carved out by dominant structures for her. Reminiscent of Bourdieu's (1991) concept of symbolic power, this suggests a notion of self-empowerment, involving pleasure and power that have been defined for the woman by her society; yet, as can be seen from the tied arms, she has little or no influence. Doubts about the efficacy of such development spectacles were raised primarily by critical scholars. Thus it was the depoliticizing approach to the universalization of women's empowerment that Chandra Mohanty (2003), Spivak (1988) and others would question with regard to westernization, modernization, orientalism and the disregard for the politics of subaltern speech.

Deconstructing the spectacle of development

One frustrating aspect of orthodox development in practice is that it is very evident that oftentimes it is typically simply a foreign international relations strategy for designing and implementing exogenous interventions. Often, these are achieved through local and national bodies and institutions. Experts take advantage of inequality, poverty and marginalization to exert their influence and thus to maintain the status quo in international politics and development agendas. The development industry is becoming increasingly reliant on specific operational strategies that comprise the law, governance order and the institutions that define and spell out, materially or ideologically, the terms of reference for those who oppress and for those who are oppressed. To deconstruct, unpack and destabilize this regime of development pornography as I have discussed, requires a comprehensive understanding of oppression and liberation. Oppression is a state of helplessness. In Mabulu's painting, this state of helplessness is symbolized by the woman who is being enslaved, or in the prevailing development context, is enslaved by a coalition of socio-political and economic forces. In an interview with Nkuna (2016), Mabulu unpacks the representation of the woman:

> The woman represents our country and all that she has to endure under this leadership. We are being milked dry, and you can imagine the torment involved when a dick is forcefully plunged into your throat, and at the same time you are being lynched. Then behind you is the hyena/colonial master, who is fucking you from behind while your breasts are being milked. How can you reconcile this type of existence with this so-called democracy? The life of a black man is sad, it is hell. And even worse is that the architects of this hell are our leaders.

As Mabulu observes, this "type of existence" is a life in which living is a form of death. All this experience, and the ritual and routine that accompanies it, is what translates into the pornography of what Mbembe (Mbembe and Esprit 2008, Interview) depicts as necropolitical force, a divine authority that subjects its citizens to Césaire's *thingification*. For the majority of marginalized non-persons their continued state of *thingification* is largely a result of the lack of power to overturn the situation that exerts oppressive conditions; or the lack of awareness by a social group to comprehend that they are living under oppression. These distinctions are significant, since they distinguish the oppressed (as in Freire) from the subaltern (as in Spivak and Mohanty). I argue that the material and theoretical distance between the oppressed and the subaltern is instantiated during the process of becoming opposed to dehumanization or *thingification*. Understanding the nature of oppression is crucial if we are to deconstruct the spectacle that is pervasive in dominant development thinking and practice. Central to the theory and practice of development are the various institutions—local and international non-governmental organizations (NGOs), bilateral donors, foreign governments and financial lending institutions (Makuwira 2014). Institutional oppression comprises the regime of rules, regulations and arbitrary considerations that hold an oppressive system and its institutions together.

The book chapters

Escobar's conceptualization of new ethnographies of development provides an opportunity for constructing what Geertz (1971) describes as a thick description of development in operation, or development at work, and not necessarily development as a structure, static and frozen in time. This allows scholars and practitioners to demonstrate the networks and relationships that govern the design and implementation of policies. Defining this approach as "hyper-ethnography," Escobar (2012, xv–xvi) discusses this new ethnography as constituting a methodological and conceptual framework that:

> allows the ethnographer to see the entire development network, investigating in depth the main sites with their respective actors, cultural backgrounds, and practical appropriation of the interventions by local groups. The result, it is argued, should give theorists and practitioners a more nuanced account of how development operates as a multi-scale process that is constantly transformed and contested. … the critical ethnographer could illuminate the conditions for more successful projects, perhaps even a more effective popular appropriation of the projects.

In the excerpt above, Escobar explains the role of the critical ethnographer as a witness and participant. As such, this book is a response to Escobar's call for a *hyper-ethnography* of actor-networks in development and it seeks to expose the socio-economic context and conditions within which development is planned and implemented. Escobar's call for re-imaging a new discursive framework is itself a challenge to explore development as a historical process. This book examines such processes through analysing the critical junctures in actor–network relationships that help us to understand how power is contested in the design and implementation of policies.

The first part of the book comprises the deconstructionist perspectives. This part, consisting of two chapters, exposes the spectacle of development and the institutions that govern its systems and language of oppression. The two chapters show the network of actors and discourses that make it hard (but not impossible) to design, experiment with, and implement realistic development interventions at the community level. In this chapter, I have provided a rationale for deconstructing the notion of the spectacle of development. I demonstrate that development is an ongoing class conflict in representation, conceptualization and implementation. During this process, antagonistic groups initiate and implement projects and programmes so as to improve livelihoods, strengthen communities and support the sustainable use of natural resources. The chapter's discussion highlights the prominence of deliberate attempts to implement dominant strategies that lead to increased unemployment, human misery and, arguably, environmental degradation. The theory of bullshit (Frankfurt 1988) has been used to conceptualize the discursive imagery that I have characterized as the spectacle of development.

In Chapter 2, "Language of oppression," the condescending and colonial attitudes that govern the conduct and behaviour of most development experts and organizations are examined. The chapter provides the characteristics of the language of oppression, which comprises the discourses, practices and strategic policies generated and produced within development spectacles. While the chapter identifies oppressors and the language they employ, it also acknowledges that within current development methodologies, even the practices and behaviours of oppressed groups can become oppressive to themselves. These are critical factors that shape the formulation and direction of prevailing development discourses and policies. Nevertheless, within these development spectacles, there are spaces of negotiation, spaces where oppressed or oppressing groups deviate from the norm and expectations, and are able to experiment with interventions that speak to local needs. Freire (1970, 1996a, 1996b) has discussed the nature and role of the radical and humanist educator in motivating communities to design and experiment with their own development, as is the case with community-based natural resources management initiatives.

The second part of the book examines the four opportunities for conceiving deliberative development with and alongside communities. These four critical junctures work as modes of deliberative development and comprise these elements: (a) the voice of the subaltern, (b) living with the people, (c) encountering poverty, and (d) pedagogy of listening.

In Chapter 3, "Capturing subaltern voices," a post-colonial feminist critique in itself, I engage in a discussion of the work of selected post-colonial thinkers: Fanon, Spivak, and Djebar, in order to explore the politics that seems to govern the formulation of alternative voices in development, even though the results are not as transformative as some expect. The central argument in this chapter is that, with or without technology, subaltern groups are already producing radical and critical voices that are themselves alternative perspectives that point the way towards the good living (*buen vivir*) that Escobar argues for. The challenge is to capture these in ways that will contribute to the formulation of policies and strategies. Yet to understand these voices, two things are paramount: First, one has to build respectful and long-term relationships with community groups in order to appreciate the socio-cultural contexts within which these views are conceived and these voices produced. Second, there has to be a deliberate process of understanding and deconstruction of the oppressor by unmasking their language and other tools of signification.

In Chapter 4, "Living with people," I explore one of the most challenging questions faced by students, scholars and practitioners of development, past and present, and that is the question of methodology. Thompson's (1963) concept of *history from below* implies a deliberate attempt by historians to study how marginalized groups live and experience history, that is, the study of history in motion. This entails mastering the skills and tools for living with people and being able to conduct rich and insightful examinations of people's ongoing attempts to make their lives better. This also calls for a new form of writing, one that acknowledges what Escobar (1995) defines as the relational and indigenous ontologies that emphasize ecological sustainability, human dignity, and social justice.

In Chapter 5, "Encountering poverty," a conversation with a renowned development scholar and practitioner, Robert Chambers (1980, 1981, 2005), is revisited, focusing on how experts make sense of poverty. It is the discovery, understanding and the explanation of poverty that prepares the groundwork for resulting development interventions (Chambers 1980, 1981, 2005; Escobar 1995). In *Rural Poverty Unperceived*, Chambers (1980, 1981) points out many biases that either enable or make it impossible for us to see and explain poverty. Like Chambers, I show that apart from certain experiences in upbringing, it is graduate training that we must pay attention to as a critical factor that shapes the way development is perceived, encountered and defined. The discussion follows an imaginary graduate in anthropology who travels from the west into the heart of a country in the south and attempts to support a development intervention within a rural community. On this journey, it is discovered that the deterministic model of development is in conflict with the relational and endogenous ontological perspectives on what constitutes well living.

In the final chapter, "Pedagogy of listening," I return to Gustavo Gutiérrez and Paulo Freire to explore listening, which is becoming a critical concept in the development literature and across a range of social and media practices. The discussion, itself a summation of the arguments in the book, addresses a simple question: what *is* listening? Listening is treated as a major factor that can and should shape how policies are made and implemented. Yet not many training or academic programmes pay attention to this practice because it is assumed that to listen requires doing little or nothing at all, that to listen all one has to do is show up or keep quiet when someone is speaking. Rather, listening is shown to be about tolerance and respect for others (Bessette 2004; Said 1978; Tufte and Mefalopulos 2009). To engage in listening is in fact an act of symbolic war, it is a struggle.

Concluding thoughts

This book offers a revised reading of Escobar's *Encountering Development*, Chambers's *Rural Poverty Unperceived*, Paulo Freire's *Pedagogy of the Oppressed* and Gutiérrez's *A Theology of Liberation*. This rereading requires much more than paraphrasing and explaining sections of their work; rather it involves entering into ethnographic encounters with the nodal points at which dominant approaches in the theory and practice of development occur. This book is a product of my conflicting experiences as a student of critical pedagogy and as one who has had to employ oppressive strategies in order to achieve certain development objectives. I felt a moral duty to write this book when it dawned on me that I was probably involved in the business of oppressing people systematically and, if I was not, I was at least complicit in the theatre of what I thought was liberation—when in actuality I was perpetuating the spectacle of development. This treatise is therefore a reflexive account of my direct and indirect interactions with the praxis of liberation.

The book is born out of the rediscovery of my voice, which had been captured and smothered under the dominant discourses and epistemologies of prevailing development theory and practice. It is a celebration of alternative ways of thinking; the unthought and illegitimate perspectives, symbolically, of telling these seemingly aberrant stories and of explaining the epistemological discomfort I have felt in reading the expositions on the periphery and on the marginalization that I have lived through. As Assia Djebar (1992) explains in the Overture to her book, it is about the resurrection of the soul to move freely and speak even if the body is imprisoned.

This responsibility is, I hope, executed with empathy, humility and an understanding of the multiple and plural stories and experiences in which emphasis is given to narrating the stories of the people standing up and not having their backs bent by the sheer weight of capitalist and patriarchal violence and cannibalism. In some sections, accounts have deliberately been dismembered, reconstituted and fictionalized to avoid initiating confrontation with the ideological Father, who, in Achille Mbembe's (2015) words, has the "shape of a goat's ass" and has a way of "staging" himself creatively as the "pagan god" of development thinking and practice. After all, in the periphery, we live life as a form of fiction, fragmented, edited and represented in policy documents, cannibalized in real life, and reconstituted in our own tales. Truth becomes performed fiction, a form of fantasy.

For Escobar (1995), Chambers (1980, 1981, 2005), Freire (1970, 1996a, 1996b), Gutiérrez (1988), hooks (1994) and most critical theorists and scholars, development is too institutionalized, too instrumentalist and too economically deterministic to provide for the totality of satisfaction that humanity needs. They seem to support the conceptualization of a praxis of liberation in which freedom implies total emancipation from oppression. Whereas development may seem to target socio-economic needs, liberation targets external and internal, material and spiritual forms of development where the aim is to achieve a "fully human life free from all forms of servitude" (Gutiérrez 1988, 71). In this case, liberation is a concept that explains the wishes, prayers and aspirations of oppressed groups who are experiencing social, economic and spiritual servitude. Liberation should also be understood as a historic process that calls on both oppressed and oppressors to create a society that is democratic, equitable, and just—for the benefit of all humanity. But importantly, for Freire, Gutiérrez, Escobar and to an extent, Chambers, liberation refers to spiritual concepts in which people's faith in God and other deities becomes central to their achievement of humanity.

As an industry, development engages numerous scholars, students, practitioners and activists, institutions, organizations and groups with different outlooks and objectives. Alongside this is the fact that numerous factors are challenging us—as students of society—to question the ethics and morality of development. The 2008 financial crisis and the resultant economic meltdown, the emergence of the BRICS (Brazil, Russia, India, China, South Africa), rising global consciousness about ecological issues, strengthening civic activism, and concerns with global terrorism call for the integration of ethnographic methodologies and class analysis in development studies curricula. A new wave of social movements and consciousness, supported by technological forms of mediation, insists on producing alternative voices and perspectives that shape the flow and contestation of power.

After all, "everything is mediated" (Livingstone 2009). Unpacking this complexity requires an investigation of development in operational practice as is the case in the chapters in this book.

The persistent spectacles of development might be explained by the fact that most project officials working in government and NGOs today have not been exposed to a critical theory and pedagogy (Makuwira 2014). The emphasis in most of graduate training is on the tools and strategies for effective development management and administration. A good manager, it is believed, is one who understands protocol, the how-to-dos of administration. Such training instils in graduates a respect for procedures, many of which are authoritarian, and a religious adherence to them often stifles organizational growth and then silences radical progressive voices. And this is the approach taken by many NGOs, who consider themselves "moral crusaders" (Makuwira 2014). Aleksandr Solzhenitsyn's (1962) *One Day in the Life of Ivan Denisovich* offers a thorough analysis of dictatorship as a strict devotion to traditions and norms, even when lives are being lost. Such a dictatorship, as a system of oppression, too often functions as a regime of regulations and behaviours in the spectacle of development.

To contribute to the liberation of the theory and practice of development, a liberatory educator or critical ethnographer must understand and embrace the theory and praxis of change. As conceived and described by Freire (1970, 1996a, 1996b), Fanon (1961, 1965) and Gramsci (1971), this educator must denounce all forms of oppression and accept that potentially, liberatory change takes place when individuals and groups confront their own prejudices, ignorance or arrogance. For this to happen, the educator must listen, since it is only through listening that an opportunity for speaking deliberative development opens up. Speaking and curating development with and alongside communities is fundamental to deliberative development, which opens up pathways for imagining possibilities of social change whose seeds will be sown when oppressed individuals and groups learn to accept that their current situation is unacceptable; that positive change itself, even the very idea of it, is revolutionary and confrontational in nature; that change is destabilizing and brutal as it involves breaking down the very violence that breeds the oppression, often spiritually and empirically. In the context of this book, critical ethnography works as a functional method for unpacking contemporary forms of development bullshit, and for exposing the spectacle that is development. It is emphasized in this chapter that even in the midst of development bullshit, alternative and radical development opportunities are being curated. To curate meaningful development, educators and oppressed groups should first learn to undermine the language of oppression because it masks the dominant paradigm, the system that characterizes the spectacle of development. The next chapter explains how language and discourse function to cement oppression within the spectacle of development—an analysis of which will provide an epistemological platform for constructing the pedagogy of listening in the second part of the book.

Notes

1 The Times Media Digital. 2016. Accessed October 7 from: www.timeslive.co.za/local/2016/10/07/Wits-protester-My-naked-breasts-show-the-power-of-a-womans-body.
2 www.cosmopolitan.com/sex-love/missionary-sex-positions.
3 www.menshealth.com/sex-women/upgrade-missionary-sex.
4 www.menshealth.com/sex-women/45-sex-positions-guys-should-know/slide/33.
5 Ibid.
6 www.iol.co.za/pretoria-news/opinion/why-the-poor-still-vote-anc-1680612.

References

Adichie, Chimamanda Ngozi. 2009. "The danger of a single story." TED Talk. Oxford University. Accessed January 20 2016. www.youtube.com/watch?v=D9Ihs241zeg.

Bakhtin, Mikhail. 1981. *The Dialogic Imagination: Four Essays*. Edited by Michael Holquist. Austin: University of Texas Press.

Bessette, Guy. 2004. *Involving the Community: A Guide to Participatory Development Communication.* Penang and Ottawa: Southbound and International Development Research Centre.

Bourdieu, Pierre. 1983/1991. *Language and Symbolic Power*. Cambridge: Polity Press.

Césaire, Aimé. 1955/1972. *Discourse on Colonialism*. Translated by Joan Pinkham. London: Monthly Review Press.

Chambers, Robert. 1980. *Rural Poverty Unperceived: Problems and Remedies*. Staff Working Paper Number SWP 400. Washington, DC: The World Bank. Accessed September 30 2016. http://documents.worldbank.org/curated/en/909311468766763144/Rural-poverty-unperceived-problems-and-remedies.

Chambers, Robert. 1981. "Poor visibility: How policy makers overlook the poor." New Internationalist website. Issue 96. Accessed January 20 2016. http://newint.org/features/1981/02/01/poor-visibility.

Chambers, Robert. 2005. *Ideas for Development*. London and Sterling: Earthscan.

Charter, Luke. 2016. "Rhodes students protest half naked against rape." *The Daily Dispatch*. April 20. Accessed April 20 2016. www.dispatchlive.co.za/rhodes-students-protest-half-naked-against-rape.

Collier, John and Malcolm Collier. 2000. *Visual Anthropology: Photography as a Research Method*. Albuquerque: University of Mexico Press.

Deleuze, Gilles and Félix Guattari. 1987. *A Thousand Plateaus: Capitalism and Schizophrenia*. Translated by Brian Massumi. London and Minneapolis: University of Minnesota. Accessed January 20 2016. http://projectlamar.com/media/A-Thousand-Plateaus.pdf.

Djebar, Assia. 1992. *Women of Algiers in their Apartment*. Translated by Marjolijn de Jager. Charlottesville and London: University of Virginia Press.

El Guindi, Fadwa. 2004. *Visual Anthropology: Essential Method and Theory*. Walnut Creek, Lanham, New York, Toronto and Oxford: Altamira Press.

Escobar, Arturo. 1995/2012. *Encountering Development: The Making and Unmaking of the Third World*. Princeton: Princeton University Press.

Fadel Fahmy, Mohamed. 2011. "Egyptian blogger Aliaa Elmahdy: Why I posed naked." *CNN Online*. November 20. Accessed January 20 2016. http://edition.cnn.com/2011/11/19/world/meast/nude-blogger-aliaa-magda-elmahdy.

Fanon, Frantz. 1961. *The Wretched of the Earth*. New York: Grove Press.

Fanon, Frantz. 1965. *A Dying Colonialism*. New York: Grove Press.

Frankfurt, Harry. 1988. *The Importance of What We Care About*. Cambridge: Cambridge University Press.

Freire, Paulo. 1970. *Pedagogy of the Oppressed*. London: Penguin.
Freire, Paulo. 1996a. *Letters to Cristina*. New York: Continuum.
Freire, Paulo. 1996b. *An Incredible Conversation*. YouTube Channel. Accessed January 20 2016. www.youtube.com/watch?v=aFWjnkFypFA.
Geertz, Clifford. 1971. "Thick description. Towards an interpretive theory of culture." In *The Interpretation of Cultures: Selected Essays* (pp. 3–30). New York: Basic Books.
Gramsci, Antonio. 1971. *Selections from the Prison Notebooks*. Translated by Quintin Hoare and Geoffrey Nowell Smith. New York: International Publishers.
Gutiérrez, Gustavo. 1988. *A Theology of Liberation: History, Politics, and Salvation*. Translated by Caridad Inda and John Eagleson. Maryknoll, New York: Orbis Books.
Hall, Stuart. 1997. "Spectacle of the other." In *Representation: Cultural Representations and Signifying Practices* (pp. 223–290). London, California and New Dehli: Sage.
Harper, Douglas. 2002. "Thinking about pictures: A case for photo elicitation." *Visual Studies*, (17)1: 13–26.
Hitchens, Christopher. 1995. *The Missionary Position: Mother Teresa in Theory and Practice*. Brooklyn, London and Paris: Verso.
hooks, bell. 1994. *Teaching to Transgress: Education as the Practice of Freedom*. London and New York: Routledge.
Lerner, Daniel. 1958. *The Passing of Traditional Society: Modernizing the Middle East*. New York and London: Free Press and Collier-Macmillan.
Livingstone, Sonia. 2009. "On the mediation of everything: ICA presidential address 2008." *Journal of Communication*, 59(1): 1–18. Accessed November 26 2016. http://eprints.lse.ac.uk/21420.
Makuwira, Jonathan. 2014. *Non-Governmental Development Organizations and the Poverty Reduction Agenda: The Moral Crusaders*. London and New York: Routledge.
Mansell, Robin. 1982. "The 'new dominant paradigm' in communication: Transformation versus adaptation." *Canadian Journal of Communication*, 8(3): 42–60. Accessed September 20 2016. www.cjc-online.ca/index.php/journal/article/view/278/184.
Mansell, Robin. 2011. "Whose knowledge counts? A political economy of the knowledge-based society/economy." Seminar Presentation. Institute of Development Studies, University of Sussex, Brighton, United Kingdom, January 26.
Marinovich, Greg. 2016 *Murder at Small Koppie: The Real Story of the Marikana Massacre*. Johannesburg: Penguin Random House.
Marx, Karl. 1852/2010. *The Eighteenth Brumaire of Louis Bonaparte*. New York: *Die Revolution* Issue 1.
Mbembe, Achille. 2001. *On the Postcolony*. Berkeley, CA: University of California Press.
Mbembe, Achille. 2015. The value of Africa's aesthetics. *Mail and Guardian Online*. May 15. Accessed March 20 2017. http://mg.co.za/article/2015-05-14-the-value-of-africas-aesthetics.
Mbembe, Achille and Esprit. 2008. "What is postcolonial theory? An interview with Achille Mbembe." Conducted by Olivier Mongin, Nathalie Lempereur and Jean-Louis Schlegel. In *Eurozine*, September 1. Accessed January 20 2016. www.eurozine.com/articles/2008-01-09-mbembe-en.html.
Moatshe, Rapula. 2016. "ANC women bare bottoms in protest." *Independent Online News*. January 19. Accessed January 20 2016. www.iol.co.za/news/south-africa/gauteng/ anc-women-bare-bottoms-in-protest-1972684.
Mohanty, Chandra Talpade. 2003. *Feminism without Borders: Decolonizing Theory, Practicing Solidarity*. Durham, NC: Duke University Press.
Mosse, David. 2005. *Cultivating Development: An Ethnography of Aid Policy and Practice*. London: Pluto Press.

Nkuna, Kulani. 2016. "Pornography of power: Interview with Ayanda Mabulu." *Culture Review*. Accessed January 20 2016. www.culture-review.co.za/pornography-of-power.

Rostow, Walt. 1960. *The Stages of Economic Growth: A Non-Communist Manifesto.* Cambridge: Cambridge University Press.

Ruby, Jay. 1991. "Speaking for, speaking about, speaking with, or speaking alongside – An anthropological and documentary dilemma." *Visual Anthropology Review*, 7(2): 50–67.

Ruby, Jay. 2000. *Picturing Culture: Explorations of Film and Anthropology*. Chicago, IL: Chicago University Press.

Said, Edward. 1978. *Orientalism*. New York: Random House.

Schramm, Wilbur. 1964. *Mass Media and National Development: The Role of Information in the Developing Countries*. Stanford: Stanford University Press.

Solzhenitsyn, Aleksandr. 1962/2005. *One Day in the Life of Ivan Denisovich.* Translated by H.T. Willetts. New York: Farrar, Straus and Giroux.

Spivak, Gayatri. 1988. "Can the subaltern speak?" In Nelson Cary and Lawrence Grossberg (eds), *Marxism and the Interpretation of Culture* (pp. 271–313). Chicago, IL: University of Illinois.

Thompson, Edward Palmer. 1963. *The Making of the English Working Class*. London: Vintage Books.

Tomaselli, Keyan (ed.). 2006. *Writing in the San/d: Auto-ethnography among Indigenous South Africans,* Lanham, New York, Toronto and Plymouth: Altamira Press.

Tufte, Thomas and Paolo Mefalopulos. 2009. *Participatory Communication: A Practical Guide.* Washington, DC: The World Bank.

UNAIDS. 2012. "Investing for results - Results for people: A people-centred investment tool towards ending AIDS." Geneva: Joint UN Programme for HIV and AIDS. Accessed September 30 2016. www.unaids.org/sites/default/files/sub_landing/files/JC2359_investing-for-results_en.pdf.

UK Government. 2008. *Communities in Control: Real People, Real Power.* London: Department of Communities and Local Government.

Williams, Raymond. 1961. *The Long Revolution*. London: Chatto and Windus.

2

"WE CAME, WE SAW, HE DIED"

Language of oppression

Setting the context

This chapter continues the discussion of Chapter 1 by exploring the ways through which language and discourse are central to the creation and sustenance of the praxis of the spectacle of development. Understanding oppression is a critical feature of an engaged pedagogy of the oppressed (Freire 1970, 1996a, 1996b; Gutiérrez 1988; hooks 1994). Oppression can be understood as a plural concept insofar as it is a behavioural category of various stakeholders, professionals and community groups within the field of development practice. The generic oppressor, the perpetrator of this regime of oppression, exists in various forms. They may be external (as in Mbembe's autocrat) or internal (as in Fanon's native elite) but what connects them is their colonial, paternalistic and condescending attitude against subaltern interests (Fanon 1961, 1965; Mbembe 2001, 2015; Wa Thiong'o 1977). The oppressor can also be a member of a marginalized group (Freire 1970, 1996a, 1996b). As such, it is almost impossible to define this oppressor in terms of personal attributes; rather the chapter discusses oppression as a behaviour that can be displayed by anyone. This chapter then extends my conversation with the aforementioned scholars to critically consider the discursive tools employed by these various forms of oppressors so as to consolidate power in the ideological and material world. Attention is given especially to the spoken word, the manners, the values and other forms of social and cultural signification.

This chapter is also a confession in itself, as it explores my experiences of *becoming* an oppressor in development contexts, thereby exposing deliberative development practice to contradictions, especially when it comes to the acquisition of subaltern perspectives. In this process, ideology becomes key in relation to consciously being aware of being an oppressor which was, in many ways, the case with my development practices. This chapter thus acknowledges two forms of oppression: the oppression by individuals who may not necessarily be ideologically aware of their role, but rather see themselves more as change agents, as pointed out by Freire (1970, 1996a, 1996b) in his exposition of the banking educator. Then there is also the oppression carried out by people like myself, who have grown up as oppressed, have acquired critical education and hence subaltern perspectives. As such, the discourse and practices of the pedagogy of liberation should also aim to rescue oppressors like me as advised by Freire (1970) and hooks (1994), so that my teaching, research and development praxes should be unmasked and liberated from my inability to speak with and alongside communities in the process of achieving self-actualization and conceiving deliberative development. In fact, the African American educator, bell hooks (1994, 2) emphasizes that learning is a "counter-hegemonic act" in which teachers and students "enact a revolutionary pedagogy of resistance."

Oppression in this case should not just be associated with individuals or institutions. Rather for Gutiérrez (1988) it should also be understood within a context of behaviours, beliefs and, importantly, the ideological structures of inequality. Carter Woodson (1933) argues that to control human actions and behaviour, all that is needed is to control thoughts. Likewise Lukes (2005) explains the three-dimensional view of power as a chain of events, which can be mobilized and set in motion and eventually require no group or institution to direct its implementation. This insight is helpful in explaining the nature of the oppression as experienced by oppressed groups. In the same vein, Bourdieu (1991) discusses the notion of symbolic power in exploring how society is organized. If speaking development locally is to be rescued from its capture by the discourses and practices of the development spectacles, oppression itself must be unmasked and deconstructed, which is a significant aspect of Gutiérrez's and Freire's critical pedagogy.

This oppression should not be understood as one side of a binary opposition to liberation because, as pointed out earlier, there are many grey areas in between; in fact, there are moments and ruptures when oppression functions as liberation. This thought is significant, because as societies work towards liberating the oppressed subaltern groups, there is conscious or subconscious use of the language and discourse of the oppressor. Freire (1996b, Interview) referred to this phenomenon and language as the "dominant syntax" and it is implicated in perpetuating and maintaining unequal power relations. Practitioners of a critical pedagogy and other development practitioners need to be aware of violence that can be associated with their discourse, even in seemingly banal assignments such as field reports, because, cumulatively, the use of the 'dominant syntax' contributes to the formulation of a regime of representation which ultimately determines the character and sustenance of policy formulation at international, regional, national and local levels. And these discourses and the representations they invoke shape the dialogue of stakeholder engagement within development contexts.

Understanding the generic oppressor

My point of departure is Gutiérrez (1988) and Freire (1970, 1996a, 1996b) who conceive of an oppressor as an individual or individuals who are, deliberately or subconsciously, opposed to liberatory practices and interventions. This means that there are various kinds of oppressors within the development chain: educators, researchers, practitioners, NGOs, community leaders, opinion makers, media institutions and the like. What this implies is that there is no homogeneous group of an oppressor and not all oppressors are the same. Yet conceptually there are certain elements and attributes that are common to all these various kinds of oppressors. To identify them I start by asking questions about the bourgeois expert who Escobar (1995, xvi) depicts as the transnationalized middle-class specialist "whose training, interests, tastes, and economic and political goals coincide enough to keep the development actor-networks going, and often well-oiled." For this discussion then, we are interested in unmasking oppression perpetuated by those who have the education and the strategic awareness and are involved in policy making and planning as well as implementation (that includes monitoring and evaluation as well). These are experts who "disseminate a normalized rationality and common sense with significant cultural and political consequences" (Escobar 1995, xvi). It must nevertheless be emphasized here that not all experts are oppressors; I am referring to the category of experts whose thinking, behaviour and practices exhibit the attributes of the language of oppression identified later in this chapter.

As such, these experts, while claiming to have a deep understanding of locality and people, often manage to perpetuate fanciful, mechanistic, deterministic and civilizational notions of modernity, albeit sometimes using new terms and concepts. Using a repertoire of scientific evidence, such experts often advise governments and other institutions—including local organizations—to dismantle cultural, economic, and political structures and processes that are in fact progressive and have been contributing to local well-being for centuries (Chambers 1980, 1981, 2005; Escobar 1995). This strategy may be enacted to foster the employment of western and modern technologies, the use of which may lead to improvement as measured by certain economic indicators, yet do little or nothing to address concerns about social justice and ecological sustainability, or indeed the spirituality that contributes to the well-being of a community. Such a category of oppressor is an important arbitrator in the creation and exchange of symbolic power within the spectacle of development. Bourdieu (1991, 168–170) defines symbolic power as that which constitutes "the given through utterances, of making people see and believe, of confirming or transforming the vision of the world and, thereby, action on the world and thus the world itself."

Central to the production and exchange of this power is its capacity to be recognized and misrecognized, hence its existence and operation depend on the ability of a group of people to submit to "the structure of the field" within which it is produced, exchanged and reproduced (Bourdieu 1991, 170).

Through analysing what is conceived as a humanist critical pedagogy, Freire introduces a framework for examining the structure of the context, Bourdieu's (1991) "field," within which symbolic power of development generates and exchanges discourses about, and of, oppression. Actually, as if communicating with Bourdieu (1991), Freire (1970, 1996a, 1996b) examines this "field" and the social contexts in which the relationships between the educators and educatees are shaped by colonial, linear and dehumanizing discourses. In the end, the rhizomatic relationship (Deleuze and Guattari 1987) that develops between the educator and educatee or the policy maker/practitioner/planner and the community is one of inequality, and thus of oppression. Here, the oppressor is both perpetrator and product of an oppressive relationship that aims to marginalize oppressed groups. So who is this oppressor? Freire (1970, 58–60) defines the oppressor as:

> The oppressor consciousness tends to transform everything surrounding it into an object of its domination. The oppressors develop the conviction that it is possible for them to transform everything into objects of their purchasing power; hence their strictly materialistic concept of existence. … The oppressors do not perceive their monopoly on having more as a privilege which dehumanizes others and themselves. … The oppressors are using science and technology as unquestionably powerful instruments for their purpose: the maintenance of the oppressive order through manipulation and repression.

This quotation helps to identify a categorical oppressor, but certain characteristics become clearer in specific situations. Drawing on Lukes's (2005) three-dimensional view of power and Bourdieu's (1991) concept of symbolic power, this chapter conceives of the oppressor on the institutional and individual levels. In the prevailing situation in development practice, there is an organized systemic discourse and set of structures that influence the way development is taught, thought about, organized and practised. The individual oppressor does not operate in isolation, but rather through this structured, orderly and symbolic set of structures and processes and systems that allow oppression to operate. The oppressor is rooted in this "field" to borrow Bourdieu's terminology.

This "field" comprises, among other attributes, the ambivalent and oftentimes contradictory discourses of colonization and humanism. Mbembe (Mbembe and Esprit 2008) points out that one justification for past and present colonization has been to spread European humanism as a force for good. Eventually, however, such European humanism mutates into a system of ideas that permeate international and national institutions and processes, which Mbembe (2015), in a new Preface to *On the Postcolony,* describes as the Father. In discussing this Father, Mbembe (2015, 1) discovers something more insidious, a necropolitical force, that "was something like a goat's ass that lived under the curse, and stood opposite the face of a pagan god—death concealed in the darkness as well as darkness in the full light of day, shining and stinking." This Father is both the oppressor and the system of oppression, with a distinct way of speaking and exhibiting a regime of discursive narratives that are inconsistent with the values of deliberative development. So, how central is language in the discursive construction of oppression?

Language and representation in oppression

Communication is central to the art and science of oppression. Sartre (1961) discusses the notion of the native elite, a localized version of Escobar's (1995) transnationalized expert. These elite experts have had their mouths "stuffed full with high-sounding phrases, grand glutinous words that stuck to the teeth," and, in the end, they are "whitewashed" with "nothing left to say to their brothers; they only echoed" (Sartre 1961, 7). Of course Sartre was discussing the teething period of political independence in Africa and the emergence of what Marx (1852/2010) conceives of as a predatory class. What is clear is that oppression survives through the structures and processes that modern capitalist systems put in place, a phenomenon that both Mbembe (2001) and Bourdieu (1991) portray as arbitrary rules and regulations. For example, the rules governing public procurement are manipulated to ensure that businesses close to ruling parties benefit. This can be coated with language and discourses of affirmative action, which on paper may seem to aim to address pre-existing socio-economic inequalities.

Like the many poststructuralists before him, Bourdieu (1991) recognizes the significance of language in constructing and perpetuating a social reality. For Bourdieu (1991, 166) symbolic power is a capability that allows the construction of the "immediate meaning of the world." In this case, language and communication are vital avenues for constructing and perpetuating an imaginary that serves to explain and validate the actions of the oppressor, which usually result in inequality and injustice. Communication does not only constitute language, but also encompasses a range of linguistic practices and activities that go beyond speaking. For instance, the clothes we put on communicate certain values and things about ourselves and our thinking. Dressing is ideological. The colour of the shoes, the shirts, jackets or neckties communicate more things about class, identity and belonging than most people care to think about. In *Letters to Cristina*, Freire (1996a) confesses to an incident during his childhood involving stealing and eating chicken with his family when they were impoverished as a result of his father's death. He describes the neighbours searching for their chicken and openly suspecting the kids from the poor neighbourhoods of having stolen it (Freire 1996a). It was their forms and manner of dressing, alongside their middle-class status that protected them from suspicion. As such, it can be argued that within development practice, dressing and other forms of self-representation are critical forms of submission to symbolic power.

In critical theory, language is treated as a system of representation (Bourdieu 1991; Hall 1997). As such, language implies organized communicative acts and actions that may either challenge or reinforce certain power structures, but always operate within the "gnoseological order" that symbolic power constructs for us.

Language is a representation system that allows humans to organize and recognize their world. Thus, language can be performed as an act of war, either as a form of defence (protecting class interests) or as a rebellion (against these interests and the status quo). The point is that language is not neutral. Our manner of speech is an important element in the construction of Bourdieu's gnoseological order.

Attributes of the language of oppression

A point of departure for a consideration of the language of oppression is former US Secretary of State Hillary Clinton's reaction soon after the former Libyan leader Muammar Qaddafi was captured and assassinated. Responding to a CBS TV News journalist's question about how she had taken the news, the smiling Hillary Clinton, who had passed through Libya a couple of days before the event, triumphantly observed, "we came, we saw, he died."[1] When asked if her visit could be linked to the assassination of Qaddafi, she gives a sarcastic chuckle and confesses, "I am sure it did." In a way, such an assumption footnotes the agency of the Libyan rebel movement that opposed Qaddafi long before the international forces started bombing the country. Likewise, President Bush speaking after the September 11 2001 attacks in New York City, contended, "either you are with us or against us," a line that had decades earlier appeared in the movie *Ben Hur*, when Messala warns Judah of the importance of supporting Roman domination and oppression of the Jews, Judah Ben Hur's people. Again, such an assertion removes any agency for the other to identify and forge a different or 'third way,' so to speak. These aspects of President Bush's and Senator Clinton's discourse offer us a starting point to examine the language of oppression within the context of development theory and practice. This chapter reviews four key attributes of the language of oppression that manifest in various contexts.

The first attribute is that often the language of oppression, humanist as it might appear in its perspective, fails to recognize the other's identity and place in history, a behaviour conceptualized by Mbembe (2015) as a kind of "goat's ass that lives under the curse." The other is the subject who is different from us whose race, gender or other social trajectories mark him or her out as being different. For Said (1978), the other is the Orient, the subject of the periphery, the one different from the Occident. In modernist and colonial humanism, the assumption is made that the other seeks to become like the Occident, the Renaissance man. In the classic text, *The Passing of Traditional Society*, Daniel Lerner (1958, 38) contends, "what the west is, the east seeks to become." Within the language of oppression western modernity is what every other being seeks to attain. As Escobar (1995) and Gutiérrez (1988) point out, development refers to the assumption that peoples of the world seek to emulate what has gone on in the west. In the quotes above, when President Bush observes that other nations in the world had only two choices, this can be construed as suggesting that there was no choice, because the other choice meant certain death and destruction. The other could not choose a third way, one of not adhering to the choices on offer—because that third choice was not on the table.

The voluntary medical male circumcision (VMMC) intervention in the south is a case in point. Not many years ago, western missionaries were condescendingly questioning the rationale in traditional societies for circumcising their young men. Even today, studies based on western scientific models seem to suggest that these traditional circumcisions are contributing to the spread of HIV—although they do not look at other socio-cultural factors that fuel the spread of the virus. Within current approaches towards HIV prevention however, the VMMC intervention is presented as a solution that offers a 60 per cent chance of protection from HIV infection, as being very modern and safe, and an advance on the traditional circumcision that continues to be regarded as fuelling the spread of the virus. This undermining of most traditional practices has its roots in both the orientalist and modernist projects.

In a revised preface to *Orientalism* written in the aftermath of September 11 2001, Said distinguishes between the practice of studying the other with empathy and understanding, and examining the other with arrogance and a general lack of understanding. The context within which VMMC is being forcibly promoted and sold by western funding agencies to uncritical policy makers in the south is a demonstration of the orientalist approaches of oppression. Even though evidence indicates a 60 per cent rate of protection, one still needs to use condoms. In areas where very few sexually active males are coming for VMMC, western institutions are still pouring in huge amounts of resources—notwithstanding the fact that Know Your Epidemic studies in various countries are pointing to unequal power relations as being a significant factor contributing to fuelling new infections. Vulnerable groups such as young women, sex workers and LGBTI groups are experiencing new infections globally, since inequality prevents them from accessing prevention and treatment services. Freire (1970, 1996a, 1996b) observes that within the contexts of oppression, the future is already a given. In this case, the privileging of a western and modernist and almost exclusively medical model seems to footnote the social inequalities within which the virus is being transmitted.

Orientalism influences the design and implementation of many development policies in which the other, the Orient, is posited as a major beneficiary. What the orientalist VMMC discourse fails to recognize is the other's previous and ongoing attempts at circumcision. The modernist VMMC initiatives disregard the traditional institutions that have circumcised sexually active males over the years, but also used circumcision as a rite of passage, in order to pass on important traditional knowledge on social, cultural and economic governance of a community. In the VMMC story, development policy and practice has reduced traditional circumcision to a mere traditional practice, without acknowledging its indigenous knowledge aspects. What this leads us to is that, as is being experimented with in other parts of the south, there have to be areas of negotiation, and not necessarily the total abandonment of the VMMC approach. Traditional circumcision has to be promoted alongside medical circumcision so that young men are no longer being circumcised to prevent HIV only, but also allow traditional systems to provide the significant social education that teaches young men to be responsible adults who respect women and men.

The second feature of the language of oppression is illustrated by the second part of Senator Clinton's response to Qaddafi's death in 2011 in the CBS TV television interview: "We came, we saw, he died." The oppressor's language is full of violence and references to violence. The scenes surrounding Muammar Qaddafi's capture, torture and assassination are well documented and available on digital media such as YouTube. Senator Clinton herself boldly implied in that CBS TV interview that she believed her visit to the country a few days earlier had something to do with Gaddafi's terrible end. Her on-air aside "I am sure it did" (suggesting her visit resulted in the capture and assassination) brings up memories of the involvement of the US and other imperial powers in the death of other southern leaders such as Patrice Lumumba, Thomas Sankara, Samora Machel and other radical leaders. Oftentimes, symbolic and material violence denotes and connotes a deliberate denial of another person's right to dignity, hence its practice can be considered to be a rejection of the humanity of the other. As Fanon states in *The Wretched of the Earth* (1961) as well as in *A Dying Colonialism* (1965), violence is a form of dehumanization.

The language of oppression makes it clear that anyone who seeks to challenge the oppressor's way of seeing and doing things should expect complete subjugation and inhumane treatment. Within the development context this is pointed out, albeit not necessarily in black and white. There are already tested models and strategies that are 'recommended.' The term that comes up often is 'available body of evidence.' Development as a system of oppression (and also of liberation) therefore seems to consider change as unidirectional—most interventions start from research, strategies and inputs while expecting outputs, outcomes and social change. The notion of 'unidirectional' here requires some qualification. It refers to more than the western-centric nature of interventions, but also to the lack of flexibility that accommodates alternative models and thinking. In this case, the language of strategies, models and policies functions as a form of symbolic power that guides the actions and thinking of policy makers, experts, researchers, educators, stakeholders and communities.

The implication is that although the *unidirection-ness* of this planned change will involve deliberative development (with elements of community participation), what is clear from Clinton's vision of change is that the oppressed have little or no agency at all in modifying the interventions. And if they attempt to go outside the box provided by the symbols of spectacles of development, then the likelihood of external funding not being made available to implement those initiatives is very high. It is in the face of this predicament that many self-funded forms of cooperative development have emerged the world over, in which local groups and external institutions and agents negotiate the kind of development that would speak to the needs of various stakeholders. The cooperatives movement that emerged in the 1980s was an attempt to solve this predicament of the unidirection-ness of dominant development—and provided local economic groups (such as farmers) with leverage in how development was conceived and implemented.

The third factor in the language of oppression is that it is also concerned with symbolic and non-material violence. Senator Clinton says, "we came, *we saw*." This kind of *seeing* is not passive. Nor is such seeing just about having sight of an event or experience. This *seeing* is the kind of seeing that precedes the death of traditional society whose passing Daniel Lerner (1958), Walt Rostow (1960) and Wilber Schramm (1964) prophesied. This is the very violence of representation. The act of seeing here seems to encompass all facets of the representation of Libya's problems by the western community. It is the kind of seeing that resulted in the United Nations Security Council Resolution 1973 (2011) that would lead to western military intervention and then to the assassination of Qaddafi. This pattern had worked in other parts of the global south.

Within the western and international media, the problems in Libya were constructed and linked to the other Arab revolutions in Tunisia, Egypt and Syria. Conferences and special journal editions in the west discussed the role of Twitter or YouTube in the "Arab revolutions." In Libya, Yemen or Syria, defining the political problems through the frame of revolution allowed the imperial forces to make a space for military intervention. In Egypt, the same western powers that supported the ousting of Hosni Mubarak allowed the country's military to depose a democratically elected president, Morsi (Kingsley 2015). General Abdel Fattah el-Sisi would be elected president in disputed elections whose processes were strategically organized to put him in power (Kingsley 2015). As a policy of containment in the Middle East, the US continues to sell fighter jets and other military hardware to the Egyptian military; after all, the US has never described what has happened in Egypt as a military coup (Kingsley 2015). On the other hand, Syria and Libya are being torn apart by sectarian violence that is being fuelled by western and regional imperialism. All these military interventions were preceded by and are a product of a regime of representation that comprises a kind of seeing and speaking, and in many cases resulting in international policies calling for all manner of positive and negative ideological and military intervention. It must be mentioned that certain military interventions are ideologically positive. Delaying military intervention in Rwanda in the 1990s resulted in genocide. The UN military intervention in South Sudan or the Democratic Republic of Congo is necessary because there are high levels of socio-political instability that could result in massive loss of lives if forces were to be withdrawn.

Nevertheless, as is the case in modernist policy making, Clinton's act of seeing can be understood to refer to the whole regime of representation—describing the problem as well as its solution. Freire (1996b, Interview) describes how this way of seeing the future comes to be treated as a fact, and as such, works as an intervention in itself. Escobar (1995) discusses how similar regimes of representation describe the problems of the south in ways that pave the way for and enable the resulting spectacles of development interventions. Likewise, Mahmood Mamdani (2007) discusses the politicality of representation in which orientalist representations in the western and international media serve as a prerequisite for certain kinds of development interventions. He draws an analogy between the tragedies in Darfur and Iraq, arguing that Darfur's tragedy is termed genocide, while Iraq's is defined as insurgency and counter-insurgency. What Mamdani is suggesting here is the strong connection between representation and ideology on one hand and development and military intervention on the other.

The language of oppression thus carries with it a kind of symbolic violence in that its representations provide a rationale for violent ideological and material interventions. Such representations often give legitimacy to unpopular or unrealistic interventions. This regime of representation encompasses television programmes on and about the south; western university centres of excellence specializing in the study of certain geographical regions; graduate students and lecturers who function as specialists on certain practices and regions in the south; consultants—Escobar's transnational middle-class specialists—hired by international development organizations; and even blogs and online entries by tourists visiting the south. Much of this information contributes to and becomes a specialized knowledge repository on and about the other and the south that eventually informs policy, strategies and decisions.

Within development contexts, an example of the oppressors' sophistication in the creation and sustenance of colonial representations is through interventions in policies and strategies. A network of transnationalized experts, donors and organizations, takes extra care in controlling national and local institutions and the processes involved in the development of strategies that will guide the design and implementation of development policies. Such tactics comprise what Steven Lukes (2005) conceives of as the mobilization of bias whereby these powerful elements ensure the control of the agenda outside the legitimate structures and institutions of policy making. This is achieved through informal conversations outside meetings (they could be over tea or dinner/lunch) in which the organizations in question emphasize to responsible officers what is expected so that they can receive the provision of financial and logistical support to specific interventions, while leaving others without any support, and all of this is achieved by bringing in international experts and advisers.

In my development work, I have encountered technical advisers provided by North American or European organizations who offered to support my professional portfolio and work plans even if I had not requested such support; I encountered easy access to resources for LGBTI programming that was not even evidence-based (even when all other interventions required to conform to the results-based management framework), and there was an insistence on certain bodies of evidence generated with the support of western organizations. What was very clear in this case was that the strategic mobilization of bias comprised institutional processes and practices by international development organizations to protect, ensure and safeguard their ideological interests within public health programming. My experience working in and with international development organizations is that an endogenous policy or strategy is often a reflection of a collection of donor perspectives about what they want to achieve in a particular sector. In my case, I had huge responsibilities for coordinating policy formulation. Sometimes a donor representative would call me at night and casually spell out very clearly what they were expecting from a series of impending meetings and processes. I understood that it was being made clear that it was up to me to steer the conversations to ensure that policy decisions reflected what had been made clear to me in the phone call.

Even if tempers were flaring and there were disagreements with the policy proposals, it was clear to us as local experts and participants that, if we wanted continued financial and logistical support, the policies had to be written in certain ways and reflect certain world views and perspectives even if there was no evidence to support them. The language of oppression thus comprises an institutionalized system that operates through teams of technical advisers and carefully chosen international consultants who guide and dictate what goes into a policy or a strategy. In practice, it is typically representatives of donors and international organizations who end up writing local strategies by fronting for local experts and programme workers. The guidelines and language governing the development of such strategies are usually set out in a way that is beyond the comprehension of most local experts and other participants at least to some extent. Even when many local people attend consultation sessions, they end up contributing little or resorting to silence when they are intellectually intimidated out of making positive contributions.

This charade of policy making therefore contributes to the organized production of specialized knowledge that Said described as orientalism. And for Said, such specialized knowledge contributes to the process of colonialism, in this case through public health interventions. Interventions designed by international development institutions as well as local NGOs seem to imagine that traditional practices are fuelling the spread of the virus, yet there is an upward spiral of new infections among young urban, educated and working groups, sex workers and other most-at-risk groups, including married people. The question to ask is why interventions focus on a factor that is least likely to contribute to the spread of HIV? This does not necessarily mean that all western interventions are colonial and oppressive and thus should be discarded. The argument here is that communicative spaces should be opened up where western organizations can learn to listen to experiences on the ground rather than work to undermine years of rights-based advocacy that has contributed to advancement in social changes on the ground. Instead of, for example, rushing to develop LGBTI-specific strategies that promote population-targeted health services, western organizations should appreciate the strategic role of the public health service model which is operative in many parts of the south, and which does not identify any demographic or social group. Unfortunately, human rights civil society organizations, competing for western and international funding, seem to make unnecessary noise that advocates for such rights and, in the process, undermines years of quiet advocacy that endogenous organizations and government departments have carved out to accommodate LGBTI rights within very hostile and homophobic environments. Developing population-specific health interventions modelled on western health financing models will only increase tensions and frictions between departments (whose governments have criminalized homosexuality) and the minority groups in question. The question is why do human rights civil society organizations engage in unproductive and confrontational advocacy even to the detriment of the welfare of the minority groups they are representing?

The answer lies in Sartre's preface to Fanon's *Wretched of the Earth* (1961). Discussing the concept of mimicry, he describes the native bourgeoisie as having been "whitewashed" and are thus able only to "echo" what has been taught to them: "they branded them, as with a red-hot iron, with the principles of western culture" (Sartre 1961, 7). In this context, mimicry is seen as a discursive process that enables the reproduction of the oppressor's manner of speaking by the oppressed. Actually, Makuwira (2014) criticizes the culture of lack of thinking, reflection and appraisal among NGOs that rarely engage in ideological reflections on some of their advocacy.

What Sartre and Makuwira are arguing is that the oppressor's social codes and semiotic structures are being taken up and reinvigorated by the oppressed. The oppressor needs qualification here. Even local organizations and individuals become oppressors. So the concept of a language of oppression does not refer only to discursive practices by some western and international organizations that exhibit the characteristics laid out in this chapter; the oppressors also comprise endogenous and local organizations that display similar attributes. It is the reason Makuwira (2014) brands such development organizations 'moral crusaders,' for while their agenda flags liberation, their programmes of action are oppressive and counter-productive to the liberation agenda. In this vein, uncritical project officers from the petty bourgeois class who Sartre defines as "walking lies" who have "nothing left to say to their brothers" tend to reproduce the orientalist development literature, research methodologies and perceptions in which southern traditions are portrayed as static and very much stuck in the past. The oppressor, who in this case ranges from a government policy maker to a western technical adviser, assumes the role of the saviour, Makuwira's "moral crusader"—in this case the project funder with financing largely coming from outside donors or the private sector, most of whom have grown up on media images and messages of pity and desperation. Most of these benefactors develop feelings of moral obligation and seem to think they are making life-saving interventions in a way that echoes what is depicted in Joseph Conrad's *Heart of Darkness*—this is discussed in detail in Chapter 5, "Encountering poverty." This is not to dismiss all development interventions by western organizations as having insidious motivations. What this chapter is questioning is the lack of empathy for how the other feels about these interventions; the lack of sincere conversations about the pros and cons of planned interventions. Building a clinic in a rural village may be a necessary biomedical intervention to curb neonatal deaths. Even if an organization has the requisite resources, it has to open up the space for critical thinking on how this clinic will be sustained by local people and organizations. It should for instance, open up a space for discussing how traditional birth attendants can work within and support this new clinic.

It should also be emphasized that the orientalist literature does not always originate in western organizations and institutions. Some of this discourse is at times generated by citizens of the south for their own socio-political or economic expediency. Perhaps for southern civil society organizations, certain issues are over-emphasized, which gives the organizations some international prominence and, as a result, enables them to secure funding for advocacy work and interventions. This is not to diminish the work of excellent rights advocacy organizations that are fighting to ensure a more egalitarian, democratic and just society. Another brand of self-orientalist literature comes from southern citizens seeking political and economic opportunities in the north through asylum or immigration. Individuals and families are known to exaggerate certain oppressive situations in home countries (crime, persecution, harmful traditional practices) in order to ensure work or asylum visas are secured in the host country. Again, to emphasize, there are numerous oppressive traditions such as genital mutilation that are practised in some (and not all) places in the south, and they require individual and collective diligence and programmatic creativity to eradicate.

The fourth aspect of the language of oppression concerns pity. Lilie Chouliraki's (2008) exploration of *The Spectatorship of Suffering* discusses the history of humanitarian communication and its epistemological foundations where the focus has been on pulling together resources to save "the other" from themselves. Building on Boltanski's notions of pity and suffering, Chouliaraki (2008) examines how images of pity towards the suffering other, especially the suffering child or the suffering mother, are used in fundraising efforts by international development organizations. She argues that the aim is not just to shock people out of their moral comfort zones as a strategy to raise consciousness in western audiences about the others' suffering. Rather the aim is to motivate them to act by donating cash or in kind to help salvage devastating situations in the south.

In this context, Chouliaraki (2008) shows how this language of pity and its tone may imitate western, eastern and indigenous deities. For western audiences donating to specific causes such as feeding the girl child, building schools or providing clean water enhances their faith and makes them feel engaged in critical challenges facing humanity. For eastern audiences, such language and acts of pity seems to bring people to Allah, Buddha or other deities they believe in. As the audiences witness the suffering on their television screens or in their newspapers, it is assumed that they will be moved to take action by donating. By doing so, they are connecting with the distant sufferer—they suffer with them like Christ himself. But as these audiences are faced with overly saturated media portraying humanitarian images on their televisions, on social media, and on the streets (where volunteers are begging for more financial resources), Chouliaraki (2008) argues that "fatigue" sets in.

The language of oppression in this case has a paternalistic tone and the voice of the oppressed is muted or absent altogether. The poor women and children in humanitarian advertisements are present and visible in their suffering, but they rarely speak; it is the voice of the oppressor that speaks for them, just as Marx (1852/2010) described in the muting of the oppressed in *Eighteenth Brumaire of Louis Bonaparte*. The public campaigns to save southern countries in one way or the other—from famine or gender-based or other forms of structural violence—create a platform for the western media to bring a discussion into northern sitting rooms, pubs and other public spaces. Mediatized campaigns such as *Kony 2012* or *Live Aid* are examples of instances where such orientalist campaigns strategically overlook the material conditions which gave rise to the problems, and worse, the allusion to pity results in *thingification* (Césaire 1955) and the absenting of the oppressed who it is argued the campaigns are for. Like the four women that Delacroix observed and painted into *Women of Algiers in their Apartment*, Chouliaraki's "images of pity" in the mainstream media mute and deny the voice of marginalized subjects. By denying the oppressed voices when they deserve to speak for themselves, the oppressed are stripped of their humanity, power and dignity. Such is the power of humanitarian communication that in its noble duty to achieve positive outcomes for marginalized groups, silencing their voices becomes a necessary marketing strategy. In the end, pity becomes a commodity and it is these images of pity that represent the oppressed to generate interest and move northern spectators to action by donating financial or human resources.

The oppressor in development contexts

As observed in passing, defining an oppressor is problematic because the concept itself refers to a process of becoming, as an ongoing engagement with empirical reality. Being an oppressor happens within human relationships. It is therefore possible for one to become an oppressor at one point and then an oppressed at another point. The production and reproduction of human relationships within Bourdieu's "field" determines oppressor–oppressed relationships. For purposes of this discussion, there are a few elements that can be gleaned from examining various forms of oppressors at a given point in human relationships. Within the development context, the oppressor is not a simplistic and static empirical category that, in some post-colonial literature (Memmi 1965), seems to be easily defined and considered as western, male and white. Of course, Escobar's allusion to middle-class experts might imply that we are dealing with the bourgeois class that has collaborated with and in some cases taken over administrative responsibilities from colonial administrators, a phenomenon explored by both Fanon (1965) and Mbembe (2001). But as highlighted so far, not all experts are oppressors and even among oppressed groups there are oppressors as well.

The first attribute of the oppressor within the development context is impunity and disregard for agreed or preferred sets of rules, policies or the law. This is not simply a disregard for the law for the sake of it, but as Fanon (1965) and Mbembe (2001) argue, it is meant to protect the privileged lifestyles of the oppressors and those who benefit from them. Here we are dealing with a network of individuals that comprises government officers, community workers, development specialists, technical advisers, NGO representatives and others who benefit and profit from the plight of oppressed groups—an issue that is a key topic of Mabulu's painting, *Pornography of Power*. In explaining dictatorial political power, Mbembe (2001) employs the notion of the autocrat; Fanon (1965) talks of the native elite and Wa Thiong'o (1977) describes a native bourgeois—all of which concepts seem to confirm that in the south, a change in government does not necessarily imply any regime or ideological change, but a change in the business elite. The capture of the state by predatory private interests or the privatization of the state often takes place before a new government is formed. It is this capture of the state that has provided a fertile ground for the germination and sustenance of the oppressor within the development context.

There are many examples of oppressors within the context of development and of the south. The Constitutional Court in South Africa found that President Jacob Zuma of South Africa failed to uphold and violated the constitution for disregarding a Public Protector's Report that criticized the over-expenditure of public resources on his private home in Nkandla (Masondo 2016). Zuma had spent about US$23million to renovate his private homestead, expenditure that was deemed to be abuse of public resources by the Public Protector's investigation, which then instructed him to pay back some of the money. South Africa's democracy is much stronger than many systems in the south, and eventually Zuma paid back some of the money (Whittles 2016). Yet there are many cases of oppressors not being held to account especially within the southern context.

This and other similar examples indicate that the native oppressor within development contexts can exhibit a deliberate disregard for the law or agreed policies because they have an exaggerated sense of self-importance bordering on self-deification. In this case, development interventions on the ground have to conform to the needs, interests and fantasies of these native oppressors. These behaviours are not just restricted to leaders and policy makers; they are mimicked by and within the chain of development practice by practitioners, policy makers, NGO representatives and even community workers.

Perhaps motivated by their own sense of over-importance and perhaps self-deification, senior officials in government and working in NGOs also manifest oppression through behavioural attributes such as their love for opulence, as observed from the luxury vehicles they use. Ministers in most poor southern countries are allocated state-of-the-art vehicles. Directors of parastatal institutions may help themselves to the latest brands of SUVs. Parliamentarians approve obscene salaries and allowances, unashamed in the face of the unthinkable poverty that they should be fighting to eradicate or reduce. The reproduction of colonial forms and structures in the organization of decolonized Africa has been explored by a host of post-colonial writers. Fanon discusses the *compartmentalization* of decolonized Africa where the primary dream of decolonized man is to take the place of the former colonizer. In fact, Fanon (1961, 1965) foretold that the new native bourgeoisie would keep intact the manners and forms of thought learnt from the colonial bourgeoisie. Similarly, Wa Thiong'o (1977) examines the moral and imperial violence perpetuated by the native bourgeoisie in post-independent Kenya that is a figurative social microcosm of the whole of Africa.

The second feature of the oppressor in development contexts is the constant reference to and use of symbolic and material violence by the native bourgeoisie. Fanon (1965) writes about the use of "class aggressiveness" in protecting positions of privilege. In *On the Postcolony*, Mbembe (2001) discusses the use of spectacle, publicly inflicted humiliation or violence to instil fear and discipline in the populace. At the time of independence within the African context, national consciousness united liberating forces in fighting against colonial oppression. But once colonialism fell, the new African native bourgeoisie was unable to provide a coherent economic programme to drive their nations' socio-economic programme of progress and development. The old tribal and sectarian hostilities that had been masked by national consciousness and struggle against colonialism begin to unravel what Gramsci (1971) described as "hegemonies in crisis." And to defend these privileged class interests, the native bourgeoisie—who have become the oppressors in their own right—then resorted to physical and symbolic violence.

A case by way of example is how the South African government unleashed its police force to kill miners who were protesting against low wages at Lonmim Marikana Mines. This massacre of 34 workers took place on August 16 2012; over 100 workers were reported injured (Marinovich 2016). Apart from the violent response of the police, the resulting investigations revealed the collusion of big business and politics (Marinovich 2016). It was reported by the world media that on August 15, 24 hours before the massacre, the deputy president of the ruling ANC, Cyril Ramaphosa, wrote to the management of Lonmin Mines observing that the wildcat strikes were criminal activities and he encouraged strong action to bring the situation under control (Marinovich 2016). Likewise in Kenya, tribal and ethnic violence ensued after the 2007 elections which left over 1000 people dead and over half a million displaced. The perpetration of violence was established to have been fuelled and funded by leading politicians.[2] Similarly, in Malawi, 20 protesters were shot dead by the police when thousands marched on July 20 2011 to protest against poor economic and political governance. In most post-colonial contexts, police are rarely taken to task for their criminal acts. The emergence of the #BlackLivesMatter Movement in the United States is a response to (and an acknowledgement) that in the postcolony, the oppressor uses the law to violently perpetuate Aimé Césaire's (1955) *thingification* of the subaltern. This is indicative of the deliberate and calculated attempt by the oppressor to keep the marginalized in their interminable state of marginality where they have no name, no identity, no history, no future and no dignity. The moment these invisible underclasses attempt to rise out of their invisibility and anonymity, they are usually met with the oppressor's carnage of violence.

The third attribute of the oppressor in the development context is the use of overt and covert discrimination. Discrimination can be versatile on the part of the oppressor. It sometimes takes the form of racism, gender discrimination, tribalism, sexism, ageism or even nationalism. The important observation is that opportunities are denied to certain social groups based on material and social trajectories that have been laid down by certain organizational cultures or by governments. Apartheid is a good example. But other forms of discrimination are so tightly interwoven with constitutional provisions that it is difficult to determine whether discrimination is taking or has taken place. Consider social mobility for example. Children coming from privileged backgrounds do have access to certain opportunities that eventually enable them climb the social ladder. Or gentrification, through which economic investment and positive changes in communities result in social dislocation of residents in low-income brackets. Attending elite universities such as Harvard, Princeton, the London School of Economics, Cambridge or Queensland can enable graduates to access certain job opportunities that are not available to others. Higher education even allows students to meet future partners from similar backgrounds and privileged circles. This is symbolic power at play; hence discrimination is most effective when covert or soft, and when it becomes ideologically interwoven with our daily practices.

One finds many variations of soft forms of oppression that can be categorized as discrimination in development contexts. An example comes from international development organizations. Allegations of prejudice against local staff surface everywhere. In many countries, international development organizations hire staff—mostly westerners—who have no prior experience of the socio-cultural conditions in which they are assigned to work. They are then awarded many privileges in comparison to the local experts who, in most cases, are well trained and experienced and have executed the same assignments, often with superior professionalism and excellence. In many meetings I have attended with officers from international development organizations, I have wondered whether some of these westerners have been employed because they come from the west or because local officers really needed technical guidance from inexperienced 'experts' who speak and reason like they have just come from universities. These experiences also reveal the imperial bullying tactics of an oppressive and undemocratic culture within these organizations. Sometimes they even illegally access the private correspondence of national staff for monitoring purposes, and there are instances of national staff members being summarily dismissed over information obtained illegally.

Despite the prevalence of oppressive practices and individuals, there remain liberatory practices that offer creative opportunities for well-meaning funding organizations, development practitioners, community workers and policy makers who genuinely care about real transformation on the ground. But it also reveals problems with certain strands of post-colonial and Marxist perspectives that seem to suggest that until real revolution happens there is no hope for experimentation with sustainable, realistic and meaningful development. That is not the case. This book argues that even if the political economy of development remains unequal, there are available opportunities that offer a platform for the construction and experimentation with deliberative development at the community level.

An auto-ethnography of horizontal oppression[3]

This section seeks to demonstrate the process of becoming an oppressor at the local level, or among oppressed groups: a phenomenon described as horizontal violence by Fanon (1961, 1965). While describing African Americans as an oppressed society after the American Civil War, Carter Woodson (1933) distinguishes the educated Negro from the uneducated Negro in his class analysis and notes the overt and covert forms of tensions between the two groups. A major argument emerging out of this chapter is that the oppressor is no longer foreign, white, male or westerner. The oppressor is actually neither here nor there (Manyozo 2010). Within the system and network of spectacles of development, we all have a capability of becoming oppressors. In fact, to implement deliberative development, planners and policy makers must study, understand, unmask and uproot the processes and networks that produce horizontal oppressors and oppression.

There is a kind of thinking prevailing among some experts that sacrifices rich narrative about lived experience for textbook theory that is often decontextualized. Theory can become a prison, limiting knowledge production by referencing a largely western scholarship. However, theory is not always inaccessible—it may offer a coherent narrative that is liberating when it captures the essence of the everyday. Post-colonial auto-ethnographic orality may use personal experience as a tool for explaining that in much development thinking the experts are typically morally and ideologically distant from local people, their knowledge, and their places. Hence, they are illegitimate representatives of the subaltern/marginalized who should not be consulted in the first place.

With the emergence of what has been called the modernization paradigm in the 1940s (Chambers 2005; Mansell 1982), post-colonialist development thinkers were already questioning the role of the expert. There are two kinds of expert—the external and the internal. The external expert is always an outsider but relies on the internal expert, mostly an educated local person who professes an understanding of people, places, and development issues. The following auto-ethnographic account indicates why the internal expert can be an obstruction to deliberative development processes.

One advantage of being raised in a dysfunctional family is that one grows up rough and tough. No matter what comes your way, life does not scare you. Families in my clan used to brew illegal traditional gin, and there were always drunken people in the compound. I grew up surrounded by noise and by lots of children. It was as if the parents were not around. Not that this bothered me, since my father used to disappear once in a while, leaving my unemployed mother with two children, a sister and myself. In our clan the absent father has always been an endemic social malaise.

I resented my mother selling traditional gin because there were so many men in our yard, and because of the noise. Nevertheless, I admired my mother for her ability to manage the shebeen business and still raise her kids in a Christian way. She has always been a wise and determined woman. When the rains washed away the only wooden bridge between our village and the primary school, almost every kid in the village dropped out of school. She would, despite my protests, wrap up my primary school uniform in a plastic satchel, escort me through the muddy waters, and then dress me in my uniform. For her, this was the only way I could "complete the white man's education."

Apart from the dramas in the shebeen, the thing I loved most was spending time with fellow goat herders. After school, every boy would take his family goats to the village forests where there was green grass. We would learn to play games, hunt mice, rabbits and grasshoppers and, of course, do what boys always do when they just want to be boys—fight. We watched traditional dances in the moonlight together as the ladies in the village performed those nice dances that involve shaking the waists and the beads, consequently shaking the manhood out of every living boy and man who happened to be watching.

Football also preoccupied our minds. We played football when we went to school. We played football during breaks. We played on the road when we came back from school. We played football all the time. The village had three teams. The big boys played in the A team, and they used the leather ball. The B team, like us the C team, used the plastic paper balls which we rolled into a spherical shape and tightened with strings. My teammates were those who I used to herd goats with. They were the same buddies I used to swim with at the village river. They were the same friends who taught me to eat stolen chicken. We were together when we received the Eucharist sacrament. Our being together all the time made up for the absent fathers, I guess.

Football was everything, because it had the ability to bring the whole village together, even though our senior team usually lost. All I remember is that when they won, there were evening "reward sessions," when they would allocate the nice girls to each other, and pair by pair they would disappear into the night. It was as if even the girls themselves always looked forward to our village's victory, because of such "rewards." As C team players, we grew up expecting to be rewarded one day, if we were to bring glory to our village.

Time seemed to move slowly. Wedding after wedding, traditional dances after traditional dances, football games after football games, funerals after funerals, we were growing up, but perhaps we were too preoccupied to notice. Most of the A and B team players must have grown older, married or moved from the village for reasons one never knows. I just know that one day we were on the pitch representing the village, using the leather ball now. We were beaten 10–0 and even jeered by our own village. We began a long losing streak.

This lasted until the days when two refugee boys came to live in the village after their families had fled from the war in Mozambique. These boys joined us in herding the goats, swimming, and playing football. One of them was a very good striker and the older one joined me in defence. They encouraged us to be much rougher with our opponents to instill fear in them. While waiting for a corner, for instance, we could slap our opponents, irritate them, and if they retaliated, we would fight them because we were good at that. Over time we started experiencing draws, and then victories followed. There was once again interest in football in the village. The key was to play rough: after all, games in those days had no referees. A corner could be contested verbally or through a fistfight between the striker who was claiming it and the defender who was arguing for a goal kick. Teams would come together, find a solution, and the game would continue. Our football team grew up together, and within a short time the Mozambican boys began to speak our language fluently. We would sit and listen to their stories about war, and about how soldiers would force women to cook and eat their own children. Between these experiences, these stories, and the traditional dances, we were becoming a feared team in the traditional authority.

Two rivers away from our village, there was another football team that was well known and had beaten our village a couple of times in the past. Whoever introduced the idea is not important, but we discussed it at length, especially knowing that it would involve money. We collected money from every willing adult in the village, as did the other team in their village. Added together, the money would be awarded to the winners.

The build-up was rife with rumours of members of both teams sleeping at the graveyard to boost their athleticism. We might have slept at the graveyard, I am not sure, but even if we did, it would not have been the first time. As a boost to our morale, a distant relative of mine who had been living in the city came for a short visit. He had been a good goalkeeper when he left. We used to call him "The Cat," because of the way he jumped to save shots that were almost going into the net. He had come back in time for the game, and we all suspected that the village storeowner had brought him back for the match.

All over the place there was talk of this match. The women and men in the fields, the girls at the river: all talked about the game. We were pumped up because we had not lost on home ground in a long time. When he joined us, The Cat started to act like our coach. It was the first time we noticed that we didn't have a coach; it was something our group had never discussed. Our strategies had always resulted from collective negotiations during the game or at half time when village elders would come and swear at us for missing this or that ball. Sometimes five of them would be talking at the same time and even though we could not remember what they actually said, we always got the point—that the second half had to be better than the first.

The Cat talked about a 4–3–3 "system," because we needed the third striker to drop and strengthen the midfield. He expressed reservations about our team being full of attacking players and he didn't think I was tall enough to be a defender. A taller and stronger boy in midfield was brought back into defence and, because of my short height, I was asked to play on the right wing and supply the crosses. To be sure, we had a strength-testing match against another village team that had caused us problems. With The Cat in goal, we had plenty of confidence and we smashed them 4–0. The new system that he introduced seemed to be working miracles. He organized our attacks and our defence and, with him in goal, we were ready to win the eagerly awaited game.

Days passed by quickly, and soon it was the big Saturday. The whole village stopped except for the shebeens. It was not only money that was at stake here. Bragging rights were also at stake. Someone may also have said that there could likely be "rewards" afterwards! The first half was a dull affair and it ended goalless. The visitors were also too defensive. The second half started the same way until halfway through it The Cat decided to take out one of the Mozambican boys playing in defence and bring in another boy, a very good striker, but who had not played with us on a regular basis. Although most of us were unhappy with the substitution, we did not protest openly; after all, The Cat was the oldest and the only one who understood "the system."

A few minutes after the substitution, we scored. The women started singing praises to The Cat. That goal, however, seemed to have made the visitors grow extra legs and they equalized. The Cat started shouting at everyone. For the first time, we started blaming each other in the middle of a game. To strengthen our defence, we tried to revert to our traditional pre-system system—pack the backline with bodies and then deliberately hurt their effective players, a tactic aimed at slowing them down. The Cat insisted that we remain faithful to the "system," and that meant going back into "our positions." They scored. The Cat made a couple of changes. They scored two more. We lost everything.

The village blamed the whole team except The Cat. If it wasn't for him the score could have been worse, it was being said. He openly criticized us after the match. We never talked about that match again, even when we went to swim or to herd goats together. Deep down in our hearts we knew that we lost the game on the day when The Cat walked into our midst as the football expert. We could not comprehend "the system," but the village blamed us for not understanding it. More painfully, The Cat seemed to have walked away from the defeat as a victor. We saw him before he left for the city, drinking and laughing with village elders. I was about to leave for high school, still a virgin.

We believed that it was The Cat's expertise and the system that were the source of the defeat because we couldn't play to our strengths. If we had lost when playing our traditional system, we might not have won, but it wouldn't have hurt so much, and maybe it would have propelled us to prepare effectively for another game.

Concluding thoughts

Like that lost game of football, the developing world is littered with the bodies of abandoned or dead development initiatives. As observed by Escobar and Mansell, the modernization paradigm continues its reincarnation within numerous participation-resistant models that depoliticize questions of power, decision-making, engagement, and local knowledge. At the centre of this problematic perpetuation of a modernist world view and the *thingification* of marginalized groups, is a network of international, transnational or native bourgeois experts, who are either external or internal, but without a comprehensive understanding of the local setting and local aspirations for living well. This chapter therefore makes certain critical observations.

The first is that the oppression referred to here is more behavioural and not an identity. The behaviour involves coming in with exogenous ideas about local economic development building on deterministic models, strategies and initiatives that do not build on local knowledge and strengths. Therefore, it should be emphasized that the language of oppression does not just refer to discursive practices by some western and international organizations that exhibit the characteristics laid out in this chapter, they also comprise endogenous and local organizations that display similar attributes. In this case, there is no homogeneous group of oppressors that stays like that forever. Within the development context, every player and stakeholder has the capability to become and *unbecome* oppressors. In one context, Hillary Clinton's exclamation "we came, we saw, he died" might seem like a reference to the liberation of oppressed peoples, especially for those who were oppressed under the terrible dictatorship of Qaddafi. But it could also be perceived as perpetuating deep-seated traditions of western interference in the south.

Secondly, this chapter has laid out some of the fundamental characteristics of the language of oppression, as well as the attributes of an oppressor. Over and above these attributes is the fact that everyone has the potential to function as an oppressor, given the context and conditions. And when they do, it is unclear in the language they use whether they are aware of what they are doing or not. Freire's critical pedagogy then targets this group of individuals because, for Freire, oppressors need to be liberated as well. The act of becoming an oppressor happens, hence it is embedded in a set of functions and activities. Within the development context, becoming an oppressor is also a process of consciousness building that occurs through engagement with social reality, one realizes that they have to employ certain practices to achieve certain goals. These actions could be oppressive. In my development work I was aware, and also very deliberate, when I employed certain strategies that I knew diminished the identity and intelligence of others, because I wanted to achieve certain organizational objectives. In that moment, I was an oppressor, or I functioned as one. The contradiction has not been lost on me, because even when I grew up in poverty and could see and experience all these oppressive situations around me, it is western education that actually sensitized and conscientized me about my oppressive material conditions.

The third observation is that even though some critical perspectives may seem to suggest that until real revolution happens there is no hope for experimentation with sustainable, realistic and meaningful development, this chapter makes a case for the availability of opportunities for deliberative development. There are spaces of liberatory practices that offer creative opportunities for well-meaning funding organizations, development practitioners, community workers and policy makers who genuinely care about real transformation on the ground. This book argues that there are available opportunities, even if the political economy of development is not conducive, that offer a platform for the construction and experimentation with deliberative development at the community level. The next section, Part II, includes chapters that expound real and imagined experiments in which various stakeholders work together to produce change.

Notes

1 CBS News, www.youtube.com/watch?v=Fgcd1ghag5Y.
2 Amnesty International. 2014. "Victims still seeking justice for the post-election violence." Accessed October 12 2016. www.amnesty.org/en/latest/news/2014/07/kenya-victims-still-seeking-justice-post-election-violence.
3 Originally published as: Manyozo, Linje. 2010. "The day development dies." *Development in Practice*, 20(2): 265–269.

References

Bourdieu, Pierre. 1983/1991. *Language and Symbolic Power*. Cambridge: Polity Press.

Césaire, Aimé. 1955/1972. *Discourse on Colonialism*. Translated by Joan Pinkham. London: Monthly Review Press.

Chambers, Robert. 1980. *Rural Poverty Unperceived: Problems and Remedies*. Staff Working Paper Number SWP 400. Washington, DC: The World Bank. Accessed September 30 2016. http://documents.worldbank.org/curated/en/909311468766763144/Rural-poverty-unperceived-problems-and-remedies.

Chambers, Robert. 1981. "Poor visibility: How policy makers overlook the poor." New Internationalist website. Issue 96. Accessed January 20 2016. http://newint.org/features/1981/02/01/poor-visibility.

Chambers, Robert. 2005. *Ideas for Development*. London and Sterling: Earthscan.

Chouliaraki, Lilie. 2008. *The Spectatorship of Suffering*. New Delhi, London and Thousand Oaks: Sage.

Conrad, Joseph. 1899/2003. *Heart of Darkness*. New York: Fine Communications.

Deleuze, Gilles and Félix Guattari. 1987. *A Thousand Plateaus: Capitalism and Schizophrenia*. Translated by Brian Massumi. London and Minneapolis: University of Minnesota.

Escobar, Arturo. 1995/2012. *Encountering Development: The Making and Unmaking of the Third World*. Princeton: Princeton University Press.

Fanon, Frantz. 1961. *The Wretched of the Earth*. New York: Grove Press.

Fanon, Frantz. 1965. *A Dying Colonialism*. New York: Grove Press.

Freire, Paulo. 1970. *Pedagogy of the Oppressed*. London: Penguin.

Freire, Paulo. 1996a. *Letters to Cristina*. New York: Continuum.

Freire, Paulo. 1996b. *An Incredible Conversation*. YouTube Channel. Accessed January 20 2016. www.youtube.com/watch?v=aFWjnkFypFA.

Gramsci, Antonio. 1971. *Selections from the Prison Notebooks*. Translated by Quintin Hoare and Geoffrey Nowell Smith. New York: International Publishers.

Gutiérrez, Gustavo. 1988. *A Theology of Liberation: History, Politics, and Salvation*. Translated by Caridad Inda and John Eagleson. Maryknoll, New York: Orbis Books.

Hall, Stuart. 1997. "The spectacle of the other." In Stuart Hall (ed.) *Representation: Cultural Representations and Signifying Practice* (pp. 223–290). Thousand Oaks CA: Sage Publications.

hooks, bell. 1994. *Teaching to Transgress: Education as the Practice of Freedom*. London and New York: Routledge.

Kingsley, Patrick. 2015. "How Mohammad Morsi, Egypt's first democratically elected president, ended up on death row." *The Guardian Online*. June 1. Accessed November 10 2016. www.theguardian.com/world/2015/jun/01/mohamed-morsi-execution-death-sentence-egypt.

Lerner, Daniel. 1958. *The Passing of Traditional Society: Modernizing the Middle East*. New York and London: Free Press and Collier-Macmillan.

Lukes, Steven. 1974/2005. *Power: A Radical View.* New York: Palgrave Macmillan.

Makuwira, Jonathan. 2014. *Non-Governmental Development Organizations and the Poverty Reduction Agenda: The Moral Crusaders.* London and New York: Routledge.

Mamdani, Mahmood. 2007. "The politics of naming: Genocide, civil war, insurgency." *London Review of Books*, 29(5): 5–8.

Mansell, Robin. 1982. "The 'new dominant paradigm' in communication: Transformation versus adaptation." *Canadian Journal of Communication*, 8(3): 42–60. Accessed September 20 2016. www.cjc-online.ca/index.php/journal/article/view/278/184.

Manyozo, Linje. 2010. "The day development dies." *Development in Practice*, 20(2): 265–269.

Marinovich, Greg. 2016 *Murder at Small Koppie: The Real Story of the Marikana Massacre.* Johannesburg: Penguin Random House.

Marx, Karl. 1852/2010. *The Eighteenth Brumaire of Louis Bonaparte.* New York: *Die Revolution* Issue 1.

Masondo Sipho. 2016. "Constitutional court's damning judgement: Zuma violated his oath of office." *City Press Online.* March 31. Accessed November 20 2016. http://city-press.news24.com/News/constitutional-courts-damning-judgment-zuma-violated-his-oath-of-office-20160331.

Mbembe, Achille. 2001. *On the Postcolony.* Berkeley CA: University of California Press.

Mbembe, Achille and Esprit. 2008. "What is postcolonial theory? An interview with Achille Mbembe." Conducted by Olivier Mongin, Nathalie Lempereur and Jean-Louis Schlegel. In *Eurozine,* September 1. Accessed January 20 2016. www.eurozine.com/articles/2008-01-09-mbembe-en.html.

Mbembe, Achille. 2015. "The value of Africa's aesthetics." *Mail and Guardian Online.* May 15. Accessed August 21 2016. http://mg.co.za/article/2015-05-14-the-value-of-africas-aesthetics.

Memmi, Albert. 1965/2013. *The Colonizer and the Colonized.* London: Routledge.

Rostow, Walt. 1960. *The Stages of Economic Growth: A Non-Communist Manifesto.* Cambridge: Cambridge University Press.

Said, Edward. 1978. *Orientalism.* New York: Random House.

Sartre, Jean-Paul. 1961. "Preface." In Frantz Fanon, *The Wretched of the Earth.* New York: Grove Press.

Schramm, Wilbur. 1964. *Mass Media and National Development: The Role of Information in the Developing Countries.* Stanford: Stanford University Press.

Wa Thiong'o, Ngũgĩ. 1977. *Petals of Blood.* London and Nairobi: James Currey.

Whittles, Govan. 2016. "Zuma pays back the money – but where did he get the R7.8 million?" *Mail and Guardian Online.* September 12. Accessed November 20 2016. http://mg.co.za/article/2016-09-12-zuma-pays-back-the-money-but-where-did-he-get-the-r78-million.

Woodson, Carter. 1933/2006. *The Mis-Education of the Negro.* Drewryville: Khalifah Publishers.

PART II
Reconstruction and recovery

3
CAPTURING SUBALTERN VOICES

Setting the context

Many years have passed since Gayatri Spivak (1988) emphasized the centrality of subaltern and female subjectivity and agency as critical components of a democratic polity. Nevertheless the question remains: how do we study the subaltern voice theoretically and then empirically explore the processes that characterize the production and integration of people's voices in the design and implementation of development policy? This chapter builds on critical feminist frameworks and insights to conduct class analyses that provide insight into defining how southern subaltern groups of women conceive, produce and consume their own voices. While rejecting the sensationalized western narratives that promote what Adichie (2009) describes as the single story narrative, the discussion aims to contribute to the fields of communication and development studies by highlighting the fragile, slippery and class politics that are at play when marginalized groups employ symbolic and material artefacts—even their bodies—as battle grounds for contesting oppressive power relationships. It should be highlighted that this chapter borrows Spivak's (1988) definition of subaltern as a position and not necessarily as an identity. Yet there are moments within this book when the subaltern as a perspective is used interchangeably with oppressed classes. This has a major implication for development thinking and practice. Even if a development practitioner is white, a westerner or an outsider, they can speak and unspeak development alongside oppressed communities so long as they acquire the subaltern perspective.

In this chapter I engage in a critical conversation with the thinkers who have been central to the coupling of post-colonial theory to feminism, that is, Frantz Fanon (1965), Gayatri Spivak (1988) and Assia Djebar (1992). I resurrect the discussion started by Frantz Fanon (1965) in *A Dying Colonialism*, picked up by

Assia Djebar (1992) in *Women of Algiers in their Apartment*, and also by Gayatri Spivak (1988) in "Can the subaltern speak?" Principally, this chapter examines the art and science of speaking by subaltern groups within the context of the south. To create a link between these three thinkers, Janie Mae Crawford, a central figure in Zora Neale Hurston's *Their Eyes Were Watching God* (1937/1998) is examined to help us understand subaltern speech and the politics that governs its production. It must be pointed out that traditional feminism, previously a domain of western thinkers and scholars, has not succeeded in significantly articulating the needs and aspirations of minority groups. This could be the reason Spivak (1988, 104) would observe "the subaltern as a female cannot be heard or read."

The discussion is structured to achieve three objectives: (a) examine how Fanon and Djebar re-insert agency and subjectivity into the identity of the 'docile' Algerian woman as a case of a subaltern group; (b) expose how Spivak and Djebar deconstruct the case of individually oppressed women who use their bodies to undermine structural violence; and (c) explore pedagogical practices in relation to the adult literacy programme in a southern village as a way of showing the challenges and opportunities of conscientizing and empowering an oppressed group. Two arguments are advanced: firstly, discursive and material violence has become a major mechanism for producing and exchanging subaltern voices. Secondly, the generation of subaltern voice often does not necessarily lead to material transformation, because oppressing classes have tended to control—and thus depoliticize—the instruments of signification with which these voices are produced and appropriated.

The political act of speaking: Fanon, Spivak and Djebar

Unlike his other attempts in which he described how colonialism and oppressors operate, in *A Dying Colonialism*, Fanon (1965) presents a manifesto for the production and consumption of subaltern voices in response to colonial oppression. Fanon recognizes that the battle against colonialism is not just fought with military hardware—rather he acknowledges that as a consequence of intellectual, cultural and empirical forms of colonial violence, the battlefield shifts from the front into the villages, into people's homes, their ways of life, and especially with how they are seen and represented. As if foretelling the contemporary contestation of signification of the place of Islam within western modernity, Fanon (1965, 35–36) observes:

> In the Arab Maghreb, the veil belongs to the clothing traditions of the Tunisian, Algerian, Moroccan and Libyan national societies. For the tourist and the foreigner, the veil demarcates both Algerian society and its feminine component. … We shall see that this veil, one of the elements of the traditional Algerian garb, was to become the bone of contention in a grandiose battle, on account of which the occupation forces were to mobilize their most powerful and most varied resources, and in the course of which the colonized were to display a surprising force of inertia.

When Fanon described this "bone of contention in a grandiose battle" in the 1960s, little did he know that this confrontation would remain unresolved for such a long time. What is essential for our discussion here is that the Arab veil, traditional clothing worn in many of the communities of North Africa and throughout the Middle East, has become a cultural battleground, a contestation of symbolic power and a feature of colonial intervention in the south. The place of Islam in modernity is currently being hotly debated in American and European polity.

In *Orientalism*, Said (1978) observes that colonialism was preceded by, and succeeded later after its consolidation by, an orientalist body of literature that supported direct colonial intervention. Fanon (1965) likewise observes that the "decisive" colonization of Algeria took place long before the Algerian civil war when the French administration constructed and defined a "precise political doctrine" of civilizing Algeria, a doctrine that would be made possible by the expertise of sociologists and ethnologists. To do this, the French administrators concentrated their efforts on rescuing the Algerian woman from the wearing of the veil, which was seen as a sign of oppression. It was within this historical context that, over a century earlier, Delacroix would produce the famous painting *Women of Algiers in their Apartment*.

As such, representation became a key feature of Algerian colonization and the subsequent liberation war. Algerian society was represented as "medieval and barbaric" and woman was represented as "humiliated, sequestered, and cloistered" (Fanon 1965, 38). It was the responsibility of the colonial administration therefore, to "defend" the "inert, demonetized, indeed dehumanized" Algerian woman and to help her discover the "immense possibilities" that awaited her (Fanon 1965).

In line with Fanon's (1965), Said's (1978), and Spivak's (1988) observations on the representation of the other, Mahmood Mamdani (2007) argues that defining and naming historical phenomena are fundamental to shaping empirical reality and, consequently, this naming produces justifications for certain development and military interventions. As Mamdani (2007) points out however, representations of crises such as the Darfur conflict by western and international media and NGOs have covert imperial and ideological motivations. He argues that compared to similar contemporary political conflicts elsewhere that have seen western media institutions and human rights organizations calling for a withdrawal of foreign troops, the conflict in Darfur continues to see overwhelming support for military intervention. This is largely due to what Bourdieu (1991) and Mamdani (2007) describe as the language of naming—which is determined by who does the naming, who is being named, and the implications of such naming. In the case of Darfur, the regime of "naming" has seen the emergence of international campaigns—to "Save Darfur"—that suffer from politicization, naturalization and demonization of the conflicts and the key protagonists (Mamdani 2007). The implication of humanitarian communication in this context is not to elicit global and public pity and compassion, but rather global and public anger, and of course humanitarian intervention (Chouliaraki 2008).

Almost as if he were conversing with Mamdani (2007), Fanon (1965) lays out the immediate consequence of the orientalist feminist literature that was produced by the French administration in colonized Algeria. He notes the proliferation of the establishment of "mutual aid societies and societies to promote solidarity with Algerian women" (Fanon 1965, 38). Other advocacy initiatives included public communication campaigns, charities to provide relief and safety net items for Algerian women. Fanon (1965, 38) then observes that in this "combat":

> Every kilo of semolina distributed was accompanied by a dose of indignation against the veil and the cloister. The indignation was followed up by practical advice. Algerian women were invited to play "a functional, capital role" in the transformation of their lot. They were pressed to say no to a centuries-old subjection. The immense role they were called upon to play was described to them. The colonial administration invested great sums in this combat.

The "indignation" that Fanon is referring to here could be considered the equivalent of Althusser's (1971/2008) ideological state apparatus. This indignation gave rise to programmatic interventions to free the oppressed Algerian woman from the domestic and cultural aggression of patriarchal institutions within which she had found herself trapped. From Fanon's perspective, the colonial institutions decided, based upon scholarly advice derived from orientalist expositions, to unchain the woman first, since this would provide the dominating powers with a trusted ally who would be in a better position to transform the Algerian man. These ideological devices encompassed workplace customs such as dress requirements, educational content and philosophies, and other forms of "the traps set by the European in order to bring the Algerian to expose himself" (Fanon 1965, 40).

Through these various modernizing interventions, the colonized responded in two ways. First, there were moments in which women would indeed become psychologically and empirically converted and, to make a point, would abandon the veil, and thus become, "symbolically unveiled" (Fanon 1965, 42). It seemed, as Fanon observes, that with more and more Algerian women becoming unveiled, the colonial occupiers strengthened their resolve and believed that the defence mechanisms of the oppressive Algerian society had been breached, and was thus "in the process of dislocation" (Fanon 1965, 42).

Likewise Lerner (1958), Rostow (1960), Schramm (1964) and many other modernist scholars observed that the western model is the only way towards achieving realistic development. They argue that for modernization to achieve economic growth, the individuals themselves have to be modernized and, consequently, the traditional societies have to abandon their native lifestyles and adopt modern living practices. These were processes that had already taken place in western cultures, when "ordinary men found themselves unbound from their native soil" and moved "from farms to flats and from fields to factories" (Lerner 1958, 47). Yet for most marginalized peoples, some of these changes were abrupt and unplanned and seemed to benefit the privileged few. As a result, in many places in the global south there were resistances to modernist development approaches.

Fanon (1965, 47) contends that "the colonized, in the face of the emphasis given by the colonialist to this or that aspect of his traditions, reacts very violently." The violent reaction that Fanon discusses is played out in scholarship, in art and of course, empirically. What is important to note is that when the struggle for liberation begins, and Fanon makes this point very clearly, the cultural struggle—in this case, the centrality of the veil—is not of much significance. Yet as the struggle undergoes what Fanon (1965, 47) describes as "important modifications," the issues of representation become critical in defining the past and future of an oppressed society. Symbolic power then becomes a critical component of subaltern struggles.

As a result of these modifications, women began to take centre stage in the Algerian revolution to mitigate the growing colonial violence and ferocity which were being recreated to inflict maximum oppression on the whole society. It is very clear from Fanon that involving the women was a strategic military decision, a "wholly revolutionary step" and not just a rationale for mass mobilization. The strategic reason to involve women in the liberation was because their daily routine gave them the capacity to act with military astuteness. Fanon (1965, 50) argues:

> It must be constantly borne in mind that the committed Algerian woman learns both her role as 'a woman alone in the street' and her revolutionary mission instinctively. The Algerian woman is not a secret agent. It is without apprenticeship, without briefing, without fuss, that she goes out into the street with three grenades in her handbag or the activity report of an area in her bodice. … It is an authentic birth in a pure state, without preliminary instruction. There is no character to imitate. On the contrary, there is an intense dramatization, a continuity between the woman and the revolutionary.

In the course of carrying out their revolutionary responsibilities and tasks, the women proved to be creative and would not be held back by cultural or colonial taboos that had governed their representation by others. For the Algerian woman, the act of going to war was therefore preceded by a battle and a victory over their fears of the occupier, and the image of the occupier in her mind and in her body. By the time she carries out revolutionary acts, she has already breached colonialism and "devalidated" it, as Fanon put it. It is through the efforts of the Algerian woman that messages were carried from one point to another; she would stand watch over a location, or transport financial and hardware resources to various revolutionary cells. In many cases, therefore, the Algerian woman functioned as the "lighthouse and barometer" for military battalions, which they would lead into battle. And there were moments when the Algerian woman would become a combatant herself and she was enabled in this by her unveiling, which, before the war, was a representation of humiliation and oppression. But now with the veil "removed and reassumed," the dressing became "manipulated, transformed into a technique of camouflage, into a means of struggle" (Fanon 1965, 59). Without the veil, the Algerian woman would move about and penetrate European cities and places without raising suspicion. Fanon (1965, 58) explains that:

> Carrying revolvers, grenades, hundreds of false identity cards or bombs, the unveiled Algerian woman moves like a fish in the Western waters. The soldiers, the French patrols, smile to her as she passes, compliments on her looks are heard here and there, but no one suspects that her suitcases contain the automatic pistol which will presently mow down four or five members of one of the patrols. We must come back to that young girl, unveiled only yesterday, who walks with sure steps down the streets of the European city teeming with policemen, parachutists, militiamen. … The shoulders of the unveiled Algerian woman are thrust back with easy freedom. She walks with a graceful, measured stride, neither too fast nor too slow. Her legs are bare, not confined by the veil, given back to themselves, and her hips are free.

Over time, as the colonial authorities learned of the participation of the Europeanized Algerian women in the revolution, stop and search tactics were employed. The Algerian woman had to change tactics. Instead of unveiling, she began to veil herself again. Fanon (1965, 62) observed that "whereas in the previous period the body had to be made slim and disciplined to make it attractive and seductive, it now had to be squashed, made shapeless and even ridiculous." As such, the veil that used to be traditional wear and marked a separation of sexes became a critical component of the struggle for liberation.

In the process, the body became mutated, was briefly abandoned, but eventually, "it helped the Algerian woman to meet the new problems created by the struggle" (Fanon 1965, 63). In the end, her active participation in military combat enabled the Algerian woman to reject the description made of her in western and eastern scholarship and traditions. Even if her body seemed, in the words of Djebar (1992, *Overture*), "incarcerated," the Algerian woman would still maintain a "soul that moved more freely than ever before." In this moment, therefore, Spivak is right that the subaltern as a female could not be heard or read—that is, she was able to structure her body in a language of the political struggle in ways that could not be decoded by the colonial authorities. Through participation in military combat, the Algerian woman destroyed the colonial institutions and traditions that resided within herself and went as far as to "knock down all the pseudo-truths that years of 'field studies' were believed to have amply confirmed" (Fanon 1965, 65).

Fanon's account of the active role of the Algerian woman in the fight for independence resonates with a long tradition of the subaltern women's involvement in socio-political struggles. Djebar (1992) recounts the folk story of another Algerian woman, a young Harazeli girl, Messaouda, who, realizing her tribesmen were almost giving up during a violent fight with an enemy tribe, "exposes herself willingly" to the enemy bows and arrows, and calls upon the men of her tribe to fight and push back the enemy, which they eventually do. Alongside Messaouda are other stories of powerful matriarchs who exhibited courage and wisdom in their leadership, thereby defying the silence that characterizes the women in Delacroix's view of *Women of Algiers in their Apartment* (Djebar 1992).

Just like the Algerian woman who—thanks to the Algerian war of independence—defiantly resurrects and reasserts her identity and individuality—from the dehumanized and oppressed object in orientalist scholarship and representations—another subjugated woman in the early 20th century India, Bhuvaneswari, similarly uses her body to reject the dominant representations. In a seminal piece, Spivak (1988) traces the orientalist history of the women in development scholarship and practice as it emerged under British occupation of the subcontinent of India, and shows how this influenced the way the Indian woman was mutilated, dismembered and spoken for by the development industry. As was the case in Fanon's exposition of the Algerian woman, Spivak's Bhuvaneswari is shown to have been an object of dominant representations, and academic and feminist programmes, until she commits suicide. It is the exploration of the politics surrounding this suicide that Spivak's article discusses.

Spivak's subaltern

It is not clear to what extent Spivak was aware of the works of Freire and Fanon when she published "Can the subaltern speak?" in 1988. But there is certainly a great similarity in how all three of them conceive liberation, oppression and colonialism. They all root their understanding of these concepts in anti-colonial theory and praxis. For both Freire and Spivak, the theoretical springboard lies with Marx, but we cannot say the same for Fanon, who throughout much of his writings did not seem to reference Marxist thinking. Nevertheless, what is critical to my argument is that all three are trying to understand the violent nature of colonization and its ideology in perpetuating a western *Weltanschauung* that is rooted in injustice and inequality.

Freire's oppressed people comprises a group of poor, vulnerable, marginalized, disgruntled individuals and groups. These are people who have either not discovered the power of their collectivity to "unspeak their world," or they are in the process of discovering their world. Thus, the oppressed are groups that are in the process of acquiring a holistic understanding of their world. This critical education is what Freire's horizontal critical pedagogy is all about—or what Edward Palmer Thompson (1963, 782) describes as the "diffusion of literacy."

The subaltern, on the other hand—described by Spivak as those without access to lines of social mobility—refers to perspectives held by oppressed peoples who have acquired a political consciousness, one that eventually enables them to begin to deconstruct imperialism and other forms of oppression that prevent them from realizing their full potential. In this case, the subaltern for Spivak does not necessarily refer to oppressed people per se, but rather she refers to a critical world view held by oppressed peoples. Spivak's concept of the subaltern, expounded in the historical essay "Can the subaltern speak" builds on a quotation from *The Eighteenth Brumaire of Louis Bonaparte*, in which Marx (1852/2010), referring to oppressed peoples without political consciousness, observes, "they cannot represent themselves, they must be represented." What Spivak argues is that the politics of representation is fraught with contestations over power—its use and misuse in society. She is also arguing by implication that there are oppressed peoples without a critical consciousness of their conditions and, as such, they have not yet acquired the subaltern perspective. Thus, for development practice, not all oppressed peoples have a subaltern perspective.

In her essay, Spivak raises three fundamental issues: (a) how western development institutions understand (or misunderstand) power and empowerment; (b) the ideological positionality of the western expert in reading subaltern voices; and (c) the politics, nature and forms of subaltern voices. Spivak is scathing in her criticism of what she perceives as naive western approaches that conceive of the subaltern in the south as helpless victims who rely on western pity, sympathy and salvation. It must be noted that "western" for Spivak does not solely refer to intellectual ideas coming from the west, but also to theories and concepts developed by scholars and liberation practitioners in the global south who uncritically build on western and westernized perspectives that are often taken out of context. As such, Spivak's "westerners" comprise external or internal experts who are culturally, spiritually and morally alienated from the socio-cultural context in which they function—hence, she refers to both the perspective and the content of that thinking.

Spivak's seminal work examines the case of Bhuvaneswari, a young Indian woman who hanged herself during the height of British colonialism in North Calcutta, India in 1926. Spivak (1988, 103–104) describes this tragic event:

> The suicide was a puzzle since, as Bhuvaneswari was menstruating at the time, it was clearly not a case of illicit pregnancy. … Bhuvaneswari had known that her death would be diagnosed as the outcome of illegitimate passion. She had therefore waited for the onset of menstruation. While waiting, she … rewrote the social text of the sati-suicide in an interventionist way … The displacing gesture—waiting for menstruation—is at first a reversal of the interdict against a menstruating widow's right to immolate herself; the unclean widow must wait, publicly, until the cleansing bath of the fourth day, when she is no longer menstruating, in order to claim her dubious privilege.

By locating menstruation at the centre of the suicide, the case of Bhuvaneswari as depicted by Spivak demonstrates that the deconstruction and undermining of oppression does not necessarily always have to be collective—as seems to be the case in Freire's critical pedagogy or in Fanon's (1965) radical decolonization programme. It is actually individuals, acting in their own capacity, who search for and find what Mbembe (2001) describes as the liminal spaces within which to dissent and undermine oppressive ideologies and structures. These forms and their presentation of voice acts usually employ popular art practice such as jokes, music, theatre and other non-verbal forms of speech. For Spivak, considering these subaltern voices is imperative if these groups are to be involved in development policy formulation and implementation, otherwise she warns "the subaltern as female cannot be heard or read" (1988, 104). What does Spivak mean?

As if conversing with Spivak, Assia Djebar examines the representation of four Algerian women by the French orientalist painter, Eugene Delacroix, based on his three-day stopover in Algeria and a few hours' encounter with an Algerian harem (Djebar 1992). This painting, a single story in itself (Adichie 2009), is a product of Delacroix's "intoxication" and encounter with the "spectacle" of women and children that would inform the backdrop of the famous painting, *Women of Algiers in their Apartment*. As he returns to France after a few days, Delacroix also takes with him a few objects, comprising "some slippers, a shawl, a shirt, a pair of trousers," perhaps as "tangible proof of a unique, ephemeral experience, traces of a dream" (Djebar 1992, 135). The resulting painting that he produces in Paris over two years contains four women, and as Assia Djebar (1992, 135) observes, the meaning of the painting is played out in the "relationship these four have with their bodies, as well as with the place of their enclosure." Delacroix would rework the painting after some years, resulting in the second 1849 version with notable changes with "less elaborate" setting, "less precise" characteristics and a widening of the angle of vision (Djebar 1992, 135).

When Spivak argues that the female subaltern cannot be heard or read, she acknowledges the challenges of deconstructing the political economy of the structures and spectacles of policies and development that silence women. Hence she quotes Marx's (1852/2010, 62) famous diction, "they cannot represent themselves, therefore they must be represented." By making the subaltern absent, Delacroix creates a rationale for orientalizing them. As such, the women represented in the painting have "remained absent to themselves, to their body, to their sensuality, to their happiness" (Djebar, 135). What this implies is that the women themselves cannot speak and are not speaking to us and, as such, we cannot know their 'distant drama' apart from the 'stolen glance' that the only witness to this event—the painting—is able to afford us. This, then, results in a forbidden gaze, all the more so considering that, as spectators, we are looking at women without their veil who, exposed like this, can normally only be seen by their husbands, brothers or sons (Djebar 1992). What this painting leads us to imagine and realize is that in the 'frozen stare' of the women, the "women's looks and voices continue to be perceived from a distance, from the other side of the frontier" (Djebar 1992,141).

This is not to argue that the subaltern cannot speak. It was never Djebar's nor Spivak's argument. Rather it is to ponder the tendency by marginalized groups to resort to symbolic and material violence in their speech that makes subaltern representation an interesting subject of critical analysis. An example of horizontal violence is the violent reaction by male street vendors against women dressing in certain 'fashionable' ways in sub-Saharan Africa. The context of the violence is that women wearing miniskirts have been objects of verbal and physical violence by largely male vendors in certain cities in sub-Saharan Africa.[1] These acts of violence generated public anger, resulting in many demonstrations across the continent in support of the harassed women but also emphasizing that these countries are signatories to various international human rights charters that celebrate freedom of expression. It must be pointed out, however, that in most of these criticisms a narrow lens on human rights was employed to analyse this sort of violence.

Questions can be raised about the relevance of examining this issue from the western humanist intellectual perspective. Understanding of this sort of violence requires the integration of class as a key historical phenomenon in the analysis of subaltern speech. It is crucial to deliberately undermine the dominant narrative that reduces these vendors' acts into a single human rights story—that of 'violence by men against women.' Human rights activists and commentators have narrowly framed such issues as a manifestation of the "savagery" of these vendors for undressing the "innocent" women, "who have the right to dress as they like." This discussion emphasizes and argues that women can wear what they want and anywhere they want, of course in recognition of the constraints within the local contexts. The violence suffered by the women should also open up a conversation about the socio-economic marginalization that social minorities experience.

These public commentaries fail to problematize the 'undressing' of the women as a political act in which marginalized groups use violence as a form of communication. Subaltern speech, for most post-colonial thinkers, is often banal and vulgar and is imbued with sporadic but politicized forms of violence, even against comrade subalterns. The "vendors" who have been stigmatized symbolically and empirically are mere objects of most public discourse: they are being spoken of, spoken for, and spoken about—reminding us of the objective of Spivak's "Can the subaltern speak"—to recover the politics in the speech of the subaltern, otherwise, as Marx already warned in the 1850s, they could end up "being represented."

What happened in sub-Saharan Africa was much deeper than just men's violence against women. It is also not just about reducing, viewing and objectifying women as mothers, as originators of life. Women are much more than their physiological organs or socially constructed traditional roles. Understanding gender politics among subaltern groups is not necessarily about deterministically perceiving the role and place of girls and women in society. It is about carefully examining how power flows and is contested within the politics of marginalization. Economic marginalization is a ticking time bomb in the south. The rising poverty and unemployment, or the lack of vocational and higher education opportunities for youth stand in stark contrast to the opulent lifestyles of many of our leaders.

One characteristic of the politics of subaltern speech is that, in its violent form, the body is elevated into a battlefield for symbolically contesting economic and political power. For instance, the Tunisian Mohamed Bouazizi set himself on fire in protest against corrupt city officials, sparking the so-called Tunisian and Arab "revolutions." Similarly, Bhuvaneswari, in Spivak's article, used menstruation to politicize what would have passed off as a simple self-immolation. In Fanon's exposition, the Algerian woman used her body as a reliable vehicle for advancing the struggle against French colonialism. In *Their Eyes Were Watching God*, Janie's journey of self-discovery is undertaken against the social expectations of how a woman of her age is viewed. In another case where a young woman used her body as a site of battle, around 2011 Mumpy Sarkar, a 12 year-old Indian girl, committed suicide in order to donate her organs to family members who urgently needed a donor, but were not being helped by a corrupt and inefficient health system—her instruction note only being discovered after her body had been cremated.[2]

To borrow Thomson's (1963) notion of history from below, subaltern speech may be considered vulgar or violent, and the associated actions seen as barbaric or deplorable. Yet these subaltern groups live in abject marginalization in which their life is a form of death in itself, to borrow from Mbembe's (2001) imagination. To study the language and voice of the subaltern requires that we stand in solidarity with their perspective. Likewise, in the seminal work, *A Theology of Liberation*, Gustavo Gutiérrez (1988) observes that friendship with oppressed groups is the only firm demonstration that a critical pedagogue can provide of his or her "authentic commitment" to liberation, equality and social justice.

The principal point here is that, within the context of the south, we should employ class and not the human rights perspective as the critical framework for studying subaltern violence because there is a danger of misrepresenting the public, 'undressing' and reducing it to a simple 'act of male violence against women.' It should be pointed out that such horizontal violence involving undressing women is also prevalent among upper or middle classes and such violence is increasingly being mediated by social media and online bullying including practices such as revenge porn. The principles of *ubunthu* as African humanism would be equally relevant as a frame of criticism because at its core, *ubuntu* is about celebrating human dignity and respect for the other. The focus should be on transforming the political economy of inequality in which women are often victims. If it is not the dressing, it is traditional and economic practices. The violence against women's dressing is just one symptom of the real inequality which is a fundamental building block of class-consciousness. European humanism should not be used as a frame to criticize this violence because, as Mbembe (2001, 2008) points out in his criticism, European humanism is also a discourse of violence and is a subject of criticism in most post-colonial theory.

Speaking alongside the subaltern: Janie Mae Crawford in *Their Eyes Were Watching God*

It must be emphasized that the subaltern speak in various contexts and often their speech is not understood, or is unheard. It is when subaltern voices become critical to development policy formulation and implementation that critical analysis has to be made of the symbolic structure and politics of voice. Marx was correct to raise the concern that the subaltern end up being represented even if they cannot represent themselves. The fact that these privileged classes are speaking on behalf of the subaltern is not really a problem on its own per se. The critical issue here is the question of authority in that the dominant classes have not been granted the authority to speak on behalf of the subaltern. The issue of authority is important because there are many cases within development contexts when oppressed classes exercise their relevant rights by making informed requests to be represented. An example occurs in *Their Eyes Were Watching God*, a novel written by the American, Zora Neale Hurston, in the 1930s.

The central figure in the story is Janie who returns home to Eatonville—an African American-only town—from a journey of self-discovery that began in this town where she was married to Joe Sparks, the mayor. In the town, news has spread that she eloped with a younger lover and the society finds her behaviour unacceptable for a woman of her age (she is 40). She has been away for about one and a half years on a journey that was undertaken with Tea Cake—the love of her life—but who she ended up shooting and killing in self-defence. Told in the first person narrative, Janie sits with her best friend Pheoby Watson and tells her story. This is a novel about a black woman who assumes authority over how she sees herself and thus attempts to rise above the narrow and deterministic prejudices of her society.

In the opening dialogue of the novel, Janie acknowledges that people have started asking questions about her moral behaviour. As can be gleaned from the excerpt below, this conversation raises three issues around the question of authority and the methodological pathway that enables individuals and groups to speak on behalf of subaltern groups. Notice how the dialogue takes place (Hurston 1937/1998, 6):

> "Ah don't mean to bother wid tellin' 'em nothin', Pheoby. 'Tain't worth de trouble. You can tell 'em what Ah say if you wants to. Dat's just de same as me 'cause mah tongue is in mah friend's mouf."
>
> "If you so desire Ah'll tell 'em what you tell me to tell 'em."
>
> "To start off wid, people like dem wastes up too much time puttin' they mouf on things they don't know nothin' about. Now they got to look into me loving Tea Cake and see whether it was done right or not! They don't know if life is a mess of corn-meal dumplings, and if love is a bed-quilt!"
>
> "So long as they get a name to gnaw on they don't care whose it is, and what about, 'specially if they can make it sound like evil."
>
> "If they wants to see and know, why they don't come kiss and be kissed? Ah could then sit down and tell 'em things. Ah been a delegate to de big 'ssociation of life. Yessuh! De Grand Lodge, de big convention of livin' is just where Ah been dis year and a half y'all ain't seen me."

From this excerpt it is clear that Janie has great trust in Pheoby as a friend. She recognizes that there is already a huge social demand for information on what has transpired between her and Tea Cake. Janie then gives her friend permission to speak on her behalf: "You can tell 'em what Ah say if you wants to. Dat's just de same as me 'cause mah tongue is in mah friend's mouf" (Hurston 1937/1998, 6). What is clear here is that Pheoby has been granted permission to speak on behalf of Janie because she knows all the facts and, more importantly, she is sympathetic to Janie's cause. The 'cause' here is the understanding that a black woman's place is not just in the home where she will have children and live in the comfort provided by her husband. This is what generations of black women, represented by Janie's grandmother (Nanny), have been brought up to believe. A black woman aspires not only to material comfort but also to abstract ideals such as independence, freedom, self-discovery and spiritual enlightenment. The ruthlessness with which Janie undertakes the journey of her life is what shocked the critics when the book was published, and shocked Eatonville too.

The dialogue between these two friends reveals something that has a huge implication for development theory and practice today. Janie challenges society at large: "If they wants to see and know, why they don't come kiss and be kissed? Ah could then sit down and tell 'em things" (Hurston 1937/1998, 6). The notion of "come kiss and be kissed" implies establishing a relationship with subaltern groups as a precursor to speaking for or on their behalf. The criticism that Spivak is raising of the reductionist approaches of dominant strands in western feminism that are operative in the south revolves around a concern about a lack of moral and intellectual legitimacy for external organizations to speak on behalf of the subaltern groups they claim to represent. If individuals and groups fail to come to "kiss and be kissed" by subaltern groups, the resultant representations will often be full of factual inaccuracies.

The excerpts of this conversation—and the novel as a whole—reveal that in order to speak on behalf of subaltern groups, researchers or change agents are required to be empathetic and sympathetic to the life and causes of the groups they seek to represent. This is Gutiérrez's "preferential option for the poor." Pheoby cautions Janie that there are some people who do not care about the truth, nor are they sympathetic to Janie's tragedy—she has just lost the love of her life, Tea Cake. Pheoby cautions Janie: "So long as they get a name to gnaw on they don't care whose it is, and what about, 'specially if they can make it sound like evil." Being sympathetic and empathetic to subaltern groups and their causes is crucial if individuals are to represent them in ways that are consistent with the local realities and needs. As if agreeing with Hurston's Pheoby, in a new introduction to *Orientalism* written in light of the aftermath of the events of 9/11, Said (1978) distinguishes between orientalist writing that is arrogant and uninformed on the one hand, and a kind of empathetic and understanding scholarship on the other.

Subaltern and oppressed

Freire's critical analysis of the notion of the oppressed has been the subject of numerous intellectual debates and reflections by community development scholars and practitioners. His work is central in understanding the deconstruction of power within various forms of development partnerships and engagements. The theme of power itself is, however, footnoted in *Pedagogy of the Oppressed*, even though the student-teacher relationship is depicted as being discursively fractured along the lines of power. Perhaps realizing this omission in his *Pedagogy of the Oppressed,* some years later Freire in conversation with Myles Horton in *We Make the Road by Walking,* confessed that he wished he had read Gramsci before writing the book (Horton and Freire 1990). Power as a form of ideology is essential to consider here. Lukes (2005) proffers a holistic perspective in his three-dimensional view; Woodson (1933/2006) identifies it as the epistemological capacity to influence and shape the mind; while Althusser (1971/2008) defines it as the ideological framework within which social, cultural and economic processes take place.

In his later works, Freire (1970, 1996) used his experiences to explain how ideology as a form of power conditioned him to behave and think the way he did. Through practice, Freire attempted to show how oppression works ideologically and that the first responsibility of a catalyzing educator is to empower oppressed peoples to challenge dominant discourses, ideologies and practices. This can only happen if oppressed people understand how ideology functions to oppress both the oppressors and the oppressed. Reflexive analysis can show that many oppressed peoples live through their oppression without recognizing their situation, cannot acknowledge its sources, and as such cannot participate in its deconstruction (Gutiérrez 1988). Critical pedagogy therefore becomes the avenue or pathway towards deconstruction, an active methodology for providing the tools and the skills to oppressed groups to empower them to understand and deconstruct their own oppression. This is the essence of Freire's and hook's (1994) engaged critical pedagogy, to "kiss and be kissed" by oppressed groups as an enlightenment process of collectively understanding oppression and then engaging in material and symbolic struggles to dismantle its discourses and structures.

Freire's pedagogy, like Fanon's radical political education, problematizes the future. For Freire, hooks and Fanon, and of course for Hurston, the future remains unknown, and therefore it can become unspoken or deconstructed. To *unspeak* is to deconstruct and then reconstruct. In this case, the future is unknown but through the actions of the educational catalyzer and the oppressed people it becomes exposed so long as the oppressed begin to understand their position in society. As such, critical pedagogy, Janie's "big association of life" or "the convention of living," becomes a journey of self-discovery by oppressed groups, empowering them to ask and answer three critical questions: (a) Who are we now? (b) Why are we what we are now? (c) How can we change our future? The third question is significant because it places agency in the hands of the oppressed and it is through this process that transformation of the oppressed into a subaltern occurs, that is, into a politically conscious class of oppressed people who want to speak and unspeak their future.

"Kiss and be kissed": The development school as subaltern voice

In this section, I reflexively explore my active participation and the involvement of local people in a development school in a rural village in Malawi, which was largely a volunteer initiative with groups of women from six villages who came together under one group with the aim of improving local livelihoods. With the permission of the senior traditional leader, I resuscitated the pre-existing but dysfunctional group with a friend, Moreen Luba, who was initially working with the women on HIV prevention. Together with the women we decided to designate its practice as a *development school* (*Sukulu ya Chitukuko*) because we had gone beyond teaching adult literacy and had started a community savings initiative. In this case, literacy was seen only as a means towards achieving certain development goals. The discussion will inertly reveal the challenges of community organizing for groups that were formed to meet specific sectorial goals.

My son and I returned to Malawi from the United Kingdom in July 2012 where we had lived and I had taught at the London School of Economics and Political Science from July 2008. This followed a one-year stint at the University of Fort Hare, Nelson Mandela's alma mater. I had just finished my PhD in Australia in 2007. By 2012, my son and I were homesick after such a long absence from Malawi but a key reason for my return had to do with my rethinking of university teaching, especially when it comes to critical pedagogy. Teaching and researching communication for development take on a distinctive form, especially when one is based in a metropolis such as London.

I had an opportunity during my time at the LSE to re-read Freire and Gutiérrez in the context of the insights into development communication that can be derived from Mbembe's, Escobar's, Spivak's and Marx's work. One great thing about London is that it is host to a number of development organization headquarters. There were numerous opportunities to talk to various experts and to attend the many workshops and seminars organized in the name of development. It was during this time that I came across Harry Frankfurt's book, *The Importance of What We Care About* (1988) and his seminal chapter, "On Bullshit" which threw me and caused me to reconsider the intellectual traditions that I had learned to venerate. Alongside the reading of the classical and post-colonial works just mentioned, I began to question my understanding of the enlightenment that is central to the praxis of critical pedagogy. I began to realize that there is a growing aesthetic and epistemological space in what I and other communication and development scholars in universities were teaching. It soon became necessary just as Janie did in *Their Eyes Were Watching God*, or as Nora did in Ibsen's (2004) *A Doll's House*, to undertake an intellectual journey of self-discovery to relearn and re-educate myself.

On a flight from a teaching exercise in Budapest, I started questioning the notion of enlightenment and came to the conclusion that critical pedagogy is in fact a *living* praxis, not something that can solely be explained to others but rather demonstrated to them. The mark of excellence in a public intellectual is not only the discursive criticism of developments in the symbolic and material world, nor simply in the narratives and syntax generated on proposed and implemented policy directions—it also requires the empirical and lived demonstration of the relevance, feasibility and realism of propagated ideals. Perhaps from the perspective of Gutiérrez (1988) enlightenment is a liberatory praxis, a process of becoming, and thus I realized that it can only be made to come alive through our active involvement in lived reality. This was my Janie moment, my experience of Nora's rapture.

This rethinking would later lead me to the realization that enlightenment, as in the translation of new knowledge into practice, is not exclusively related to the creation of new ideas and the innovations that may follow from them. It crucially involves the translation of ideas into practice, whether this occurs in the sciences, social sciences or through lived experience. In some cases, these experiments do not work. For example, between 1997 and 2001, I was involved in the creation of community communication projects that used participatory village theatre as a vehicle for generating development radio (Manyozo 2012). A frustrating experience occurred when I led a team of researchers to pre-testing radio stories and episodes collected within the community. Yet the communities who had initially provided the input rejected these stories and their relevance. It would not be until years later that I would realize that the praxis of enlightenment is fraught with contradictory power relations. In this case, communities had seen through our manipulation to generate certain preferred storylines on public health that they did not like. I would also realize that the 'fantasy' world of development manuals, templates and models become increasingly irrelevant over time, especially if a practitioner does not experiment with these models and approaches at regular intervals.

Organizing the oppressed to find their voice

By August 2013, I contacted Moreen to help me identify a rural community where together we would teach adult literacy. The Ministry of Gender and Community Development had produced a textbook in the 1990s, which we intended to use in our teaching. No one forced us to use the book but it was the only available guide with which to frame our teaching and learning experience with the group. It combined language literacy and functional numeracy. The book's approach was rooted in the agrarian policy orientation of the Malawi independence government and the topics were oriented towards subsistence agricultural production, including nutrition.

As we (both myself as an educator and the educatees) progressed in our learning and teaching, we started to explore other methods of teaching and learning involving the use of radio programmes and participatory mapping. It was during these experiments that the group opened up to accommodate those who were not living with the HIV or AIDS virus but wanted to learn how to read and write. We explored ways of tackling growing poverty, and focused especially on issues such as the narrow domestic income base. We employed the assistance of a small and medium enterprise development expert, Mirriam, from a small and medium enterprise initiative, partly because the group had managed to raise about US$2,000, which would be used to give out small loans to members. Mirriam's involvement allowed the group to explore various forms of income generation activity and together we discovered the benefit of adding commercial farming to our portfolio. A large farm was identified to rent and we agreed to grow crops that would yield a good income. This involved doing participatory baseline research on market opportunities.

At the time of writing, a year later, and now that I have left this initiative, all is not necessarily rosy, as it never is in the imperfect world of development theory and practice. Some participants have not paid back the money they borrowed from the funding pot. There are cases of conflicts between certain individuals. There were moments of hiatus, when the group would slow the pace of meetings and joint work, especially when people had moved out of the community to look for better economic opportunities in other cities or simply lost interest in the group and the hard work that development always requires. The group under the leadership of Moreen continues to soldier on nevertheless.

An important element in our *development school* was village mapping. We toured the village in order to "re-learn" it. About 25 of us usually walked as a herd might do, talking to other villagers about their understanding of the village and how they saw its future. The school participants suddenly took over the process and instead of just asking questions of other villagers, they started engaging in heated debates on development interventions in the village and how they could improve them. This experience was reminiscent of a scene in Ngũgĩ Wa Thiong'o's *Petals of Blood*, during which the teacher and the students go out to learn about plant biology but end up discussing questions about the unidirectional worm's feeding of the flower and how this is very similar to exploitation in society (Wa Thiong'o 1977). Likewise, the conversations during our village tours often revolved around power, politics, sex and gender issues. We argued over the question of domestic violence; we questioned the social welfare system in our country where we find many elderly people lying sick without help; we wondered about the absent fathers when we saw many kids playing unattended to—and importantly, we also noticed that three boreholes in the village were constructed only on one side, marginalizing the other side of the village.

Our participatory baseline information and mapping techniques offered more effective ways of teaching our students than formal lectures or seminars could hope to achieve. The eyes begin to visualize the things that existed before in different ways; the mind begins to question the banal, the usual, the everyday; the ear begins to hear the same songs or sounds very differently. Life takes on a new rhythm, a new tune and a new ambience as doubt creeps in regarding what we initially regarded as normal and as 'best practice' tradition. We realized that when doubt arises, questions emerge, and tradition gives way to critique, education can begin. As such, education is no longer about the acquisition of specific facts or techniques. It is a gradual process of allowing doubt to elicit questions and new insights that become an active part of our epistemological identity. When doubt was allowed to unsettle our intellectual comfort zone, knowledge arising through praxis was able transform education into a site of conflict, embracing ignorance, tradition (the norm) and reality.

To go back to the development school: the class once read an article about a woman whose incarcerated husband had broken her arms during a domestic altercation, but she pleaded with the magistrate not to sentence her husband heavily—since he was the breadwinner—while acknowledging that she realized that what he had done was wrong. Interpreted through a reductionist feminist perspective, the woman might seem disempowered. But the development class noticed that the woman understood that what her husband had done was wrong, even though it was a common occurrence within her community. The woman in this case is economically disempowered and a simple feminist development approach might be to suggest that the woman acquire a business so that she can get rid of the man. Our class noted, however, that the stability of a social system largely depends on stable relationships and institutions, including marriage. Empowering women economically is just one facet of this challenge. For the class, a key component of any intervention would be to improve the way women negotiate and contest power within such relationships, not simply releasing them from them. Our group shared the opinion that many ideologically informed off-site interventions miss the essence of the problem when it comes to the issue of women's empowerment. Yet it is significant to note that even this perspective is also problematic.

Concluding thoughts

The development school in this rural southern village is not perfect; there are many pitfalls and it is not a perfect model of deliberative development. In its current form, it has not achieved many of its objectives of radically empowering a subaltern and oppressed group to use their voice in curating their own development. Yet it continues to contribute to the experimentation with local people's own endogenous deliberative development, and not necessarily to challenge the modernist development discourse. In Eugene Delacroix's *Women of Algiers in their Apartment*, and other orientalist policies and reports, the forgotten black servant, symbolically representing those left behind, such as women, homosexuals, the unemployed and subjects on the periphery are stripped of their subjectivity and agency and hence they are oftentimes represented and spoken about in dominant discourses. In contrast, the "development school" discussed above, however imperfect its form, is nevertheless allowing a process of deconstruction of the dominant syntax of development spectacles—in the case of gender relations. Spaces are being opened up to allow the *speaking* of development in which individuals and groups are building their consciousness as they formulate and clarify their interests and positions. In the words of Janie Mae Crawford in *Their Eyes Were Watching God* (Hurston 1937/1998), the school is enabling all the participants to "kiss and be kissed" by the villagers themselves. As if emphasizing this approach, hooks (1994) discusses the notion of engaged pedagogy that is itself a radical process that empowers teachers and students resulting in their achieving self-actualization. This is, as indicated in previous chapters, a process of becoming, that is, the formulation of what Deleuze and Guattari (1987) conceive of as a social rhizome. Such interventions provide spaces for marginalized communities to enter into a dialogue with dominant discourse communities, thereby allowing them to create the ideological polities within which to question top-down development interventions and their associated discourses.

Like the militant Messaouda in Algerian folklore and the other Algerian women in the war of independence discussed in this chapter, who seemed to willingly engage in the symbolic and material political struggles, the voices of marginalized communities are not 'products' that can be packaged to suit various policy-driven scenarios. Such voices are best understood as the moments of communicative acts through which marginalized groups learn and come to understand and appreciate the depth and breadth of their oppression. Voice comes to be lived, it becomes a form of lived reality, a critical actuality, a conversational and dialogical pathway through which the oppressed begin to question their socio-political and economic reality. The frozen stare of the four Algerian women in Delacroix's painting is—through this process—being reactivated, brought back to life. In the excerpt from *Their Eyes Were Watching God*, Janie talks about having been a "delegate to the big association of life, a big convention of living." This is Janie's acknowledgement that she has discovered herself through an educational process that has seen her have experience with different men. Telling this story requires someone who is sympathetic to her journey of self-discovery. To produce a voice that tells this kind of story requires that we join Janie on her journey. The resulting narration can therefore represent Janie's interests and perspectives, and applied in other contexts such as the development school experience, it is as if Janie has rented us her tongue. Subaltern voice has to come alive if it is to make sense. It has to be made alive. That is the essence of development interventions that build on subaltern speech, as in the case of the development school project.

There are also moments, like with Messaouda and the Algerian woman in Fanon's *A Dying Colonialism* and the Indian woman, Bhuvaneswari, in Spivak's "Can the subaltern speak," where the subaltern themselves assume authority over the production of their speech. In these cases they refuse to be represented, but decide to represent themselves. The production of this speech is not solely intended to answer back to a dominant or orientalist discourse. What it suggests is that oppressed groups are constantly engaged in socio-cultural and political struggles and that they are often exploring ways of undermining and defeating oppressive power structures. And, of course, there are moments when they do so and moments when they do not.

Subaltern speech in these contexts should not be viewed as single events isolated from the politics that produced them. Rather, development interventions must be sympathetic to subaltern speech as a process of political engagement. The crucial role of a liberating educator is to engage in this political process and to provide the subaltern with creative tools and skills, so that they may produce better and more politically conscious voices. The speech of the subaltern can be an authentic platform for constructing effective development interventions, especially when it comes to eradicating structural violence, because, like Janie Mae Crawford, they have been to "de big convention of livin'" and others, including ourselves, have not.

Notes

1 For further reports, see Malm, Sara. 2014. "Woman is stripped and beaten by group of men because she was 'tempting them' by wearing a miniskirt in Kenya." *Daily Mail Online*, www.dailymail.co.uk/news/article-2837884/Kenyans-march-against-attacks-women-mini-skirts.html. See also BBC Online 2012. "Malawian women protest over 'trouser attacks'." www.bbc.com/news/world-africa-16645594; *Mail and Guardian Online* 2008. "Outrage over attack on mini skirt-wearing woman." http://mg.co.za/article/2008-02-19-outrage-over-attack-on-miniskirtwearing-woman.

2 Poddar, Ashis. 2011. "Girl ends life to donate eyes to dad." *The Times of India*, July 4. http://timesofindia.indiatimes.com/india/Girl-ends-life-to-donate-eyes-to-dad/articleshow/9092271.cms. See also, *The Huffingtonpost*, "Mumpy Sarkar, 12-year-old, commits suicide to donate organs to family" at www.huffingtonpost.com/2011/07/07/mumpy-sarkar-suicide-organ-donation_n_892287.html.

References

Adichie, Chimamanda Ngozi. 2009. "The danger of a single story." TED Talk. Oxford University. Accessed January 20 2016. www.youtube.com/watch?v=D9Ihs241zeg.

Althusser, Louis. 1971/2008. *On Ideology*. New York: Verso.

Bourdieu, Pierre. 1983/1991. *Language and Symbolic Power*. Cambridge: Polity Press.

Chouliaraki, Lilie. 2008. *Spectatorship of Suffering*. New Delhi, London and Thousand Oaks: Sage.

Deleuze, Gilles and Félix Guattari. 1987. *A Thousand Plateaus: Capitalism and Schizophrenia*. Translated by Brian Massumi. London and Minneapolis: University of Minnesota. Accessed January 20 2016. http://projectlamar.com/media/A-Thousand-Plateaus.pdf.

Djebar, Assia. 1992. *Women of Algiers in their Apartment*. Translated by Marjolijn de Jager. Charlottesville and London: University of Virginia Press.

Fanon, Frantz. 1965. *A Dying Colonialism*. New York: Grove Press.

Frankfurt, Harry. 1988. *The Importance of What We Care About*. Cambridge: Cambridge University Press

Freire, Paulo. 1970. *Pedagogy of the Oppressed*. London: Penguin.

Freire, Paulo. 1996. *Letters to Cristina*. New York: Continuum.

Gutiérrez, Gustavo. 1988. *A Theology of Liberation: History, Politics, and Salvation*. Translated by Caridad Inda and John Eagleson. Maryknoll, New York: Orbis Books.

hooks, bell. 1994. *Teaching to Transgress: Education as the Practice of Freedom*. London and New York: Routledge.

Horton, Myles and Paulo Freire. 1990. *We Make the Road by Walking: Conversations on Education and Social Change*. New Market: Highlander Research and Education Centre.

Hurston, Zora Neale. 1937/1998. *Their Eyes Were Watching God*. New York: First Perennial Library.

Ibsen, Henrik. 1879/2004. *A Doll's House*. Translated by Kenneth McLeish. London: Nick Hern Books.

Lerner, Daniel. 1958. *The Passing of Traditional Society: Modernizing the Middle East*. New York and London: Free Press and Collier-Macmillan.

Lukes, Steven. 1974/2005. *Power: A Radical View*. New York: Palgrave Macmillan.

Mamdani, Mahmood. 2007. "The politics of naming: Genocide, civil war, insurgency." *London Review of Books*, 29(5): 5–8.

Manyozo, Linje. 2012. *Media, Communication and Development: Three Approaches*. New Delhi: Sage.

Marx, Karl. 1852/2010. *The Eighteenth Brumaire of Louis Bonaparte*. New York: *Die Revolution* Issue 1.

Mbembe, Achille. 2001. *On the Postcolony*. Berkeley, CA: University of California Press.

Mbembe, Achille and Esprit. 2008. "What is postcolonial theory? An interview with Achille Mbembe." Conducted by Olivier Mongin, Nathalie Lempereur and Jean-Louis Schlegel. In *Eurozine*, September 1. Accessed January 20 2016. www.eurozine.com/articles/ 2008-01-09-mbembe-en.html.

Rostow, Walt. 1960. *The Stages of Economic Growth: A Non-Communist Manifesto.* Cambridge: Cambridge University Press.

Said, Edward. 1978. *Orientalism*. New York: Random House.

Schramm, Wilbur. 1964. *Mass Media and National Development: The Role of Information in the Developing Countries*. Stanford: Stanford University Press.

Spivak, Gayatri. 1988. "Can the subaltern speak?" In Nelson Cary and Lawrence Grossberg (eds), *Marxism and the Interpretation of Culture* (pp. 271–313). Chicago, IL: University of Illinois.

Thompson, Edward Palmer. 1963. *The Making of the English Working Class.* London: Vintage Books.

Wa Thiong'o, Ngũgĩ. 1977. *Petals of Blood.* London and Nairobi: James Currey.

Woodson, Carter. 1933/2006. *The Mis-Education of the Negro.* Drewryville: Khalifah Publishers.

4

LIVING WITH PEOPLE

Setting the context

In *A Theology of Liberation*, Gutiérrez (1988, 67) emphasizes the need for radical and humanist educators to embrace "human experience of human relationships" with groups and communities. Building on this observation, this chapter primarily concerns itself with demonstrating how to speak and unspeak development with people in their own communities. It is one thing to sit in an office and imagine the meaning of concepts and then perhaps make proposals on strategies and approaches that should be used to engage people in the making of history. But it is quite another thing to go out in the community and work with people to implement such proposed policies and strategies in ways that satisfy them as well as the policy makers and development organizations. Gutiérrez (1988) proposes that doing liberation—or in the case of this book, speaking development—requires an awareness and experience of human relationships. What he seems to be calling for here is the active involvement of critical educators in a historical process that entails working with marginalized groups to design and implement development. This approach is summarized in one of Gutiérrez's observations, a "preferential option for the poor." As such this chapter examines one of the most contentious concepts in development today, "living with the people." What does it mean?

The chapter explores this notion by examining how the integration of new knowledge technology within a development context provides a communicative space that enables marginalized groups to contribute to deliberative development. The discussion in this chapter continues my conversation with some southern scholars of communication for development, in this case especially with one of the pioneers of communication for development in Africa, Chris Kamlongera (1988), and a Latin American theorist and practitioner, Alfonso Gumucio Dagron (2003). The exposition engages Gumucio Dagron's (2003) critical analysis of information and communication technologies (ICTs) in development alongside Tufte and Mefalopulos's (2009) notion of living with the people. For Gumucio Dagron (2003) the exponential growth of the ICT industry in the south has opened up avenues for innovative, participatory and sustainable implementation policy planning and development. These are processes that require a well-rounded humanist educator with great skills in living and engaging with people (Freire 1970; Kamlongera 1988). For Tufte and Mefalopulos (2009) to design and effectively implement a critical pedagogy, a facilitator must acquire the pertinent skills and tools to ensure they ask the relevant questions in a collective learning process that involves unlearning various biases and prejudices. For Kamlongera (1988), the emphasis has been on listening to communities as a priori to the collaborative act of speaking development. Though there exists many social science disciplines that attempt to train students to live and engage with people, it is Communication for development (C4D) that has become synonymous with communicating development at the local level.

Communication for development

Most contemporary communication for development definitions largely emanate from Nora Quebral's (1975, 1) early definition of the field, which elaborated the "art and science of human communication, applied to the speedy transformation of society." Following Quebral's pioneering definition and subsequent theorization, numerous definitions and conceptualizations have emerged (Gumucio Dagron and Tufte 2006; Gwin Wilkins, Tufte and Obregon 2014; Hemer and Tufte 2005; Obregon and Waisbord 2012; Scott 2014). In spite of these, it can be argued that the field cannot be understood without acknowledging the schools and approaches within the field. My consideration of these approaches and schools of thought yields a redefinition of communication for development as the method-driven, theory-informed, learning-based and evidence-driven employment of media and communications to interrupt and transform the political economy of development in ways that enable individuals, communities and societies to determine their own history (Manyozo 2012). It is important to mention that all kinds of history are ideological and contextual, and their objectivity can be questioned. Yet, in this case, it is a people's history written by them and for themselves. For Gutiérrez (1988) and Escobar (1995), transforming the political economy, the culture and the social traditions of a society is fundamental for the attainment of human liberation, so that individuals can reject the undercurrents of *thingification* (Césaire 1955), and instead become active agents in the creation of the dialectic of history (Marx 1852/2010).

Various schools of thought contributed to pioneering experiments in communication for development. Broadly, these were the Latin American, Bretton Woods, African, Indian, Los Baños and Communication for Development and Social Change (C4D&SC) schools (Manyozo 2012). The first, the Latin American School, had its origins in the regional meetings of the Catholic Bishops after the Second Vatican Council in 1963 leading to the Medellin Agreement, the liberatory theology of Father Gustavo Gutiérrez of Peru and Bishop Oscar Romero of El Salvador, Colombia's Radio Sutatenza, Bolivia's Miners' Radio Stations, Miguel Sabido's entertainment-education experiment in Mexico, and other grassroots social change interventions (Gumucio Dagron and Tufte 2006). The second, the Bretton Woods School had its origins in the development project of the post-World War Two Marshall Plan, the establishment of financial institutions such as the World Bank, the International Monetary Fund, the European Development Bank, the African Development Bank, the Asian Development Bank and other regional banks. Alongside these financial institutions, international and transnational development organizations emerged, including United Nations institutions and organizations such as Oxfam and Save the Children, as well as government departments such as the UK Department for International Development (DFID). The third, the Indian School emerged from development journalism experiments and other projects aimed at developing ICT applications within rural contexts. The fourth, the African School evolved from the theatre for development experiments produced collaboratively by universities and local communities starting in the 1950s. The fifth, Los Baños, evolved from research work at the University of the Philippines, where academics in the College of Agriculture were exploring creative ways of communicating agriculture and rural development information to rural end users. The sixth, the C4D&SC School emerged in the 2000s as a collaboration involving southern and northern partners. A possibility of a seventh school might include work undertaken by scholars and practitioners in the former USSR and China, Cuba, and past and present communist countries which do not subscribe to the dominant development paradigm. The debates and scholarship in the communication for development field have largely footnoted the scholarship in communist Eastern Europe, China, Cuba or the former USSR, at least as judged by publications throughout the post-war period.

These schools are not necessarily exclusive but, in one way or another, through funding and the transnational reach of experts, they have informed one another. The early instructional technology experiments in India, for example, were often funded by Bretton Woods institutions, and the first communication for development scholars at the University of the Philippines—such as Nora Quebral, Juan Jamias or Felix Librero—were trained in western universities. It has to be mentioned, however, that from the late 1950s, the International Association of Media and Communication Research (IAMCR) would then establish a section to explore communication for development issues, and many scholars were engaged with southern scholars working in the field.

The three approaches

Through a critical analysis of these schools, it is possible to identify three main approaches that have informed the theory and practice of communication for development: (1) those focusing on communication *content*, (2) those emphasizing media practices and *structures*, and (3) those focusing on communication *processes*

(Manyozo 2012, 2016). For example, analyses of the establishment of the miners' radio stations in Bolivia tend to emphasize structure, and similarly, the establishment of Radio DZLB at the University of the Philippines involved a structural intervention. The establishment of the radio listening clubs in India involved efforts to initiate a process (the aim was to horizontalize the radio broadcasts), as did Don Snowden's participatory video experiments under the *Fogo Process* (Manyozo 2012). The entertainment-education experiments of Miguel Sabido in Mexico tended to emphasize content, similar to the theatre for development experiments in Africa. And it is from this categorization that the three approaches can be named and defined.

The first approach focuses on content, and is also conceptualized as the *media for development* approach; it typically refers to the collaborative production of media and communication content with the aim to teach, educate, and mobilize communities to undertake specific actions within development contexts the world over. The 2008 financial crisis ruptured binary oppositions between south and north and the key oppositions are now better characterized as being class distinctions rather than organized around geographical space. In the western world, there is an increasing presence of homelessness, inequality, domestic and gender-based violence, alcoholism, drug abuse and poverty. As such, the south is there even in the north. In its early days in the 1950s/60s, this approach was largely informed by: development journalism experiments of the Philippine Press Institute and the Asian Media and Information Centre (AMIC); agriculture communication and extension experiments in South East Asian universities; rural journalism experiments in India; entertainment-education initiatives of the Mexican state television station; and later by public health communication institutes in North America, as well as by many rural educational experiments in the south. It is this specific approach that, in my opinion, has been captured by development industries, as it provides them with the epistemological space to design and implement the modernist, empiricist and positivist programmes that can yield them the scientific results desired to construct a change narrative that Mansell (1982) defines as the dominant paradigm.

The second approach—focusing on processes, is generally a *participatory communication* approach with a concern for geographical or ideological community, in which a facilitator often leads participants in a consciousness-building session, with the aim of allowing everyone to contribute towards making history. This is the approach that liberation theology thinkers such as Gutiérrez or Freire talk about in their theories of critical pedagogy—it is about the facilitator, the educator being present through their semiotic *firstness* with communities, and discussing and planning development together. This is achieved through a participatory-action research process "based on two-way communication methods and is most effective in investigating, assessing and uncovering key issues" (Tufte and Mefalopulos 2009, 15). It also requires the creation of an informal public sphere that promotes dialogue and action in which the "empowerment process is based on reflection on problems, but also on integration of action—the attempt to act collectively on the problem" (Tufte and Mefalopulos 2009, 11). It is the deeper analysis of this participatory communication approach that this book is about: To question how power figures in relationships that shape the design and implementation of development policies in and within the community.

The third approach—concerned with practice and structure—is a *media development* approach. It has its roots in the pre-Industrial Revolution period when newspapers came to the fore. The media development approach is often concerned with strengthening journalistic practice; building or consolidating media structures and institutions; and establishing and enabling legislation to protect freedom of speech. Media development refers to organized and strategic efforts aimed at supporting and building the capacity of media institutions through policies, structures and practices used as pathways towards consolidating good citizenship and governance, building democracies in fragile states and enhancing sustainable development (Manyozo 2016; Scott 2014). Such media assistance aims to close gaps between socio-economic centres and peripheries through the provision of universal access to media hardware and software (Manyozo 2016; Scott 2014). The assumption underpinning this approach is typically that increased access to and participation in the creation, sharing and utilization of information will eventually strengthen the role of civil society as a space where citizens/people can actively participate in democracy and hold authorities to account. Sustainable financial investment in building media capacity—whether through structures, skills, literacies, or policies—is expected to trigger the improved quantity and quality of media content and increased public participation in media production and consumption, which will result in the improvement of governance through enabling marginalized groups to contribute to development discourses. Of course, such efforts are constantly mediated by politics and international relations, socio-economic environment, literacy levels, culture, access to technology or the quality of what Mansell (2011) designates as the knowledge societies. For Mansell (2011), knowledge societies can be conceived of as the socio-economic and political context within which institutions and groups employ available software and hardware to generate, exchange and utilize information and communication resources and data to improve governance and development. The plurality signalled by 'societies' is intended to signpost diversity in contrast to a universal feature that is seen or should be seen in every society.

Four major works have established the conceptual frameworks for these three components of the communication for development field. These are *Media and Global Change: Rethinking Communication for Development* (Hemer and Tufte 2005); *Communication for Social Change Anthology: Historical and Contemporary Readings* (Gumucio Dagron and Tufte 2006); *The Handbook of Global Health Communication, Development and Social Change* (Obregon and Waisbord 2012); and *The Handbook of Development Communication and Social Change* (Gwin Wilkins, Tufte and Obregon 2014). The last two readers have helped to bring the field from the margins of influential scholarship into wider recognition and have helped to encourage a major turn in communication for development training.

Nevertheless, the problem with past and current scholarship in the communication for development field is that the work is propounded within the broad framework of western economic determinism and modernity which assumes that, "what the west is, the east seeks to become" borrowing again from Lerner's *The Passing of Traditional Society* (1958, 38). Recently, it has become imperative that the teaching, research and practice of communication for development should first and foremost involve the contestation of the notion of development itself, as is currently the case in some academic training programmes, journals and books. The concern is that many such programmes and publications seem to have been captured by the economic determinism models, and this is a feature that is also shared by other social science disciplines (Post-Crash Economics Society 2014).

People, ICTs and development

Apart from being deemed to be important in strategies for conceiving and implementing communication for development—reflecting any of the three approaches mentioned above—it is important to appreciate that ICTs are often seen as technologies that are important for development interventions more generally (Gumucio Dagron 2003; Mansell 2011). They are often seen as providing an opportunity for creating linkages between the centre and periphery within countries and at national and regional levels. An expanded ICT production and usage sector is frequently expected to increase opportunities for the inclusion of marginalized groups and to increase the involvement of the majority of the middle and lower classes in what has been called "the knowledge societies" (Mansell 2011). ICTs may be claimed to offer a development platform for new ways of creating and sharing wealth, and the opportunities that come with it. In some cases, it is noted that ICTs themselves are not ideologically neutral (Mansell 2011). This has implications insofar as they support communicative spaces that may allow for the imagining of realistic development narratives and dialogues born of local aspirations and needs. As such, the use of ICTs may expand opportunities for speaking, for creating subaltern speech, and subsequently for integrating such speech within dominant development narratives, which is the first step towards undermining spectacles of development. The argument here is that radical approaches towards development do not have to discard and dismiss dominant development bullshit, but, rather, also work within the system and curate interventions that respond to community needs. ICTs also offer symbolic tools for the production and exchange of alternative communicative action that may be deliberately and strategically able to undermine and reform the dominant development syntax.

These opportunities, however, are often undercut by a problematic political economy of development that gives rise to digital illiteracy, social and economic inequality, financial, institutional and social unsustainability, the absence of community ownership, scarce local content, inappropriate technology, and linguistic and cultural irrelevance. In rejecting ICTs as a solution to problems of poverty and underdevelopment, for instance, Gumucio Dagron (2003, 28) cautions:

> A bit of historical perspective could help to avoid the same old mistakes and better understand the deep roots of poverty: the real causes of

> underdevelopment are social injustice, exploitation of poor countries by rich countries as well as the poor within each country by the rich upper classes that control government, financial institutions, services and the productive sector.

Building on Gumucio Dagron's essential factors that need consideration in the theory and practice of any approach to deliberative development, I discuss these factors in the context of an imaginary local community in a region not far from a major road that connects the region to a capital city 450 km away. This community assumes the collective identity of many marginalized communities that I have been privileged to visit and live in the world over. The names of places have been modified but the events in this story are real—in what follows they are narrativized into a chronology to emphasize the importance of communication as an epistemological space for the contestation of power relations in a community. This discussion is intended to illustrate the extent to which ICTs themselves are not neutral, but are semiotically linked to the socio-cultural context within which they are introduced, and I draw upon my own recollections of what happened.

Visiting the village

There is a small dusty road that meanders from the main tarmac road, down the village forest. The road then slithers its way through the mostly grass-thatched houses and disappears into the endless oblivion of the unresolved, uncontested and shocking poverty. This village would become a significant intellectual platform that enabled Everson Banda, the headmaster at the local primary school, to provide a different kind of education to numerous development researchers and practitioners who were fond of visiting this village. No one can remember how or when all this started, but this village was considered 'lucky' by many surrounding villages for its ability to attract white people who, it was whispered openly, were bringing lots of monies for development.

Everson Banda was not from this area, but ended up here when he slept with and impregnated Amina, the then fellow student at the district secondary school where he had been studying. He failed to go to the university, but instead was enrolled in a teachers' training college where, after his diploma, he was sent to this rural school. His uncle had raised Everson after his parents passed away from a strange protracted illness that wasted the patient's skin and bones. As one of the few people who spoke English in this remote area, the foreign, white, development experts often visited the village through him, and it would be he who would translate for the local village chief and other village elders.

When he started teaching, he brought Amina to live with him, a kind of marriage in the traditional sense. Over time, Everson took on a second wife, the chief's niece, which allowed him some sort of ethnic validation, considering the covert animosity between various ethnic groups in this country and region. Marrying a local woman, especially a chief's niece, provided him with honorary ethnic status as a local, more so than if he had mastered the local language. As such, it fell upon his shoulders to introduce and guide development experts who came into this community.

It is this dusty road into the village that would become another classroom for Everson Banda as he guided the many development experts who visited the village.

"On the left, as you can see, is a dilapidated building that used to be a majestic market in those days, funded by the government of Germany. This was built in the late 1970s."

"Why would anyone build this market?" the slim, tall, young white male with a goatee sort-of asked.

"This derelict structure was originally meant to be a mini farming-produce market, which would offer communities an opportunity to market their produce and animals. The place had thrived in the 1980s but once the government constructed a major bridge and the tarmac road with funding from the European Union, villagers could transport their products to far and distant markets."

Even in this dilapidated state, the mini market shows great architectural conceptualization, and seems to have cost millions in local currency to build. Over the years, the traditional court utilized the space, but more recently, it has become a playground for children. Even when the local assembly tried to force the local farmers to move into the market structure, their efforts were unsuccessful. Very dirty but happy children can be seen playing an unfamiliar traditional game to visitors, running through the building or jumping through the broken windows while trying to hit each other with a fruit that seems to be a pear. On the other side of the market building, we see a group of young men who are skinning the carcass of a pig. Some of them are boiling the blood, as is the custom here, which they will use as stew for a traditional dish with their families.

Past the market, the entourage, which is headed towards the village headman's compound, passes a broken down water pump. A group of women are walking towards the village well that was dug deep in the ground to ensure a steady supply of drinking water, near the banks of the local river.

"This water pump was installed three years before by an organization whose European name cannot be recalled nor pronounced by locals here," continues Banda, who then goes on to provide an abridged history of local development. When the pump was initially installed, many villagers stopped drawing drinking water from the popular drinking well because of the new pump, which provided fresh water. A big ceremony had been organized to launch this water project. The local Member of Parliament (MP) and other important government dignitaries had come to attend the launch. It was all happiness in the village. The water pump also became a meeting point. Traditional dances were organized around its installation. People would wash at the water pump because it was said that the freshness of the water strengthened the garments. People took baths at the water pump. Then one day the pump broke down and even the smart Everson Banda did not know how to fix it. The numerous visits to the district offices to establish how to fix the water pump yielded nothing. A government engineer was sent to take a look and write a report. He took some of the "broken parts" and no one heard from him again.

Eventually the villagers accepted that maybe it was not meant to be after all, "When God gives something, He can take it back," and that is what the white preacher, Pastor Richardson who visited every month had said.

For Everson, travelling with the white external development agents allowed him to teach things he really believed about life. The dusty roads into the village allowed him to take education—which he normally delivered in class—out into the community. He liked walking in front of his delegation, stopping to explain things that he felt were important. He took on this role like the famous Scottish Missionary Dr. David Livingstone, who Banda believed must have done the same in the late 1800s. The villagers would congregate outside their houses and watch in amazement as Everson explained things in a language they could only dream of. "He speaks to these people in their own languages."

It was often said by the many extension workers who had come to work in this community that this was a "barren" space—no matter what interventions the government and development partners introduced, nothing ever came of them. The initiatives eventually died a silent death—unlike the pomp and fanfare that had characterized their introduction—or to paraphrase Alfonso Gumucio Dagron, these interventions had become cemeteries of development. Perhaps what the rural development planners had overlooked was scenario planning, thus they did not factor in changes in local socio-economic attributes and indicators. The new road and bridge had changed the dynamics of mobility. The road and the vehicles that passed by enabled people to be both rural and urban at the same time. So this community was no longer rural, and therefore rural development interventions here seemed misplaced.

The radio station in the village

The discussions at the village headman's place were long and went on into the dead of the night. The visitors sat around the fire and listened to wonderful tales of how the local people migrated into this valley. In the distance, young girls and men could be heard performing tribal dances. It seemed the village had the temerity to come alive in the moonlight. Some of the young men and women were huddled in pairs under the dark shades of trees whispering to each other of their dreams yet to be lived. The young men believed they could travel to the city, make some money and come back to marry their brides.

At the village headman's compound, food was shared and it was time for Everson Banda and the visitors to leave. The visitors had come to experience life in the village but would actually be housed in one of the classrooms at the school. But there was an agreement in terms of their assessment of the local communication landscape. One of the visitors would make an important record in his diary entry the next day:

> It is very clear that this valley of villages confronted by massive social, cultural and economic challenges, which calls on us, the West, to continue providing

> development assistance to the global south, much of which is experiencing a rapid exponential growth of the telecommunications and ICT sectors. In these valleys and other peripheries however, the spoken word and its orality remain powerful articles and conventions for the generation, exchange and consumption of social meanings and their reference frames. From girls' education to subsistence farming, public health to other development challenges, governments and institutions have struggled to engage with rural and regional populations, especially those whose reliable means of producing and exchanging meanings remain traditional and indigenous forms of communication.
>
> In reality, these socio-economic factors do place a huge responsibility on media to inform, empower and challenge the many rural, poor and illiterate citizens to actively engage in the formulation and implementation of policies affecting their lives. Unfortunately for these of the valley communities, there is minimal access to the national broadcaster, whose reception is very poor. A little less than 40% of the local population has access to radio sets, which rely on dry cells that are increasingly becoming expensive. It is therefore an open secret, and the chief agreed with our conversations, that we should establish a radio station to ensure that we bring these people into the communication society of the 21st century. There is need to seek funding for the purchase of radio equipment, so that this community will have its own radio station. This is going to enable local people to actively engage in the reconstruction of their lives, through the facilitation of local dialogical and dialectical communications.
>
> Preliminary discussions with community leaders seem to overwhelmingly support the introduction of this radio station, which we believe could open up many windows for further development of this impoverished area.

In the ensuing weeks there were further consultations with community groups and it was agreed—or rather suggested by the visitors—that the community radio should be for women only. It would become the first women-owned and run community radio in the region. The visitors emphasized that women were oppressed and that their voices were ignored and not heard in policy forums. Everyone agreed, including the men—after all this was being suggested by the visitors, the white visitors, so it was true.

It would take another two years for the radio station to finally come to the community. There was indeed a huge fanfare. Local communities had contributed bricks and their labour to the construction of the station near the school, close to the major electricity grid that came from the city and went on to the border town, another 300 km away. The local member of parliament—who local people rarely saw—would contribute iron sheets and cement. Technical specialists who had come with government people would install the equipment and before long electricity would be installed. Everson Banda and the village headman would select the first group of young women from the village who would be trained in radio broadcasting by a women journalists' group from the city. Wind-up radio sets donated by the Freeradio Foundation would be distributed everywhere.

There was celebration in the communities. The radio station seemed to have given a new lease of life to civil and public life. Women's income-generating groups popped up. Financial advisers would visit the village to talk about village banking and other strange concepts that implied that women starting social enterprises would benefit them. It was a great period to be a citizen in this valley. The storeowner took advantage of the bringing of electricity to the school to install electricity in his shop, and alongside he opened a small video house, installed a television screen and DVD player. This place would enable villagers—after paying a small fee—to watch American and Nigerian movies. And at night when the storeowner was asleep, the village headmen and some of the elders would sneak into the village cinema with their local gin brew in order to watch pornographic movies. In essence, the radio station had indeed changed the face of the community, perhaps as prophesized by Schramm (1964, 20):

> No one who has seen modern communication brought to traditional villages will ever doubt its potency. Once in an isolated village in the Middle East I watched a radio receiver, the first any of the villagers had seen, put into operation in the headman's house. The receiver promptly demonstrated that knowledge is power. It became a source of status to its owner; he was the first to know the news, and controlled the access of others to it. From him and all others who heard, the noisy little receiver became a magic carpet to carry them beyond the horizons they had known. But the most impressive demonstration of the impact of that radio was the scene when a group of villagers—who had previously known higher government chiefly through the tax collector or a soldier—heard for the first time a spokesman of their leaders invite them to take part in governing their country.
>
> No one who has heard the happy shouts with which a cinema van is greeted in an African village is ever likely to forget the experience. Less quickly, less dramatically, the impact of communication is seen when a road is newly opened to a village. Strangers come in with goods to sell and ideas and news to exchange. Villagers travel to the nearest city and bring back new standards and customs. And change begins.

During daytime, outside the radio station, many people would assemble just to talk and chat. A maize mill was also being installed by the storeowner, and it would make grinding flour much easier for local women, since they had to use traditional means of pounding the corn. In the meantime, without anyone noticing, gradually the radio station, with the beautiful voices of local girls, became an ambience within village life.

Then one day, just like that, the radio was off-air. At first people thought it was going to be for a short time. When there was no radio programming for the entire morning, the whispers and rumours started circulating. Equipment had been stolen, it was being said. It must be Kapesi, the local gangster. That bloody Kapesi! It must be him. He had a way of looking at the radio station when he was drunk.

The village had enough of him. He would be made to pay. Then another rumour started circulating. Slowly, people were assembling at the station. There was a vehicle outside the station. Inside, there seemed to be a meeting going on. Everson Banda was there, arguing with two guys in yellow and green overalls who didn't look interested or convinced. Then they drove off. Then word got out, it was the electricity bill. Electricity bill for what? Isn't this a development project?

The station had accumulated a huge electricity bill over a period of time. The MP had paid the bill for the first three months, but he would leave it to the local community to source funding to pay for themselves. It was their radio station and they had to take responsibility. How much was the bill? It was a very huge bill, and that afternoon there was a meeting at the village headman's place. It was a heated meeting because there was the suggestion of everyone contributing. It was not yet harvest time and the villagers did not have any money. Another group of men said they would not contribute to the station because it was a women-owned radio. But, the chief argued, all of you listen to it. The MP would be informed, and a week later the electricity would be reconnected, as there was huge political pressure on the electricity provider, due to the presidential and parliamentary elections that were being held in the near future.

A couple of weeks later the radio would be off-air again. After extensive consultation and with the assistance of a commercial broadcaster, the local community learnt that there was a problem with the transmitter and antenna. No one knew what that equipment was, really. Another meeting was held in the community, where it was agreed to send a delegation to the regional government offices. The local MP had stopped picking up calls from the community. The delegation to the government was meant to seek financial support. The group of female journalists from the city would come and pick up the four-person delegation. The meeting at the regional government offices was unfruitful. There were no finances for the radio station in the local budget and, in fact, the officials didn't know a radio station had been established. What about the white people who established the station? Everson Banda had sent them a message but they had not replied.

Another meeting in the village resolved that the station should no longer be for women only but involve men as well and thus it would be a community radio and not a rural women's radio. A committee was set up to look into management issues including revenue generation. Someone suggested that local businesses should pay to have their businesses advertised. The problem was that much of the business in the community took place after harvest. Then the volunteers working at the station said they wanted some form of remuneration because, instead of working in the gardens, they were researching and producing stories and then broadcasting them. Someone suggested that the five bicycles that were brought with the equipment to help with journalists' mobility should be sold to generate funds. This proposal was rejected as being too short term in its focus. It was becoming clearer during these conversations that the radio project was a huge responsibility and highly problematic because no one had sat down to think carefully as to what having a radio station actually implied. A management committee was eventually set up and tasked with the responsibility of drawing up a strategic plan for the station's financial and institutional sustainability. In the distance, a drunken Kapesi was walking past and he could be heard, like a sleepwalker, wondering whether the local community really needed the radio station.

The women's development group

In the aftermath of the radio project, a period of peace and quiet seemed to emerge in the villages. The village cinema continued to provide local entertainment and football also demonstrated its ability to bring villagers together. Alongside the cinema in captivating local people, were the traditional dances and the "family role playing" that involved adolescents and young adults having sexual relations in the gardens. These are some of the practices that the women's empowerment group, established by the wife of a white pastor, Pastor Richardson, who visited the village once a month, would focus on eradicating.

The pastor's wife, Alyssa, believed that very oppressive traditions, inequality and low economic status were holding the women back from realizing their full potential. It was her dream to establish successful social enterprises with groups of local women. Key components of these women's groups were income-generating activities and, of course, adult literacy. In this particular community, a young girl, Luthando, a recent city high school graduate—but who was still unemployed—was drafted to be the adult education teacher. Alyssa, or Madam Alyssa as local women fondly called her, would organize a two-week capacity building training course in the capital city for Luthando, so that she could offer her lessons more effectively.

The women's group would grow in strength, even if there were some doubts about their focus on women's empowerment, which implied advocating an end to some of the local customs, placing the group at odds with some of the established institutions such as the village council or the traditional school councillors who initiated the village girls into adulthood. With a little start-up capital from Alyssa, the group would struggle for over a year, with some members dropping out and new ones coming in. Then as time passed they began establishing businesses together and they would bank and reinvest the profits. The ground rules put in place would include confiscating household items if anyone failed to pay back the small loan she secured. There was a huge fight and it involved the village mediation process when one woman, Nasela, failed to pay back what she owed the group and eventually the group confiscated her husband's bicycle. The husband's argument was that he had nothing to do with his wife's financial endeavours, but the village mediation process—probably under the influence of the village headman's wife, who was also a member of the women's development group—ratified the confiscation of the bicycle and its eventual sale to recover Nasela's debt. The sale of this bicycle impoverished Nasela's family further as the husband's small business of buying and selling small fish, which relied on cycling to distant markets, also died off.

To inspire the women further, Madam Alyssa asked the women if they wanted to learn to use a computer. Though no one really knew what one looked like, they all agreed it was important to learn to use the computer. Again, Luthando, the adult literacy teacher, would be sent to the city to learn how to use the computer herself so she could teach the others. The computer would be brought to the village but was housed at the school because that was the only place where there was electricity, apart from the storeowner's, who would charge the group to use the power and his location. "Development is supposed to be free, why we have to pay for electricity anyway?"

Once a week the women would assemble around the computer and watch Luthando type things that Madam Alyssa had requested. It was a great experience for them just to watch this machine take in all the instructions it was being given and then, even after it was switched off and then on again, Luthando would be able to find what she had been working previously. As time passed, the Internet would be connected to the computer and an email account opened which helped Luthando connect with Alyssa on a regular basis. But it also allowed Luthando access to the wider world. She could read online news and was able to browse for job vacancies.

One challenge the women faced when learning the computer was the language. Everything on the computer was in English while their adult literacy classes only taught them to write and speak their own language. Eventually the women agreed that they really didn't need to learn to use the computer because Luthando was around and she could do whatever was required on their behalf.

Back on-air

On a sunny afternoon, a white 4×4 Toyota van stopped at the school and out came two Middle Eastern-looking, and dressed, men who would converse with Everson Banda for some time, before being led to the village headman's compound. There was a lot of whispering in the village regarding these new visitors. Then Luthando was invited to the chief's compound where discussions seemed to go on and on. These men had responded to an email that Luthando had written to their organization, seeking support to resuscitate the local radio station. They were from an Islamic charity organization with a name not many could pronounce properly. They were interested in working with rural communities and, especially, in helping orphans. The village would have an orphanage where all the orphans would live and they would be provided with education and food. One village elder wanted to know what would happen to orphans who wanted to live with their extended families but attend the orphanage school. It was emphasized that the children had to reside at this orphanage; after all, some elderly women in the community would be trained to cook and care for the children.

It seemed a welcome proposal, considering that the 'slimming' disease had destroyed the social fabric of these communities. There was now an increased frequency with which people were dying every week. With regard to the radio station, the charity organization would pay for the maintenance of the transmitter and the antenna. And because there were unsettled electricity bills, the charity would pay off the bills as well. The only thing they wanted in return was that the station should be co-managed by one of the charity people, that half of the station's programming should be Islamic religious programming, and that the charity would pay the community volunteers who worked at the station. It was a very awkward situation for the community because, to start with, there were no Muslims in the valley communities and most people were either Christians, animists or both.

Eventually, a solution was arrived at. Luthando would manage the station with a local management committee that included the Islamic charity, whose local office was going to be located within one of the storeowner's unused block of shops, thus generating for him some much-needed cash. The charity also brought in a young man from the city, a professional journalist who was publishing some materials in the charity's public relations office. It was this young man who would present the Islamic programming that was largely comprised of recorded Arabic language sermons and music. Once in a while, he would feature a recording of broadcasts of Islamic prayers that were prepared by the capital city office, even though locally there were no Muslims, yet. Even if it was a weird situation for the community, it was acceptable and understandable, for it ensured that the station was back on-air.

Before long, the orphanage was built. Huge trucks had brought the bricks and other building materials. The village provided a piece of land for the orphanage next to the school and church. A group of six local women would be trained in childcare and management. Madam Alyssa would express her concern about these new developments. She openly mentioned to the women she did not like the idea of Muslims coming into the community.

"Our radio is back on-air, and at least our orphans are being looked after," said Luthando. "The rest of the stuff does not matter, so long we have our radio back." But Madam Alyssa was still not convinced and would begin to trust Luthando less still when she learnt that it was Luthando that had written to the organization seeking assistance.

Living with the people

Madam Alyssa picked up a publication from Banda's bookshelf, flipped through the pages, half reading, and half dreaming: "Living with the people is a process that requires skills and tools." This quotation seemed to remind her of a familiar publication she could not recall. Mmmmhhh. "I wonder what this means." She tried to ignore it, instead focusing her thoughts on the Mosque that was being built. She could not understand how the villagers could willingly offer their land for the construction of a Mosque. These people needed Jesus and she felt they were letting Jesus down by accepting the construction of the Mosque. Rumour had it that there were four recent Muslim converts in the local community, including Kapesi, who was now sober, had stopped stealing, and was a wonderful and reliable member of the local community. She tried to ignore what she was reading but the question still came back to her. What kinds of skills and tools does one need? She flipped the pages, and there it was:

> Living with the people is a process that requires skills and tools. It requires a communicator's willingness to learn indigenous knowledge systems. On the part of the people, it requires that they be properly informed as to what the project is all about and why it is important. And this is where most projects stop because the information experts are interested in marketing development projects to communities. Genuine participation however, requires that communities be in a position to question the need for the project, be it a school, a hospital or a rural growth centre, because they are the ones to use it. Most planners consult community leaders, arguing that these leaders represent their communities. It is important to remember that in a multiparty democracy, the legitimacy of representation is often being compromised by bribes, illiteracy, unfounded fears and mistrust, worsened further by the politicization of traditional decision-making structures. Consulting the village headman, therefore, does not mean consulting the whole village because, when the water pump breaks down, the village headman will not single-handedly be responsible for its repair. Or when an antenatal clinic is built, it is not the village headman who will deliver in there. Consultation therefore requires making constant contacts with the majority of the beneficiaries themselves, without manipulating them to accept outsiders' thinking towards a particular problem. Listen to this communicator: "We have observed that this village does not have a clinic; as a result, many women and children are dying during delivery. If we build a clinic here, women will have safe deliveries. Funds are available and we are ready to help you build this clinic if you are interested." Then listen to another communicator: "We would like to discuss your thoughts and see what we can do together with regards to official reports showing rising deaths of children and women during deliveries."
>
> The first communicator is obviously selling a clinic project, by linking the deaths of women and children during delivery to the absence of clinics. He is actually asking villagers to offer ground for the construction of the clinic. The second communicator converses communicatively with his audience by not mentioning the clinic, but instead pointing them to extant numerical evidence about the deaths during deliveries, and motivating them to do something about it. Such consultation enables communicators and their listeners to develop a mutual understanding, which will lead to the establishment of causes of and solutions to a particular challenge. Consultation is therefore an ongoing communicative process through which intended beneficiaries are motivated to initiate a project. Consultation goes on even after the project has been implemented. Participation on the other hand, is the beneficiaries' actual social input towards that particular project in from of commitment and opinions.[1]

Alyssa tried to remember where she had first read these words. They sounded very familiar. Some of the words sounded similar to Proverb 15:22, "Plans fail when there is no consultation, but there is accomplishment through many advisors." She contemplated the words. What is it that the Islamic charity had done right and she had failed at? The women's group had more defaulters now and its survival was very hard to foresee. Another women's banking group had been formed by a rural banking organization and many of her members had gone over to join in. Her trusted local change agent, Luthando, had found a job in the city, thanks to the computer and the Internet. It seemed that the pastor's wife had to start over.

Everson came back with bread and milk. They started drinking tea and the silence between them spoke volumes. After many years of ministering in this region, Alyssa and her husband were returning to Europe. Her mother in law had cancer and she wanted to be close to her before she passed away. Her husband had mentioned in confidence to her that Everson would make a great pastor and that he needed to be trained so that he could take over the local church. For them it was imperative that they leave the church with someone they could trust. What did Everson think? Everson Banda himself smiled and said nothing.

The door opened. Everson's second wife, who Pastor Richardson—Alyssa's husband—had requested Everson divorce and have only one wife to be in good standing with the Lord, walked in. She had made fritters for him and brought a plate to the table. Everson produced some money, gave it to her, and informed her that he was going to spend a night at the other wife's place. More silence.

"Living with people is a process that requires skills and tools." Where had she read this? What did it actually mean? Then the question came out of her mouth even though she had tried hard to suppress it: "I thought you had divorced her? You know that Christ doesn't want a man to have two wives." There was a long silence—Everson drank his tea silently with a smile on his face.

"Alyssa," he began. The 'madam' was no longer there. "You have been living in this country, and I have known you for over ten years. But you haven't learnt anything."

"What do you mean? I have been here all this time." Then she switched to the local language that she spoke quite well. "What do you mean I have not learnt anything?"

"You don't listen."

"What are you talking about Everson?" He shifted his position, faced Alyssa, looked at her as he had never done before and began explaining something he felt he should have done a long time back.

"Jesus teaches us that listening is an act of faith. It is an act of faith in the people we work with. Listening does not just imply keeping quiet when someone is speaking as we are doing now. It is a politically conscious decision to enter into a communion with other people. Yes, you have been here all these years but were you able to actually see what was going on in front of you?"

"I have always been here with you all, haven't I? Is there anything I am missing, Everson?"

"It is all about living with the people. It is about listening with our hearts, and not our eyes. This community has been undergoing gradual changes all this time. If you had the inquisitive mind of the snail, you would have seen that." All this wasn't making sense for Alyssa.

"Haven't I been listening, then? I thought it was the reason I have been here all these years?"

"I can see how you despise my second wife."

"I don't despise her. You know a man cannot have two wives if you value your relationship with Jesus."

"That is exactly my point. If I divorce her, who is going to look after the children I have with her?"

"But what about Jesus? What about the church?"

"Inna Lillahi Wa Inna ilaihi Raji'un."

"That's Arabic. You are speaking Arabic?"

"From Allah we came, and to Allah we will return."

There was a long silence interrupted only by the eating of the fritters. Then he began, again, and from Alyssa's point of view, he was not like the same understanding, docile, smiling Everson Banda she had known all these years. He looked more philosophical but also lost, speaking from a place that she could not understand. She was confused.

"My point is that listening to others implies that we get out of our epistemological comfort zones and be humble, learning to live with different people with the aim of enriching our understanding of them."

She was the pastor's wife and she loved the people in these villages. That is what she had been doing over the last ten tears. How could she have been wrong? What was going on in the mind of Everson? As he mumbled on, her eyes drifted to his bookshelf. Frantz Fanon, Paulo Freire, Karl Marx, Edward Said, Vladmir Lenin, Malcolm X, the Qur'an. It was the books! She just knew it! It was the books! She felt pity for him. Tears began to form on the edges of her eyes.

"Everson, please, you really need to receive and accept Jesus as your Saviour."

He kept quiet. His eyes were a little teary and he smiled a little. There was silence and the sound of eating.

"Alyssa, you are just who you are and you will never understand this place and its people." She left. Very broken, carrying with her the burden of a wasted ten years. The words kept ringing in her mind: living with the people is a process that requires skills and tools.

Living with people, rethinking graduate training

One critical observation emerging from this discussion is that there is a need for coherent training programmes that provide university students with skills in living with people. This has been the case in communication for development training. Yet, as Silvio Waisbord (2005) demonstrates, there is a growing chasm between the theory and practice of communication for development. Between the 1960s and

1970s, it was only the University of the Philippines at Los Baños (UPLB) that was offering programmes in communication for development (C4D). From the 1990s, other C4D degree programmes would spring up, first in the South East Asian Region, then in Africa, and then in Latin America, which also has an equally deeper and richer experience with C4D (Ramiro Beltran, 1993/2004). In the mid 2000s, numerous programmes would emerge in Europe and North America especially at Ohio, Malmo, East Anglia, the London School of Economics and Political Science, City University, Westminster and others.

Communication for development training

Also known as development communication, development support communication, or more recently, as communication for social change, communication for development was first articulated by Quebral in the 1970s (1988, 2011). At that time, the College of Agriculture was already offering development communication as a major within its Master's Programme in Agriculture Communication. It was only in the 1974/75 school calendar that the UPLB began offering Bachelor's degrees in the field, making it the first training institution in the world to do so. Later, when the College of Development Communication was established, a series of graduate C4D programmes were introduced. There were four areas of focus—development broadcasting, educational communication, development journalism and science communication. These were meant to provide students with a holistic understanding of development issues in the global south and from that understanding to enable them to develop effective communication interventions that would address them (Quebral 1988, 2011).

It was clear from these early days of C4D training that development and communication were two separate theoretical entities, but as concepts they were perceived to be interdependent (Quebral 1988, 2011). Nevertheless, to be a C4D specialist, one is required to understand development holistically, and using that knowledge, to bring one's communication expertise to bear, in order to initiate communication programming that could empower people to find solutions to their development challenges. As such, studying and understanding development was a must (Quebral, 1988). In an email conversation to advise on a proposal for a C4D Master's Programme that I had put together at the University of Fort Hare, Quebral (in Manyozo 2012, 9) elucidated C4D as:

> A systematic education with objectives, methodologies and outcomes but which happens outside the formal school system. It does not promote only one course of action for everyone but instead offers an array of choices from which the users of communication select what is right for them, given their needs and circumstances. [C4D] must help equip the users, however, with the capability to choose and the information and knowledge base from which to choose. … For people to dialogue, they must have both a knowledge base and the capability to choose.

Quebral's training approach emphasizes dual engagement—the C4D graduate should be able to engage with theoretical perspectives but also with empirical reality. When it comes to training in C4D however, it is the relevance of the curricula to field practice that is of a major concern. Waisbord (2005) spells out his vision for communication curricula that respond to the needs of the field by emphasizing the centrality of power around which C4D training should be built.

Two training models

Two dominant perspectives towards conceptualizing and defining communication for development training are being propounded. These are the development communication and the communication for social change perspectives.

The development communication model

The development communication model emphasizes the location of C4D training within development paradigms. Quebral (1988, 8) argues that C4D "is coloured" more by how we define development, which is "the stronger principle in the tandem" to an extent that any change in the definition of development automatically changes the meaning of C4D. As many C4D training programmes demonstrate, the development theory perspective offers parallel comparisons between the evolutions of the field in relation to western development theories. And this means seeing the field through western lenses. C4D therefore is presented as a response to both development theories and the criticisms that such development theory receives (Gumucio Dagron and Tufte 2006; Hemer and Tufte 2005; Gwin Wilkins, Tufte and Obregon 2014; Obregon and Waisbord 2012).

Informed by and married to dominant development thinking, this training model has its roots in the agricultural extension programmes of the UPLB and other South East Asian universities, Bretton Woods institutions (especially the World Bank) and North American Universities, especially Cornell, Wisconsin, Guelph and other land grant institutions. The early training experiments would produce graduates whose expertise was in creatively developing and disseminating agricultural knowledge to rural farmers. As a training model, development communication recognizes the challenges of underdevelopment as a result of colonialism and imperialism. The UNDP's Bangkok Office would establish the Development Support Communication Unit in the 1970s. Under the influence of the UPLB, other universities have employed a similar C4D training model in designing their own graduate programmes. Such universities include but are not limited to: Kasetsart University in Thailand, Govind Ballabh Pant University of Agriculture and Technology in India, University of Malawi at Chancellor College, or the University of Reading in the UK.

The social change model

The social change model is largely associated with the Latin American School of communication for development, with roots in post-colonial critiques of development theory, liberation theology, the experimental works of community radios and other community-based civil society institutions (Ramiro Beltran 1993/2004). But in modern times it is associated with the work of the Rockefeller Foundation, especially the 1997 and 2004 Bellagio Conferences (Rockefeller Foundation 1997). The 1997 gathering was funded by the Rockefeller Foundation, and brought together a small group of 22 professionals "to explore the vast possibilities of new communications for social change" (Rockefeller Foundation 1997, 5). This Conference would lay the groundwork for the first and only World Congress on Communication for Development that the FAO would organize and host in Rome in 2006. The Bellagio Conferences and the World Congress worked to ensure the institutionalization of C4D within international development organizations.

Communication for social change (CfSC) as an alternative concept to C4D emerged from these meetings. The Rockefeller Foundation introduces and discusses an integrated model of communication for social change as "an interactive process where community dialogue and collective action work together to produce social change in a community" so as to improve the health and welfare of communities (Figueroa et al. 2002, 5). Other theoretical contributions have come from entertainment-education as developed by Miguel Sabido and the Population Communication International, and further elaborated by the Johns Hopkins University. For this model, there is also an increased emphasis on issues of human rights and democracy.

Major advocates of this model have been the Communication for Social Change Consortium and the Journalism and Communication Programme at the University of Queensland, where Jan Servaes would, in the early 2000s, establish the Centre of Communication for Social Change (CfSC). The CfSC Consortium has been publishing *Mazi*, a CfSC Report (a resurrection of the defunct Development Communication Report), and has facilitated the creation of the network of universities specializing in communication for social change. This network, REDECAMBIO (www.redecambio.org), is now based at the Corporacion Universitaria Minuto de Dios UNIMINUTO, in Bogota, Colombia (Gumucio Dagron and Tufte 2006; Hemer and Tufte 2005).

This model has usually been built on bodies of work in critical theory, democracy and good governance, media effects research, or even cultural theories, with the interest being in showing how strategically designed communication systems and programmes provide public and democratic spheres, where people generate critical and deliberative dialogues leading to the strengthening of civil society, empowerment and social action. It is about exploring, as Sonia Livingstone (2009, 1) says, "the mediation of everything." Building on such theoretical terrain, the social change model can thus be seen to attempt to formulate a C4D paradigm that is relevant to both developing and developed societies.

This model should be understood within the political context of the intrusive and, oftentimes, political and military involvement of the US government in Latin America, which resulted in undermining successive leftist governments and in the seeming support for military and political dictatorships. Conceiving deliberative development within such conditions was, and is, inconceivable, hence the emphasis on the social change model which called for the total transformation of society. Examples of graduate programmes promoting the social change model include the Catholic University of Peru's MA in Communication for Social Change Programme and a host of other Master's Programmes in the region, from Mexico to Chile, which may not be categorically known as communication for social change. What should be understood, however, is that the development of this kind of training was taking place alongside other paradigm shifts. These included the failure of the modernist paradigm of development, the Latin American post-colonial critique of modernization, the emphasis on alternative communications, and the institutionalization of more horizontal and participatory communications within civil society advocacy (Ramiro Beltran 1993/2004).

Some graduate training programmes

A brief survey of established programmes in the field suggests that most of the graduate programmes are located in media, communication or journalism schools and departments. This is not a problem in itself, but it suffices to say that if, as expected, a graduate should acquire knowledge and skills in development, then collaborations with development studies departments would become a necessity. Some notable graduate programmes are: Malmo University in Sweden (MA in Communication for Development); University of Reading in the UK (MSc in Communication for Innovation and Development); London School of Economics and Political Science (MSc in Media, Communication and Development); University of Ohio in the US (MA in Communication for Development); University of Queensland in Australia (MA in Communication—Communication for Social Change); UPLB (MSc in Development Communication); Catholic University of Peru (MA in Communication for Social Change); University of East Anglia (MA in Media and International Development); Johns Hopkins University (Master of Public Health). The fact that it is perhaps only East Anglia and Reading universities that offer these programmes within development studies-related departments says much about how development studies view communication for development.

A communication for development specialist

A host of organizations continue to explore and experiment with communication for development in various ways. Within the three C4D approaches there are various professional portfolios that require different skills sets, knowledge and expertise. Central to these skills is living with people. Since media, communication and journalism programmes could not produce this specific kind of graduate and because there were insufficient training programmes in communication for development to produce these graduates, development organizations chose the easy option. They would recruit graduates in agriculture communication, extension, journalism and communication. Then they would provide them with short-term training through on-the-job workshops. Over time, with increasing numbers of journalism graduates being recruited for these jobs, there grew a false conception that journalism or public relations students could also double as development communicators. Gumucio Dagron and Rodriguez (2006, 10) observe, "communication positions within development and social change projects are filled with people doing posters, newsletters, radio and video programmes, and public relations." There is thus a focus on media production skills without understanding the development context within which these skills and the resultant media content will be produced.

A training programme in C4D is different from mainstream journalism, public relations and communication programmes not just in content, but also in the kind and quality of graduates that they produce. So who is this graduate who emerges from a university training programme in CfSC or C4D? Gumucio Dagron and Rodriguez (2006) mention four key attributes, namely: (a) the strategic vision to use communication processes to facilitate social change; (b) field experience; (c) appreciating communication technology as just a tool and not an end in itself, and (d) the comprehensive understanding of power, culture and change. Likewise, Quebral (1988, 2011) sees this communicator as a facilitator who moderates dialogues among stakeholders in development processes. To produce this graduate, a training programme should be guided by the ideal attributes of the communicator of development and social change. A good example of these attributes comes from a generic C4D specialist job description, as elucidated in Table 4.1.

It is very clear that the package of knowledge and skills emphasizes understanding of human behaviour, managing stakeholder relationships, social and behavioural sciences, motivational psychology, planning for behaviour development, and psychology. This demonstrates that behavioural research skills are becoming a must in this field. As such, C4D training has to open up to contributions from social psychology, development management, and also from public health. In terms of the qualifications and knowledge, media and communication programmes should collaborate with other disciplines to ensure graduates are well rounded in the sciences of human behaviour and community engagement. The Johns Hopkins University's Master's in Public Health, and perhaps other similar programmes, seem to have what the media and communication programmes need.

With regard to skills and tools, again the job description above has three that stand out: (a) organizing the research, development, pre-testing, and production of culturally relevant communication materials; (b) developing and enhancing strong partnerships with community groups, leaders and other partners in the community and civil society – for promotion of participation in social and behavioural changes

TABLE 4.1 Communication for development specialist job description

Skills (duties and responsibilities)

- Designs, manages, and facilitates the implementation of programme communication strategy, plan of action and activities for strategic communication and promotion for social and behavioural change in support of country programme delivery;
- Organizes the research, development, pre-testing, and production of culturally relevant communication materials;
- Develops and enhances strong partnerships with community groups, leaders and other partners in the community and civil society for promotion of participation in social and behavioural changes supportive of programme goals;
- Develops training materials and activities to build capacity for participatory and behaviour change communication;
- Provides effective coordination and technical support to government counterparts and other partners in the development and strategic use of communication for social development;
- Monitors and evaluates programme activities and pre-evaluation reports. Exchanges findings, experiences, lessons learned and new methods with partners;
- Participates in budget planning and ensures compliance and the optimal appropriation of allocated programme funds.

Technical knowledge

- Education: Advanced university degree in the social/behavioural sciences (Sociology, Anthropology, Psychology, Health Education) with emphasis on strategic communication planning for behaviour development, social mobilization, participatory communication, and research;
- Knowledge of current developments in the fields of: communication theory, motivational psychology, adult learning theory, indigenous media, community organization and participation, strategic communication planning, behaviour analysis, formative research and evaluation of communication interventions;
- Knowledge of inter-disciplinary approach in programme development and implementation in programme communication, social mobilization and behavioural change;
- Knowledge of and experience in emergency operations and management;
- Knowledge of and skills in programme communication networking, advocacy and negotiation;
- Knowledge of training/facilitation and impact evaluation of communication intervention;
- Knowledge and experience to organize and implement training, including development of curricula and methodologies. Knowledge of community capacity building;
- Knowledge and experience in the methods of communication to clearly and concisely express ideas and concepts in written and oral form and to listen to and acknowledge others' perspectives and views;
- Computer knowledge, skills and practical experience, including Internet navigation, network, telecommunications and various office applications.

Source: UNICEF (2016).

supportive of programme goals; and (c) developing training materials and activities to build capacity for participatory and behaviour change communication. These skills require that training be oriented to ensure students are offered the opportunity to work with communities, to ensure they understand the science of influencing behaviours, and how to measure the link between C4D interventions on the one hand and the impact, on the other. It should be remembered that graduate programmes are intended to produce a development specialist (or in some cases, a public health specialist) who has relevant communication skills. Therefore, it is not an overstatement to argue that what we are interested in is to have a graduate who understands the process of development and how communication can facilitate the involvement of people in that process (Peirano 2006; Quebral 1988; Ramiro Beltran 1993/2004), and not the other way round. In this case then, it is vitally important to have a component of development theory in the curriculum. The proposal below spells out the minimum package of a skills set that graduate programmes in C4D should ensure is part of their output.

Knowledge and skills set for a C4D specialist

To provide the necessary skills in terms of living with people, C4D training programmes should combine both the theoretical perspectives and practical components. With increased marginalization even within developed-world contexts, there are ample field-based training opportunities that will offer students and their educators an opportunity to test some of the ideals in practice. For this discussion, the chapter presents two aspects of such C4D training. The first concerns knowledge and expertise which should ideally comprise the following: (a) *critical perspectives in development theory and practice* (covering dominant, critical and alternative perspectives); *theory and practice in C4D or CfSC* (covering all the traditions and schools of thought); and (c) *critical reflections on power* (through courses in media and communications or sociology but covering significant conceptual frameworks of power, ideology, gender, mediation, etc.).

The second aspect of the training concerns the *minimum skills set* that should be delivered in the form of studio-based formats, and is also very practical. These should comprise but not be limited to: (a) *communication for development research* (paying attention to investment thinking, monitoring and evaluation, and situation analysis); (b) *engaging with stakeholders and communities* (skills in collecting oral histories, listening, consultation, public speaking, advocacy); and (c) *leadership skills* (demonstrating empathy, understanding, tolerance, change management, driven by results).

This requires that training providers re-evaluate course content, teaching methodologies and their theoretical paradigms. Communication for development training has to begin listening and responding to innovative thinking that is shaping the practice on the ground if the curricula is to stay relevant. Such training has also to create stronger linkages with development studies departments to ensure that students understand what they intend to communicate about.

Concluding thoughts: An engaged C4D pedagogy

Granted these proposed minimum packages of elements necessary for a comprehensive communication for development training, how should these be taught? Since, apart from the technical knowledge of the subject, the training objective is to produce social change communicators who have mastered the art, science, tools and skills of engaging with people, how should C4D training be delivered? This is an important question because, from experience, one encounters experts, scholars and practitioners who are very much sexist, colonial, racist (not openly), paternalistic, and exhibiting all the traits that Freire (1970) associates with the banking educators whom hooks (1994, 11) elaborates as "those who are smart in book knowledge." Rejecting the mechanistic, commodified and orthodox bourgeoise educational structures and approaches that emphasize the 'dictatorship' of the professor and the linear transfer of knowledge and information, bell hooks proposes the practice of engagement pedagogy. In this approach, hooks (1994, 21) provides a manifesto of what she considers a holistic learning framework that is:

> The practice of freedom, [in which] students are not the only ones who are asked to share, to confess. Engaged pedagogy does not seek simply to empower students. Any classroom that employs a holistic model of learning will also be a place where teachers grow, and are empowered by the process. That empowerment cannot happen if we refuse to be vulnerable while encouraging students to take risks. Professors who expect students to share confessional narratives but who are themselves unwilling to share are exercising power in a manner that could be coercive.

For hooks therefore, the content of C4D training is important, but the role of the educator who delivers that content is crucial, as is the teaching style. hooks discusses two critical roles of radical and progressive teachers. First, this kind of teacher has the responsibility to transgress and transform the curriculum to ensure that it does not perpetuate dominant thinking that reinforces domination and structural violence. Second, the progressive teacher deliberately uses the classroom as a "site of resistance." The first objective concerns the content of the curriculum that comprises the selection and combination of readings employed in teaching the topics. This implies teachers going beyond what is celebrated as dominant and accepted structure and content on the subject, replacing and transgressing authoritative pieces on the subjects, and bringing in critical scholars who will destabilize dominant thinking. The second aspect is about transforming the world view of the student, and this combines the radical curriculum, the questions asked of students in class, the activities and assignments, but also the way we allow the learning process to celebrate the experiences of the students themselves. These are important things to consider because with the increasing institutionalization of C4D by international and local development organizations, focus has been placed on understanding templates, strategies and models by leading organizations and institutions, as if these are being considered in a political and ideological vacuum.

I was privileged to be a student of the late Chris Kamlongera during my undergraduate studies in theatre and history in the 1990s. There is a dusty road that meanders from the university, my alma mater, slithering its way through the mostly grass-thatched houses and disappearing into the valleys and hills. This village would become a significant intellectual platform that enabled the late *Prof*, as we students fondly called him, one of the pioneers of the African School in communication for development, to provide a different kind of education.

Instead of sitting in class and teaching us theories and concepts, as is expected of the orthodox, and the "banking," approach to education (Freire 1970), Chris herded our class into these villages on foot. He divided us into small teams and asked us to engage with villagers. We would go from house to house, talking to residents about local development issues. Chris discouraged any note-taking, instead emphasizing that we join the villagers in whatever activity they were undertaking.

"You have to listen, and learn to engage" was his mantra at the beginning of each field exercise. Upon returning to our classrooms, we would analyse the issues and then come up with plays. On an agreed date with the village leadership, we would perform these plays, which also included local participation. If Chris was concerned with the direction of a particular scene, he would join the scenes as a drunken character to ensure we captured villagers' perspectives in the performances.

This was my entry into the world of communication for development. For Chris, the practice was always more about the democracy of the communicative process and its transformative capacity. He saw ICTs and the media only as tools which, if required, might facilitate that engagement. This is the essence of the understanding that Chris instilled in us while we were seated in the village arena, singing and performing with local people.

As students we did not know that we were part of a larger intellectual scheme, that we were contributing to the radical deconstruction of the dominant syntax in communication for development. For Chris Kamlongera (1988), his objective was to mobilize universities to embrace non-classical and alternative theoretical frameworks and paradigms in order to offer students a holistic understanding of development and the world. For his students, this intellectual journey had occurred much earlier in this and in other villages where he took us during various participatory action research endeavours. Genuine education for Chris lay in capturing the hopes and aspirations of local people. It meant that we had to learn to listen. His was therefore the pedagogy of listening, a pedagogy of engagement, a pedagogy of living with people.

I had the rare honour and privilege of knowing him as a teacher, as a friend and as a colleague. Like Gutiérrez and Freire before him, Chris's pedagogy challenges all of us to actively intervene in creating a society that is more equitable and democratic by walking this symbolic road to the village, to wherever communities are. This is where we will engage in a pedagogy of living with people, in which experts and subject-matter specialists use relevant skills to empower people to get involved in the historical process of making and unmaking their world.

Note

1 Manyozo, Linje. 2004. "The power of community consultation." *Drum Beat* 265. Republished. Accessed January 20 2016. www.comminit.com/tamboratv/drum_beat_265.html.

References

Césaire, Aimé. 1955/1972. *Discourse on Colonialism*. Translated by Joan Pinkham. London: Monthly Review Press.

Escobar, Arturo. 1995/2012. *Encountering Development: The Making and Unmaking of the Third World*. Princeton: Princeton University Press. http://edition.cnn.com/2011/11/19/world/meast/nude-blogger-aliaa-magda-elmahdy.

Figueroa, Maria Elena, D. Lawrence Kincaid, Manju Rani and Gary Lewis. 2002. *Communication for Social Change: An integrated model for measuring the process and its outcomes*. Communication for Social Change Working Paper Series. New York: Rockefeller Foundation. Accessed November 20 2016. www.communicationforsocialchange.org/pdf/socialchange.pdf.

Freire, Paulo. 1970. *Pedagogy of the Oppressed*. London: Penguin.

Gumucio Dagron, Alfonso. 2003. "Take five: A handful of essentials for ICTs in development." In Bruce Girard (ed.), *The One to Watch: Radio, New ICTs and Interactivity* (pp. 25–44). Rome: Food and Agriculture Organization.

Gumucio Dagron, Alfonso and Clemencia Rodriguez. 2006. "Time to call things by their name: The field of communication and social change." *Media Development*, LIII(3), 9–16.

Gumucio Dagron, Alfonso and Thomas Tufte. 2006. *Communication for Social Change Anthology: Historical and Contemporary Readings*. South Orange, NJ: Communication for Social Change Consortium.

Gutiérrez, Gustavo. 1988. *A Theology of Liberation: History, Politics, and Salvation*. Translated by Caridad Inda and John Eagleson. Maryknoll, New York: Orbis Books.

Gwin Wilkins, Karin, Thomas Tufte and Rafael Obregon (eds). 2014. *The Handbook of Development Communication and Social Change*. Hoboken, NJ: Wiley-Blackwell.

Hemer, Oscar and Thomas Tufte (eds). 2005. *Media and Glocal Change: Rethinking Communication for Development*. Buenos Aires: CLACSO.

hooks, bell. 1994. *Teaching to Transgress: Education as the Practice of Freedom*. London and New York: Routledge.

Kamlongera, Christopher. 1988. *Theatre for Development in Africa*. Bonn and Zomba: University of Malawi Fine and Performing Arts Department and German Foundation for International Development.

Lerner, Daniel. 1958. *The Passing of Traditional Society: Modernizing the Middle East*. New York and London: Free Press and Collier-Macmillan.

Livingstone, Sonia. 2009. "On the mediation of everything. ICA Presidential address." *Journal of Communication*, 59(1): 1–18.

Mansell, Robin. 1982. "The 'new dominant paradigm' in communication: Transformation versus adaptation." *Canadian Journal of Communication*, 8(3): 42–60. Accessed September 20 2016. www.cjc-online.ca/index.php/journal/article/view/278/184.

Mansell, Robin. 2011. "Whose knowledge counts? A political economy of the knowledge-based society/economy." Seminar Presentation. Institute of Development Studies, University of Sussex, Brighton, United Kingdom, January 26.

Manyozo, Linje. 2004. "The power of community consultation." *Drum Beat* 265. Republished. Accessed January 20 2016. www.comminit.com/tamboratv/drum_beat_265.html.

Manyozo, Linje. 2012. *Media, Communication and Development: Three Approaches*. New Delhi: Sage.

Manyozo, Linje. 2016. "Sustainable livelihoods and governance in media development." *DW Akademie*. Accessed October 21 2016. www.dw.com/en/sustainable-livelihoods-and-governance-in-media-development/a-35959426.

Marx, Karl. 1852/2010. *The Eighteenth Brumaire of Louis Bonaparte*. New York: *Die Revolution* Issue 1.

Obregon, Rafael and Silvio Waisbord (eds). 2012. *The Handbook of Global Health Communication, Development and Social Change*. Hoboken, NJ: Wiley-Blackwell.

Peirano, Louis. 2006. "Developing a unique proposal for communication for development in Latin America." *Mazi Online*. Accessed October 8 2016. www.communicationforsocialchange.org/mazi-articles.php?id=298.

Post-Crash Economics Society. 2014. "Economics, education and unlearning: Economics education at the University of Manchester." Accessed January 20 2016. www.post-crasheconomics.com/download/778.

Quebral, Nora. 1975. "Development communication." In Juan Jamias (ed.), *Readings in Development Communication* (pp. 1–11). Laguna: UPLB College of Agriculture.

Quebral, Nora C. 1988. *Development Communication*. Laguna: University of Philippines Los Baños.

Quebral, Nora. 2011. "Development communication, Los Baños style." Public Lecture, London School of Economics and Political Science during an Award of an Honorary Doctorate in Media and Communication, December 20. Accessed October 8 2016. www.lse.ac.uk/media@lse/events/pdf/Professor%20Nora%20Cruz%20Quebral%20Dec%202011%20lecture.pdf.

Ramiro Beltran, Louis. 1993/2004. "Communication for development in Latin America: A forty year appraisal." Accessed October 8 2016. www.southbound.com.my/communication/cul-ch.htm.

Rockefeller Foundation. 1997. "Bellagio Conference Report – Communications and social change: Forging strategies for the 21st Century." Accessed October 8 2016. http://web.asc.upenn.edu/gerbner/archive.aspx?sectionID=114&packageID=560.

Schramm, Wilbur. 1964. *Mass Media and National Development: The Role of Information in the Developing Countries*. Stanford: Stanford University Press.

Scott, Martin. 2014. *Media and Development*. London: ZED Books.

Tufte, Thomas, and Paolo Mefalopulos. 2009. *Participatory Communication: A Practical Guide*. Washington DC: The World Bank.

UNICEF. 2016. "Communication for development specialist, UNICEF, Job advert." Accessed October 30 2016. https://jobs.undp.org/cj_view_job.cfm?cur_job_id= 63013.

Waisbord, Silvio. 2005. "Five key ideas: Coincidences and challenges in development communication." In Oscar Hemer and Thomas Tufte (eds), *Media and Glocal Change: Rethinking Communication for Development* (pp. 77–90). Buenos Aires: CLACSO.

5

ENCOUNTERING POVERTY IN THE *HEART OF DARKNESS*

Setting the context

How do we encounter and study poverty in places that are geographically, culturally and epistemologically different from us? My analysis in this chapter brings together a combination of post-colonial narratives and prose, in order to critically examine the orientalism of the infrastructure that underpins the political economy of the spectacle of development. By juxtaposing texts from Joseph Conrad's novel and Robert Chambers's (1980, 1981, 2005) scholarly work, my post-colonial argument will be that perceiving, comprehending, and constructing representations of poverty is fundamentally a political, moral and aesthetic struggle. To really see and study poverty requires a critical analysis of the structural and economic factors that produce that poverty.

To encounter, understand and deconstruct poverty in the development context requires that scholars and practitioners be intellectually open-minded, empathetic, understanding, and display epistemological compassion towards others and their ways of speaking and thinking. My exposition aims to creatively weave certain strands of development theory and ethnography into a narrative about an imaginary anthropologist who travels into a rural area to find poverty and bring about development. This chapter seeks to make a contribution to development theory and practice (and this includes communication for development), due to the increasing demand by civil society groups and communities to exercise their agency in planning and implementing interventions.

As in the preceding chapters, I conduct a reflexive conversation with Robert Chambers, who, writing in *The New Internationalist* (1981), discusses the biases that lead to the failure of policy makers to encounter and understand poverty. Chambers has been a leading thinker in rural development since the 1970s and, outside teaching and researching, he has consulted and worked with major development institutions and organizations. Though he is a westerner, his critical perspectives have, over the years, contributed to and shaped the radical rethinking of development theory and practice. Chambers (1980, 1981) observes that instead of a careful and empathic examination of rural poverty, policy makers tend to engage in rural development tourism, that eventually "favors roadsides and projects, elites and men" and in the process, "rural poverty remains unseen." Chambers presents various kinds of biases that make it almost impossible for the experts, whom he describes as "urban-based outsiders" to see and understand rural poverty.

For Chambers, seeing poverty implies that we must also see the structural and economic factors that produce such poverty. It requires that we stand in solidarity with the people who live through that poverty (Gutiérrez 1988). In addition to the forms of bias discussed by Chambers, I suggest that graduate training is a significant contributing factor because it so often fails to prepare students with the relevant tools and skills they need to understand how the oppressor contributes to the oppression that produces poverty. Instead of equipping students with the tools and skills for studying people and places, some western graduate programmes in the development field and other areas of the social sciences only provide a one-sided and unbalanced view of the world (Post-Crash Economics Society 2014). As a result, some of these training programmes are producing students who are uncritical of the dominant development paradigms and are, instead, intellectually fascinated by their journeys into the orient as noted in Chapter 3 in Assia Djebar's (1992) criticism of the orientalist painting, *Women of Algiers in their Apartment.*

I also write this chapter as a response to the behaviour of some of the most arrogant, self-aggrandizing, self-centred, egotistical, ideologically myopic, culturally insensitive, and intellectually orientalist development experts and researchers. There are of course exceptions, as there are scholars who are empathetic in their research and scholarship and who are genuinely interested in studying the other world and its peoples as a way of enriching their knowledge. It is the other experts, however, who replicate the methods and approaches of the French orientalist painter, Eugene Delacroix, yet who have such a hold over the theory and practice of international and community development. These are the brains behind the production of present and future development experts. When it comes to poverty, they cannot see, refuse to see, and therefore understand nothing, save their orientalist perceptions, which they have been exposed to in universities and scholarship. To see, understand and, more importantly, teach about poverty and development requires that critical lecturers and experts reject what the American scholar and public intellectual, James Baldwin (1986) described as 'the view from here'. hooks (1994, 13) characterizes the orthodox and banking education as a form of "rote, assembly-line" approach to education. Critical lecturers and experts "transgress" these approaches, in which the classroom is transformed as a site and experience of radicalizing learning for the self-actualization of both the teacher and the students (hooks 1994).

It is within this epistemological context that I chronicle the journey of an anthropologist—who I do not identify here—herself a development expert, who was drafted in by an international development organization to assist with a community participation component of a rural micro-hydroelectric power project in the south. I argue that to encounter poverty, the expert must break her links with the ideologies, networks and institutional structures that have educated and employed her through engaging with reflexive and critical pedagogy. Such a break does not have to be revolutionary, meaning a complete break from universities and the organization she is working with, but it requires a willingness to engage with alternative scholarship and empirical reality.

The crisis in teaching development

At the time of writing this chapter, there is an ongoing debate within the UK higher education system. After the 2008 financial crisis, the Post-Crash Economics Society (PCES) was formed in 2012 at the University of Manchester by a group of economics students. The formation of this society was partly a response to the financial crisis, but also to a 2011 conference organized by the Bank of England, "Are Economics Graduates Fit for Purpose?" During this conference, the curriculum for undergraduate economics training was put under the spotlight (Coyle 2012; Ward-Perkins and Earle 2014). Of all the cases for a radical rethink of the economics syllabi in British and western universities, one case particularly stands out. The PCES (2014, 9) contended that:

> Economics education at Manchester has elevated one economic paradigm, often called neoclassical economics, to the sole object of study. Other schools of thought such as institutional, evolutionary, Austrian, post-Keynesian, Marxist, feminist and ecological economics are almost completely absent. The consequence of the above is to preclude the development of meaningful critical thinking and evaluation. In the absence of fundamental disagreement over methodology, assumptions, objectives and definitions, the practice of being critical is reduced to technical and predictive disagreements. A discipline with a broader knowledge of alternative perspectives will be more internally self-critical and aware of the limits of its knowledge. Universities cannot justify this monopoly of one economic paradigm.

Thus, in traditional training programmes, largely built on neoclassical economics theories and paradigms, alternative ways of seeing, reflecting and understanding the world are hidden from the students, thereby denying them the opportunity to acquire a holistic understanding. Years earlier, Mansell (1982, 44) had expressed the concern that the preponderance of North American neoclassical models of development "went largely unquestioned." And for students being taught these paradigms and models, they are not provided with theoretical antidotes; and if they are taught any alternatives, the teaching is often stripped of its historical context, depoliticized, and executed in a way that obscures the underlying assumptions and critical frameworks. In whichever case, the PCES students are concerned with how symbolic power is shaping the current education ideologies and curricula. It is not uncommon for instance to find western degree programmes teaching courses on subaltern politics and power without academic recourse to fundamental theoretical frameworks drawn from Marx, Fanon or Spivak, for example, thereby depoliticizing the very essence of these academic programmes and courses.

A corollary is that such training then prevents the student from acquiring a holistic understanding of the world, and renders their training irrelevant in other parts of the world. They are thus denied the acquisition of analytical tools with which to, in the words of Freire (1970), speak and unspeak the world. The PCES also notes that students and professors alike have been unable to explain the factors leading to the financial crisis on the basis of their research (Ward-Perkins and Earle 2014). For example, during the opening of a new building at the London School of Economics and Political Science in 2008, Queen Elizabeth II asked a question that no one at the time could answer. Probably commenting on the shockingly unstable behaviour of international markets, the Queen had asked: "Why did nobody notice it?" (Pierce 2008).

From the perspective of the PCES, one explanation for the expert failure to predict and explain the crash might be attributable to professors with little or no industry experience, academics with little or no understanding of the world of the other, and the commodification of education leading to competition for high-fee-paying students, especially in the fields of finance and economics. These factors are symptomatic of the orientalist nature of British and other western universities in which the "other" and the other world are noted in passing, not seen as civilizations that must be studied in their totality in order to attain a fruitful and enriching understanding of the world. In the next sections, I seek to show the relationship between what Chambers (1980, 1981) describes as development tourism biases and Said's (1978) orientalism. The argument is that, in both cases, most development planners who do not ask difficult questions will fail to see the real poverty which will, in the end, contribute to their production of orientalist scholarship and knowledge.

The prologue[1]

Departing from Oxford train station, Sarah Mendez Casper, an anthropology graduate, waved her family goodbye. The hour-long train ride to London seemed like an eternity. Her boyfriend, Chris, was waiting in London to help her with last-minute shopping and packing before she departed for Southern Africa. She had travelled to this wonderful continent many, many times during her fieldwork. She knew lots of places, lots of people. She strongly believed—and this she repeated to friends, colleagues and family—Africa to be her first home. She felt at peace there.

She remembered the days when she was pursuing her Masters at the School of Oriental and African Studies and then a PhD at Oxford. For three years after finishing her doctorate, she worked with a renowned development anthropology professor from Harvard. Their collaborative research had focused on indigenous knowledge systems, and how they could be incorporated into development initiatives in the south. Such expositions had built on the work of Clifford Geertz (1971), Jay Ruby (1991, 2000) and the United Nations Economic Commission for Africa (UNECA). They had published papers together, and for the most part, at least in conferences and seminars, their peers considered their work to be ground-breaking.

Course after course, reading after reading, the Harvard Professor, who visited Oxford often, and had now settled in Kidlington (about 5 km outside Oxford), had emphasized that to understand people, one needed to understand the relationships that allowed for the sharing and contestation of power. Then things had moved too fast. A German company (with a subsidiary in London) was sponsoring the construction of micro-hydroelectric power stations in some African countries, but was facing some challenges in working with communities where the projects were to be located. The technocrats at the energy company could not understand how demographic groups—marginalized by the formal economy—without access to clean water and electricity, could still hesitate when opportunities arose to bring light and 'civilization' to their villages. It was important for the company to invest in community relations. Tennysons, the retired Harvard Professor, was consulted, and, as one might expect, he recommended Sarah.

Tennysons had travelled to and lived in many countries in Africa. He had spent much of his 35-year teaching career in Uganda, Kenya and Rwanda, conducting field research at least three or four months of every year. After his divorce, he had married an Ethiopian woman. Tennysons knew Africa and he loved talking about it. Deep inside, he seriously believed he had been a black man in a previous life, and would feel happy if such sentiments were thrown his way. Even though he did not say it openly, anyone who interacted with him knew that it was what he was thinking: "Look, I even married an African woman." He understood and enjoyed African music. On one of his many shelves, he had a collection of Baaba Maal, Hugh Masekela, Mirriam Makeba, Maryan Mursal, Tabuley, Mbilia Bel, Ali Farka Toure, and lots of traditional African music. Over the years, he had collected indigenous masks, drums, bows, arrows, spears, clay pots and other artefacts. He spoke excellent Swahili, Zulu, Shona and Amharic.

In honour of the field of development anthropology to which he had contributed over 20 books, countless papers in peer-reviewed journals, book chapters and conference presentations, Oxford University had named a lecture theatre after him. His publications had, over four decades, provided a springboard for London's and Brussels' engagement with sub-Saharan Africa. He was one of the leading critical voices who lobbied for military intervention in Darfur, when a host of leftist thinkers, including Mahmood Mamdani, appalled at the spiralling horizontal violence in Iraq and Afghanistan, had argued against. In fact, Mamdani (2007) had argued that the politics of naming and representation had contributed to defining Darfurian violence as genocide, and, hence, worthy of military intervention. Professor Tennysons considered what was happening in Darfur as genocide, and argued that, after independence of the South from the rest of Sudan, the peace-keeping mission should be stationed along the border as in the case of the Korean Peninsula, because he contended that the North and the South Sudan would remain in a state of permanent conflict, even if there were to be no open warfare.

In an open letter to the Secretary General of the United Nations and members of the Security Council, published in *The Wall Street Journal* in the US, *The Guardian* in the UK, *The Sydney Morning Herald* in Australia, and official papers in China and Russia, Professor Tennysons had argued that the Al-Bashir government would continue sponsoring violent rebellions against the Juba government, and that China, Iran and Syria would be at the centre of this orgy of military violence. It was also Professor Tennysons who had advised the Ugandan and Nigerian governments that to combat the rising threats of religious terrorism in their countries they had to invest heavily in the areas where the terrorist organizations such as the Lord's Resistance Army and the Boko Haram came from. He strongly believed that economic marginalization creates conditions for 21st century terrorism, and contexts akin to Joseph Conrad's "dark places":

> "And this also," said Marlow suddenly, "has been one of the dark places of the earth." He was the only man of us who still "followed the sea." The worst that could be said of him was that he did not represent his class. He was a seaman, but he was a wanderer, too, while most seamen lead, if one may so express it, a sedentary life. Their minds are of the stay-at-home order, and their home is always with them—the ship; and so is their country—the sea.
>
> *(Joseph Conrad 1899/2003,* Heart of Darkness, *5)*

It was Professor Tennysons who had written an iconic field guide to the practice of development anthropology, a treatise that was being treated as the Magna Carta in anthropology and other social science departments the world over. It had been published in the 1980s but revised in 2008 after the financial crisis. Tennysons had noted the following in the revised introduction, and this is what Sarah remembered as she prepared for her working trip to Africa:

> It must be remembered that, despite the expansion of its middle class, the exponential growth of the ICT sector and the unavoidable impact of globalization and modernity, resulting in multiparty politics and the entrenchment of the neoliberal market economy, Africa is largely an informal economy. This is a continent whose people—with very strong ties to the land, the environment, and the spiritual world—are bound together by ethnic identities and relationships. By and large, Africans are one, perhaps with the exception of the largely Muslim and Arabic North, which often strategically affiliates itself with the Middle East. After a careful study of the Zulus or Xhosa, Shonas or Ndebeles, Gikuyus or Luos, Bagandas or Nyankoles, the Hausas or Yorubas, one cannot help but notice the obvious similarities. They speak the same language; they dance to the same rhythms; their smiles, laughter or cries are very genuine and motivated by their collective respect for the human soul and the land. The land, yes, the land is their mother but also their god. …

> While education has produced a class of the literate and educated, who have embraced globalization, Africans remain rooted to their traditions. Most of these traditions are the fuel that drives the African hopes, inspirations and frustrations. Yet there also exists a huge body of harmful traditional practices and beliefs, that we should feel obliged to transform, since, in their current form, they undermine the dignity and humanity of the most vulnerable groups, especially women and children, gays and lesbians, the disabled, and the ethnic minorities. …
>
> Without wishing to sound colonial and paternalistic, what I have learnt all these years of researching, working and living in the continent, is that Africa is so innocent, it is beautiful, it is very pure like a child. Exploring Africa is like exploring God Himself. Africa is strange yet familiar, aggressive but friendly, deep and at the same time shallow; Africa is inviting but also distant, it is a smile that cries, a shout that whispers. There is always a lot to know about this place, but the key fundamentals of what makes Africa, such as human behaviour, art, music, or philosophy, have remained the same over the years.

Sarah contemplated this introduction as she prepared to board her flight to Southern Africa. Within herself, she wondered whether Professor Tennysons's observations amounted to orientalism. She recalled that Said (1978/2003) had contended that such problematic representations stripped the south of its historical diversity and pluralism. Could it perhaps be, she wondered further, that it was an instance of Bakhtin's (1981) notion of multiple voices or *heteroglossia* being discursively flattened, made static, and confined to stereotypical definitions that conflate space and time? But she could not raise her doubts openly, after all, who was she to question the professor's scholarly wisdom? She really needed this job.

She understood that German and British engineers had conceived the programmatic blueprint for the rural hydroelectric power stations during a climate change conference in Geneva. The conference presentations had attracted the interest of a German-based company, Africa Energy Limited, which funded pilot experiments in Kenya and Nigeria. Many lessons were learned from the pilot trials but two stood out. The first was that for such projects to succeed, they had to deliver economic gains and benefits to the local community—this meant that implementation had to be preceded by comprehensive business plans. Such plans should allow for the integration of private capital, no matter how minimal—as this might ensure financial sustainability without continuously relying on exogenous donor funding. The second lesson was that such a power plant needed to be driven by local people, hence setting up and sustaining it required across-the-board community engagement, community building and a leadership strategy. It is these two lessons that compelled Africa Energy Ltd to bring in technical expertise from the development anthropology field in order to strengthen the community aspects of the project. The second phase of the project was being implemented in Malawi, Mozambique, Zambia, Angola and Tanzania. Sarah's involvement was meant to support the engineering teams who were already on the ground. She saw herself as a small but critical proverbial cog in the complex development puzzle.

By the time Sarah was being flown to Africa, Africa Energy Ltd had already completed environmental impact assessments in all the targeted communities and, in all cases, little or no anticipated risk to the local environment or the livelihoods had been identified. All indications were that the project would create jobs, stimulate economic growth in rural towns, and encourage financial inclusion for women and girls. In an international development class, one of her professors had emphasized that unplanned urbanization was a ticking time bomb in many southern cities, since it bred rising unemployment, social unrest, vagrancy, prostitution, housing and sanitation problems, new HIV infections, and a host of other social problems. The future of development in the south, the professor had argued, lay in developing rural and regional towns, which he believed would also, in the long run, alleviate and then eradicate urban poverty. Since physical infrastructure is the basic foundation when it comes to spurring economic growth, it was considered important for western development institutions to invest in rural industries and, in this case, in clean energy, which would provide jobs and open up socio-economic opportunities that would subsequently improve rural people's lives. Kids would be able to study at night under electric lights; the local hospital would treat women and children better; qualified doctors would not hesitate to work in rural health centres. Villagers would buy refrigerators and others would bring televisions, allowing local people to be transported to worlds beyond their imagination, as had been propounded in dominant development theories and models (Lerner 1958; Rostow 1960). For a long time, some of these villages had wanted their own radio station—electricity would make this possible. Sarah's excitement grew as she contemplated the diffusion effects of infrastructure development. After all, wasn't this what Lerner and Schramm had, in the 1950s, contended would occur, in line with the economic growth model?

With just one investment the face of the village would change. In this case, Sarah strongly believed now, even though she had thought about this for some time, that real development should invest in interventions that can benefit local people financially and also spiritually. The villagers would benefit financially because they would own 50 per cent of the shares through local cooperatives that Sarah would help them establish. Government and private investors would hold the other 50 per cent. But there would also be spiritual benefits for the villagers, as the project would bring a sense of satisfaction that they were benefitting from the fruits of their own labour. This is how she understood Amartya Sen's work, *Development as Freedom* (1999). For Sarah, this was a very important mission. Her parents were Baptist missionaries spreading the message of Jesus Christ in Bolivia and had instilled in her the virtues of bringing light to the world. Light for Sarah meant bringing the villagers both Jesus and electricity. As she thought about this and these prospects, Sarah began impatiently to look forward to her work in Africa. She believed that if the five community-based and run micro-hydroelectric power plants could indeed successfully spur local economic growth, she would have found

Jesus, and consequently, she would have found the long-sought formula for developing the south—after all, the news from the two pilot projects was very encouraging. The two schemes were operational: the villagers had embraced them, albeit with a little resistance that was quelled by the police, and the first tranche of revenues was being collected from the end users. Things were looking good.

In the heart of darkness

As the plane landed at the international airport, Sarah's heart missed a couple of beats. This was it then. The plane was finally heading to its parking hanger. "Ladies and gentlemen, welcome to …" Sarah could not wait to hear the rest of the welcome message. After a few minutes of waiting, she alighted from the Boeing 737 with her hand luggage and went straight to Immigration. The queue was long, with a mixture of nationalities and races; of course, there were more South East Asian and Middle Eastern nationals. There was a huge colourful billboard with welcome messages in English and Chinese. Africa was changing, and always in transition.

> Now when I was a little chap I had a passion for maps. I would look for hours at South America, or Africa, or Australia, and lose myself in all the glories of exploration. At that time there were many blank spaces on the earth, and when I saw one that looked particularly inviting on a map, I would put my finger on it and say, "When I grow up I will go there." …. There was one yet—the biggest, the most blank, so to speak—that I had a hankering after. "True, by this time it was not a blank space any more. It had got filled since my boyhood with rivers and lakes and names. It had ceased to be a blank space of delightful mystery—a white patch for a boy to dream gloriously over. It had become a place of darkness." … And as I looked at the map of it in a shop-window, it fascinated me as a snake would a bird—a silly little bird.
>
> *(Joseph Conrad 1899/2003,* Heart of Darkness, *9–10)*

The only immigration officer on duty seemed bored or frustrated, even disinterested. He would slowly look at each passport, flip through the pages, look at the holder and then take his time to stamp the passport. Other immigration officers were seated in the lobby watching what sounded to be an English Premiership football match. By the looks on their faces, the team they were supporting was losing or under pressure. Sarah remembered the brochures she had read about this country; they all said local people are always smiling and charming and are eager to help tourists and visitors. The queue moved at a snail's pace.

An impatient, tall and hairy white man asked the football-watching officers if they could help their colleague. They looked at him and continued watching the game. Five minutes. Ten. Twenty. The heat was becoming unbearable. The air conditioners, if there were any in the building, were not working. Suddenly there was a huge roar from the football-watching immigration officers. They hugged and congratulated each other. "I always knew Gerrard would score," said one. "At least a draw is much better, especially knowing this is Arsenal," chipped in another. "I think Wenger should be sacked, we are tired of these senseless draws. We have lost two points here," said a younger officer who was wearing an Arsenal-branded wristband.

"Is Liverpool playing this afternoon?" Sarah inquired, out of curiosity; she was a lifelong West Ham supporter.

"No, this was just a replay of last week's match," came the reply from one of the officers.

"Lunch is over guys" shouted the only immigration officer who was working, trying to remind his colleagues, who were by now, slowly and reluctantly, walking to their workstations. Sarah looked at her watch—it was 1300 GMT, meaning 1500 local time. What a long lunch break! The queue then moved more quickly. Finally.

That evening, during a welcome supper organized for her by the energy company country office, Sarah would listen to many stories about the communities she would work with. These stories comprised the experiences of the engineers who had been flown in to train local community groups and work with them to install the power plants. The Church of Scotland, which had long and deep experience of working in these communities, had initially acted as the link with the local government and traditional structures. By now the engineers had surveyed the local topographical terrain and had established the sites where the water flow would be diverted from the river to the yet to be constructed canal and then taken downhill using gravity, hitting the turbines, and flowing back into the river. It was expected that each micro-hydropower plant would generate no less than 150 kilowatts and would serve a population base of not less than 50,000.

"The traditional chiefs are well out of their mind," retorted the senior engineer, who had spent the last 15 years in Africa and Asia.

"What's wrong with the chiefs?" inquired Sarah, sipping her non-alcoholic wine. There was a momentary silence and then collective laughter from the engineers.

"The thing is, Ellen ..." Rachel, one of the only two female engineers started to reply.

"The name is Sarah, not Ellen. Pleasure to acquaint myself." Sarah extended her hand, trying to be friendly, which Rachel ignored.

"Okay Sarah, we can see you are new to this shit," continued Rachel. Sarah could see the doubts and dislike the engineers had for her and perhaps for her role in the project. "You see, these villagers are so stuck in ignorance and the past that they don't see the benefits this power plant is going to bring to their lives and these communities."

"But they are not ignorant" Sarah said as she tried to use her anthropological background to argue her case.

"Mmmhhh, so you are the smart one, yeah? If it's not ignorance, how do you define a phenomenon in which people are resistant to the changes that are going to transform their lives?" asked Rachel sarcastically before another engineer agreed with her.

"Does it make sense to refuse a project because of a sacred mountain that hosts some unknown spirits, the spirits that cannot bring them electricity?" The engineers laughed together. Sarah composed herself.

"I think it is important to try to see the world from their perspective" said Sarah recollecting scholarly thoughts of cooperative and deliberative development by authors she had studied, such as Clifford Geertz (1971), Gustavo Gutiérrez (1988), Jay Ruby (1991, 2000), and Paulo Freire (1970, 1996a, 1996b).

"It's that very perspective that has kept them in the dark and so backward all these years," observed the senior engineer. Sarah realized this conversation was becoming difficult.

"Have you ever spent time with them?" she asked, meaning the villagers.

"You just arrived and you seem to believe you understand them. We have been here over six months," argued Rachel.

"But you are not living within and alongside the community."

"What's your point Sarah?" asked another engineer who by now was somewhat drunk and badly needed a good night's sleep. "We already work through the relevant local government structures. Some chiefs are with us; others are still on the fence."

Sarah remembered reading Jay Ruby's (1991) article on cooperative anthropology. Her response somehow paraphrased Ruby but also emphasized her own ideas about deliberative development. She added, "I think it is still vital that we experience and appreciate the point of view of the local people. Seeing the world from their perspective could change the way we view this project and also them as a people."

"How long would that take? Two days? One week? A month? Six months? A year or even years?" asked Rachel.

"And what if they say no to this wonderful project? We pack up and go? Wasting all these resources?" continued the drunken engineer.

"To add to that," continued Rachel, "we already work with the local government and traditional structures, as we cannot achieve anything if we spend precious time listening to every person. Consultation is not in my job description." She lit her traditional cigarette, which smelt like marijuana, walked over to the small radio set in the corner and switched it on. Bob Marley's 'Exodus' was playing.

"That is exactly why we have a community participation component in the project, to try to bring people on board." No one was interested in listening to Sarah but nevertheless the arguments continued late into the night and the two parties could not agree on anything. Sarah needed a good rest, since within two days, she had an appointment with two chiefs in the valley who seemed unenthusiastic about the proposed power plant. The engineers continued drinking and they would later be joined by the District Commissioner and a few other teachers who were championing the micro-hydroelectric power plant project in the valley.

The smell of poverty

Two days after her arrival, Sarah would be picked up on a Thursday morning by the District Commissioner (DC) and then driven to the villages in the valley. She had been assured that the villagers and chiefs would be waiting for them at the local school. The two-hour drive deep into the mountainous regions was wonderful, as it provided Sarah with the opportunity to reflect on how she would approach the local communities. She had re-read Clifford Geertz's (1971) chapter on thick description, Alessandro Portelli's (1991) concept of collective memory, Guy Bessette's (2004) notion of participatory development communication, and crucially Paulo Freire's (1970) *Pedagogy of the Oppressed* and *Letters to Cristina* (1996a).

They arrived at the school around 10 a.m. Two local women were pounding in one wooden mortar. A couple of naked children could be seen chasing each other. A man and what looked like his wife walked by. They seemed to be coming from the garden. The man was carrying a child on his back and had two hoes in his hands. On the man's chest hung a small radio that was tuned to one of the stations. The radio announcer was talking to someone who had called the station to support the outlawing of homosexuality by a new bill enacted by parliament. The woman was carrying a load of firewood on her head and was eating a piece of raw cassava. The couple walked on and disappeared into the 'theatre' of village activities.

"They will come soon. Villagers are always late," the District Commissioner assured Sarah, who by now was seated in the middle of the front chairs wearing her African *chitenje* wrapped around her waist in an effort to connect better with local people. Reminiscent of 'Anthropology 101,' some 30 minutes later, the head teacher of the primary school appeared, accompanied by three nurses from the local health centre. "They will come," mumbled the DC to Sarah, who understood from her field guidelines that Professor Tennysons had shared with her and which contended that local people in this part of the south had little or no concept of time and appointment. Another 30 minutes. An hour. Another hour. It was beginning to get hot. The DC by this time had openly declared his impatience and whispered something into the ears of the head teacher, and they then drove away together into the village, reappearing after 30 minutes with two chiefs. After the exchange of greetings, one of the chiefs, speaking in excellent English, turned to Sarah:

"Our sincere apologies. I think there was a miscommunication. The meeting cannot take place because we need to finish consultations."

"Couldn't we bring everybody to this ground and talk about things here, and if there are any misunderstandings, we could work them out together?"

"My lady, there are serious concerns from some locals. Were you not briefed?"

The DC then interrupted, "No we were going to brief her today. But the most important point is that the government wants this project to be implemented, and it will be." He was looking a little impatient and unhappy.

There was now overt tension in the air. Sensing that there were many unresolved issues, Sarah tried to find a way forward in the conversation, looked at the DC, and said:

"Mr. District Commissioner, this is okay. Let's give people more time to conduct horizontal consultations." The local MP who was also driving by, stopped and greeted everyone. He asked after the progress of the micro-hydroelectric power plant. He then emphasized that, whatever was the case, he wanted the project to be implemented, especially considering that elections were coming in two years' time: the government needed a good story. The two chiefs insisted that they needed another week to complete their consultations and everyone agreed to that, except for the DC. As they left, Sarah exchanged phone numbers with the chiefs, nurses and the head teacher. Just in case.

"Villagers do not understand development. This project is for them and is going to benefit them," argued the visibly annoyed DC as they got into his car.

"Still, I think we should give them this week to see what they say."

"These people have been giving excuses for six months now."

"Six months?"

"If not more. The story is the same. They want more time for consultations. What kind of consultation takes six months?"

"I have read of consultations that take years."

"This country does not have the luxury of resources to conduct protracted consultations. Why do we even bother consulting ignorant villagers as if they understand the complexity of development questions?"

"I remember one of the books I read saying that once local people are consulted the project gets local ownership, legitimacy, and is assured of local support and investment."

"With due respect my lady, this is not a book. This is real life and we need electricity in this part of the world. I also studied at the university for my undergraduate degree. What makes us development planners assume that local people know what is best for them?" It was very clear that the DC was under immense pressure from politicians to deliver this development project within a given period of time.

After being dropped off at the camp, Sarah freshened up and joined the team of engineers for afternoon drinks. She was now beginning to understand their frustrations. Later in the afternoon she would phone the chief and the head teacher. She arranged to meet them after two days, but the two insisted it would be preferred if she came without the DC or any government officials.

The project would provide a driver and she eventually departed for the village. This time the chief looked jovial, so too the head teacher. In fact the head teacher had seemed a man of few words but this time he had lots of stories about the village and the various development projects. The chief's wife had prepared a local dish that looked appetizing and delicious. After eating, Sarah would be taken to the sites of the planned micro-hydropower station. She requested her driver to return for her after a few days. She really needed to explore things for herself.

> The best way I can explain it to you is by saying that, for a second or two, I felt as though, instead of going to the centre of a continent, I were about to

> set off for the centre of the earth. … There it is before you—smiling, frowning, inviting, grand, mean, insipid, or savage, and always mute with an air of whispering, "Come and find out." … The edge of a colossal jungle, so dark-green as to be almost black, fringed with white surf, ran straight, like a ruled line, far, far away along a blue sea whose glitter was blurred by a creeping mist. The sun was fierce, the land seemed to glisten and drip with steam.
>
> *(Joseph Conrad 1899/2003,* Heart of Darkness, *18–19)*

The project site was located high up the hill and offered the naked eye a picturesque view of the Valley of a Thousand Villages—the name the colonialists had given to this area. The Lichenha River starts in this range of mountains and meanders through the dense forests of the plains, snaking out to the Zambezi River. The forest is comprised mostly of indigenous trees. Life in these villages seemed to revolve around the mountains and the river. As she toured these places, Sarah was told many stories that revealed that these villagers were an ethnic minority and had been driven from their land in the 1800s by a genocide perpetrated by groups of Bantu-speaking militant refugees from Central Africa. Even after settling in the country in the mid 1840s, they were further pushed away to the infertile mountains by other dominant ethnic groups who were being supported by the British colonial authorities as part of their divide-and-rule strategy. By the time the country achieved independence in the late 1950s, this ethnic group was further marginalized by successive central governments that never bothered to provide basic social services. The only external governance known to this Valley of a Thousand Villages was the Scottish Mission which had, from the 1850s, built schools and health centres.

> "The chief of the Inner Station," he answered in a short tone, looking away. "Much obliged," I said, laughing. "And you are the brick maker of the Central Station. Everyone knows that." He was silent for a while. "He is a prodigy," he said at last. "He is an emissary of pity and science and progress, and devil knows what else. We want," he began to declaim suddenly, "for the guidance of the cause entrusted to us by Europe, so to speak, higher intelligence, wide sympathies, a singleness of purpose." "Who says that?" I asked. "Lots of them," he replied. "Some even write that …"
>
> *(Joseph Conrad 1899/2003,* Heart of Darkness, *39)*

Until five years ago the plains were very quiet and there was much tranquility, and the villagers seemed to prefer to be forgotten by the outside world. The people had become more independent and resilient. Then certain white people and Indians—accompanied by government officials—came to tell the villagers that there were geological experiments that a foreign company wanted to conduct in the mountain. Over the course of two years they drilled holes in the mountainside and blasted with explosives, collecting rock samples. Truckloads and truckloads of the samples were taken away. No one knew what the experiment was about and after two years of disturbing the peace of the villagers, the white men and Indians left, leaving some of their equipment behind. They said they were going to return. Months after their departure, part of the mountain collapsed and the resulting flash floods destroyed much of the valley.

Over 200 people, mostly children and the elderly lost their lives—livestock, crops and other property were destroyed. In the aftermath of this tragedy, no government official came to give condolences to the families. Much of the humanitarian assistance had come from the Scottish missionaries. It was within the context of the flash floods that Patrick Machava would apply for early retirement from his prestigious position in the military to help rebuild the Valley of a Thousand Villages. Patrick, named after the Irish patron saint, was a well-travelled man. He had been to France, Italy, the United States, China, Russia, Spain and much of Africa on security missions. He had fought in Iraq and Afghanistan as an officer for a private American security firm. A couple of years before his early retirement, his grandfather, who had fought alongside the British in the Second World War, passed away. The villages had unanimously designated him a senior chief to replace his grandfather. His military and global experience accorded him huge respect among fellow chiefs. He once shouted at an MP in English. He could talk to the white missionaries and other foreign visitors in English, French, Spanish or Portuguese. His house was powered by solar electricity, the only one with power, save for the health centres which used generators once in a while. He owned a huge grocery and a two-ton truck that also served as the village ambulance.

Since Patrick's return, a couple of NGOs had come to operate in the Valley of a Thousand Villages. World Vision and Save the Children were, respectively, running a livelihoods and a nutrition project to eradicate infant stunted growth. World Vision was working with local farmers to practise crop diversification and eradicate food insecurity. Opportunity Bank was opening up a rural branch in order to work with women's groups in village savings loans. What Sarah noted in her short stay and, of course, through conversations was that, much as the local people would work with international and local development organizations, they nevertheless remained cautious and suspicious. She understood why the consultations over the micro-hydropower plant were taking so long. But she also realized something very important, something that would have a profound effect on her career and how she saw her role in her current work.

She wondered whether it was necessary for her to have come here. She felt that development was already here even before she arrived. Sarah realized that real development lay in understanding the complex relationships that were governing human interactions, and not just in bringing technology and new thinking.

> It had become so pitch dark that we listeners could hardly see one another. For a long time already he, sitting apart, had been no more to us than a voice. There was not a word from anybody. The others might have been asleep, but I was awake. I listened, I listened on the watch for the sentence, for the word,

> that would give me the clue to the faint uneasiness inspired by this narrative that seemed to shape itself without human lips in the heavy night-air of the river.
>
> *(Joseph Conrad 1899/2003,* Heart of Darkness, *43)*

Sarah began to question whether her graduate training had prepared her for these complex traditional politics. It was imperative that Patrick be convinced of the positive contribution of the micro-hydroelectric power station to the local economy. Yet it was clear that unless Patrick found something financially, spiritually or socially beneficial to him, then the project would not take off. Perhaps, Sarah wondered, Patrick was feeling that the project would rob him of his political power that originated from being the only person with electricity in the village. But why would he work hard to bring NGOs into the local communities if he didn't want the communities to develop? Were there any people she had not talked to? Homesteads she had not visited? Rains began to fall. It was the rainy season. As she ran into the shade, she remembered Robert Chambers' advice about the poor visibility of poverty and how it can be hard to find and talk to the people who are really steeped in poverty. Perhaps she had made a mistake in affiliating herself with Patrick's family. Chambers's (1980, 18–20) caution rang in her memory:

> "Elite" is used here to describe those rural people who are less poor and more influential. They typically include progressive farmers, village leaders, headmen, traders, religious leaders, teachers, and para-professionals. They are the main sources of information for rural tourists, for local-level officials, and even for rural researchers. They are the most fluent informants. It is they who receive and speak to the visitors; they who articulate the village's interests and wishes; their concerns which emerge as the village's priorities for development. It is they who entertain visitors, generously providing the expected beast or beverage. It is they who receive the lion's share of attention, advice and services from agricultural extension staff. It is they too, who, at least at first, monopolize the time and attention of the visitor. Conversely, the poorer or the poorest do not speak up. With those of higher status, they may even decline to sit down. Weak, powerless and isolated, they are often reluctant to push themselves forward. …
>
> Tourists also tend to visit places where activity is concentrated, easily visible, and hence easy to study. Children in school are more likely to be seen and questioned than those who are not in school; those who use the health clinic more than those who are too sick, too poor or too distant to use it; those who come to market because they have goods to sell or money with which to buy more than those who stay at home because they have neither; members of the cooperatives more than those who are too poor or powerless to join it; those who have adopted new agricultural, health, or family planning practices more than those who have not. Again and again it is the underprivileged who are overlooked.

Once she recalled Chambers's (1980, 1981) advice she realized what she had not paid attention to all this time. How could she have forgotten? How could she have been so silly? But the word *power* kept coming up in her mind and she wished she had enough time to study how it operates at the local level. How could she have missed it, crucial as it was to her work?

Power.

She recalled Pierre Bourdieu (1991) and his notion of symbolic power as the power that helps people construct and organize their social reality, thereby enabling them to acquire a coherent understanding of things, that is, time and space. She also remembered Steven Lukes's (2005) three-dimensional view of power and she thought that elements of non-decision-making might be relevant here considering that, within this community, there was a concerted effort by powerful families to mobilize and reinforce certain biases. It was almost impossible to do anything.

Then it occurred to her. Why hadn't she realized this all along? Chimamanda Ngozi Adichie's (2009) "The danger of a single story" came into her mind. Perhaps the whole project was based on a single story about this rural village. In literature and in project documents, policy makers had conceived of this place through the economic indicators that showed that the people were in need of an economic stimulus in the form of infrastructure development—the hydropower plant. "The danger with the single story is that it creates stereotypes, and the problem with stereotypes is not that they are untrue, but that they are incomplete," Adichie (2009) had observed. Perhaps she needed a new perspective. Her eyes lit up. Sarah's face glowed. And suddenly it dawned on her. This village was not poor and the villagers were not poor people after all. How could she not have seen all this?

Concluding thoughts: Finding the village but missing the poverty

> Marlow ceased, and sat apart, indistinct and silent, in the pose of a meditating Buddha. Nobody moved for a time. "We have lost the first of the ebb," said the Director suddenly. I raised my head. The offing was barred by a black bank of clouds, and the tranquil waterway leading to the uttermost ends of the earth flowed sombre under an overcast sky—seemed to lead into the heart of an immense darkness.
>
> *(Joseph Conrad 1899/2003,* Heart of Darkness, *130)*

The foregoing engages with Robert Chambers's (1980, 1981) insights into the challenges faced by outsiders and insiders as they attempt to encounter poverty in their quest to deconstruct it. What this narrative shows, using illuminations from Joseph Conrad's *Heart of Darkness*, is that development practitioners might have the best of intentions. The challenge lies in ensuring that those intentions are shared with local communities. In the process of trying to do just this, exploitative groups take advantage of people's lack of information to manipulate development narratives and initiatives for their own needs. The sincere efforts and the honest dreams end up like Kurtz in Conrad's account: someone who had so much hope but then after his death, "of all his promise, and of all his greatness, of his generous mind, of his noble heart, nothing remains—nothing but a memory" (Conrad 1899/2003, 128).

As Marx (1852/2010) observed in *The Eighteenth Brumaire of Louis Bonaparte*, working classes without pertinent political consciousness end up being spoken of, spoken for, and represented by oppressing classes. As such, even though civil society organizations exist that claim to be inspired by Marx's ideal of an equal, just and free society that agitates for social and democratic change, such activism cannot really be transformative unless it is undertaken with the interests of local people at heart, because they can sustain that effort. The key here is to speak development with and alongside individuals and communities, and not to speak *for* them. Perhaps that is what Patrick, the chief, part of the local elite in Chambers's (1980, 1981) analogy, might seem to represent. The implementation of a comprehensive radical education that engages oppressed peoples in a journey of self-reflection and critical consciousness is a key characteristic of this organic intellectual-educator. Perhaps as a local elite, with resources and being financially well off himself, transforming this community might not seem a critical agenda for Patrick. Yet Sarah still believes that Fanon (1961, 1965) and Freire (1970) were spot on in observing the significance of collective consciousness as being central to the process of decolonization.

Patrick has the education and understanding to appreciate the need to develop his community. And he seems to understand what it will take to develop his community. But he doesn't seem to want to go in that direction. Sarah, on the other hand, might be a foreigner but this gives her the advantage of acquiring a holistic understanding of how local politics is stifling local development. The challenge is that there is a covert tension between how Patrick and Sarah view poverty, its causes and how to deconstruct it as means of finding a pathway towards achieving sustainable local development. Perhaps there was no poverty warranting this kind of intervention in the first place. By moving into this community, and perhaps by prolonging her stay, Sarah is beginning to deconstruct dominant development systems here, which Patrick seems to be part of. Sarah's openness, empathy, understanding and respect are opening up opportunities to work with the people to reimagine a new discourse, which will destabilize the current status quo. But she has to find a way to work with Patrick. Then the word came to her in a form of a vision like Saul's on the road to Damascus.

Listening.

Note

1 The following sections are based on collective experiences with western scholars, international development experts and growing up in poverty. The events have been fictionalized and so are the identities and personalities of Professor Tennysons and his student, Sarah Mendez Casper. But the tensions, conflicts and scenarios happened.

References

Adichie, Chimamanda Ngozi. 2009. "The danger of a single story." TED Talk. Oxford University. Accessed January 20 2016. www.youtube.com/watch?v=D9Ihs241zeg.

Bakhtin, Mikhail. 1981. *The Dialogic Imagination: Four Essays*. Edited by Michael Holquist. Austin: University of Texas Press.

Baldwin, James. 1986. National Press Club Speech, 12 October 1986. Accessed March 20 2017. www.youtube.com/watch?v=CTjY4rZFY5c.

Bessette, Guy. 2004. *Involving the Community: A Guide to Participatory Development Communication*. Penang and Ottawa: Southbound and International Development Research Centre.

Bourdieu, Pierre. 1983/1991. *Language and Symbolic Power*. Cambridge: Polity Press.

Chambers, Robert. 1980. *Rural Poverty Unperceived: Problems and Remedies*. Staff Working Paper Number SWP 400. Washington, DC: The World Bank. Accessed September 30 2016. http://documents.worldbank.org/curated/en/909311468766763144/Rural-poverty-unperceived-problems-and-remedies.

Chambers, Robert. 1981. "Poor visibility: How policy makers overlook the poor." New Internationalist website. Issue 96. Accessed January 20 2016. http://newint.org/features/1981/02/01/poor-visibility.

Chambers, Robert. 2005. *Ideas for Development*. London and Sterling: Earthscan.

Conrad, Joseph. 1899/2003. *Heart of Darkness*. New York: Fine Communications.

Coyle, Diane. 2012. "Are economics graduates fit for purpose?" *VOX CEPR Policy Portal*. Accessed November 20 2016. http://voxeu.org/article/are-economics-graduates-fit-purpose.

Djebar, Assia. 1992. *Women of Algiers in their Apartment*. Translated by Marjolijn de Jager. Charlottesville and London: University of Virginia Press.

Fanon, Frantz. 1961. *The Wretched of the Earth*. New York: Grove Press.

Fanon, Frantz. 1965. *A Dying Colonialism*. New York: Grove Press.

Freire, Paulo. 1970. *Pedagogy of the Oppressed*. London: Penguin.

Freire, Paulo. 1996a. *Letters to Cristina*. New York: Continuum.

Freire, Paulo. 1996b. *An Incredible Conversation*. YouTube Channel. Accessed January 20 2016. www.youtube.com/watch?v=aFWjnkFypFA.

Geertz, Clifford. 1971. "Thick description. Towards an interpretive theory of culture." In *The Interpretation of Cultures: Selected Essays* (pp. 3–30). New York: Basic Books.

Gutiérrez, Gustavo. 1988. *A Theology of Liberation: History, Politics, and Salvation*. Translated by Caridad Inda and John Eagleson. Maryknoll, New York: Orbis Books.

hooks, bell. 1994. *Teaching to Transgress: Education as the Practice of Freedom*. London and New York: Routledge.

Lerner, Daniel. 1958. *The Passing of Traditional Society: Modernizing the Middle East*. New York and London: Free Press and Collier-Macmillan.

Lukes, Steven. 1974/2005. *Power: A Radical View*. New York: Palgrave Macmillan.

Mamdani, Mahmood. 2007. "The politics of naming: Genocide, civil war, insurgency." *London Review of Books*, 29(5): 5–8.

Mansell, Robin. 1982. "The 'new dominant paradigm' in communication: Transformation versus adaptation." *Canadian Journal of Communication*, 8(3): 42–60. Accessed September 20 2016. www.cjc-online.ca/index.php/journal/article/view/278/184.

Marx, Karl. 1852/2010. *The Eighteenth Brumaire of Louis Bonaparte*. New York: *Die Revolution* Issue 1.

Pierce, Andrew. 2008. "The Queen asks why no one saw the credit crunch coming." In *The Telegraph Online*. November 5. Accessed January 20 2016. www.telegraph.co.uk/

news/uknews/theroyalfamily/3386353/The-Queen-asks-why-no-one-saw-the-credit-crunch-coming.html.

Portelli, Alessandro. 1991. *The Death of Luigi Trastulli and Other Stories: Form and Meaning in Oral History*. Albany, NY: State University of New York.

Post-Crash Economics Society. 2014. "Economics, education and unlearning: Economics education at the University of Manchester." Accessed January 20 2016. www.post-crasheconomics.com/download/778.

Rostow, Walt. 1960. *The Stages of Economic Growth: A Non-Communist Manifesto.* Cambridge: Cambridge University Press.

Ruby, Jay. 1991. "Speaking for, speaking about, speaking with, or speaking alongside – An anthropological and documentary dilemma." *Visual Anthropology Review*, 7(2): 50–67.

Ruby, Jay. 2000. *Picturing Culture: Explorations of Film and Anthropology*. Chicago: Chicago University Press.

Said, Edward. 1978. *Orientalism*. New York: Random House.

Sen, Amartya. 1999. *Development as Freedom*. New York. First Anchor Books.

Ward-Perkins, Zach and Joe Earle. 2014. "Economics students need to be taught more than neoclassical theory." *The Guardian Online*. Accessed January 20 2016. www.theguardian.com/commentisfree/2013/oct/28/economics-students-neoclassical-theory.

6 PEDAGOGY OF LISTENING

Setting the context

This chapter summarizes the discussions in the preceding chapters as a context for discussing the praxis of listening as curated by Freire and Gutiérrez. The first chapter explored the predicament created by the prevailing view of the material and symbolic culture of knowledge, values, attitudes and practices in development practice, and the second chapter examined the role of the oppressor and how this oppressor employs language which frames a certain kind of development as the only pathway to modernity. The third chapter explored the politics of enabling the voices of subaltern groups to be heard and how challenging it is to incorporate their voices within policy formulation. Incorporating marginalized voices in mainstream policies could be considered less radical and less revolutionary, but it is the position of this book that destabilizing dominant syntax should not wait for an overthrow of an entire social system. The fourth chapter investigated the crucial question of living with people and why relevant communication tools and skills should be a feature of any development training programme. The fifth chapter provided a narrative in the form of an imaginary encounter between local groups and a recent development anthropology graduate who is sent on a civilizing mission to a rural community in the south, as they begin to question their training, prejudices and their concept of development itself.

Perhaps the social-change critique did make sense in Latin America where it emerged—and it made sense because of the successive military and dictator-led governments that were being propped up by western governments, as a way of stifling socialist and left-leaning governments. In many instances in the south, there is relative democracy, with its serious challenges, and it is not a question of instituting social changes, rather it is about transforming the current thinking and practices. As Jonathan Makuwira (2014) has observed, it is about conscientizing and transforming the behaviours and practices of policy makers, NGOs and other decision-taking bodies within the development industry chain.

This chapter engages in a critical appraisal of a pedagogy that Gutiérrez (1988), Freire (1970, 1996a, 1996b), Escobar (1995), Chambers (1980, 1981, 2005) and other critical students of society have advocated—the pedagogy of listening. Much of the participatory development literature emphasizes the bottom-up production of marginalized citizens' voices and their incorporation into policy formulation, implementation and evaluation. But as the preceding chapter has shown, by drawing from Chambers, not all marginalized people are equal. Those marginalized individuals with a few more resources, opportunities and better access to opportunities for social mobility, whom Chambers (1980) conceives of as the "local elite," always have access to voice and socio-economic opportunities. They display a sense of great comprehension of the relationship between local groups and outsiders. Hence, Chambers (1980, 19) describes them as being the "most fluent informants." Much as deliberative development debate is beginning to discuss questions of listening to voices from below, rarely is there an emphasis on listening as a deliberate process of seeking out those with inferior status and who are subordinate to other marginalized individuals and people. It has, nevertheless, to be acknowledged that there exists a body of research that emphasizes integrating what experts consider to be views and opinions of local people in the creation of socio-economic policies. Yet the kind of listening I am referring to, in contrast, builds on Chambers's (1980) caution against project biases that prevent a holistic perception of poverty as well as the key insights in Freire's (1996b) interview on the idea of listening as both a virtue and practice of tolerance. Freire observes:

> It is through the exercise of tolerance that I discover the rich possibility of doing things and learning things with different people. Being tolerant is not a question of being naïve. On the contrary, it is a duty to be tolerant; an ethical duty, an historical duty, a political duty. But it does not demand from me that I lose my personality.

For Freire, tolerance allows any student of society to appreciate learning and doing things with other people if they engage in the active practise of listening. This concluding chapter is a self-reflective and auto-ethnographic exposition through which I present these forms of listening: (a) listening to evidence, (b) listening to ourselves, and (c) listening as a form of speaking. The aim is to reject 'the view from here', which is itself a neo-liberal and western-centric positionality that assumes and emphasizes a privileged perspective in looking at and defining the world. My contention is that, as development practitioners, we need to build our capacities to practice all three forms of listening if we are to work with others in designing and implementing policies that seek to improve lives and communities in ways that are consistent with their aspirations. I write this chapter in the context of the proliferation of online and offline mechanisms for producing subaltern voices. The objective of developers and users of many of these platforms is to celebrate democratic possibilities and new opportunities for producing and exchanging voice.

Community engagement discussions and models are increasingly becoming technologically deterministic especially in relation to the role of social media facilities such as Facebook, Twitter, Instagram, YouTube, Weibo, and other forms of participatory media. Thus, proponents of neoliberal models of democracy are rejoicing at the ability of citizens to speak and be heard. The transformative nature of these voices should also be taken into consideration. Yet for a holistic and nuanced understanding of the transformative potential of these voices, there is a need to listen to and understand what these voices are all about.

With the emergence and consolidation of community media, Indy media and other micro forms of speech production, the public sphere is no longer seen as a homogeneous mediascape, if it ever was; and in some accounts is therefore no longer monopolized or refeudalized by the bourgeois as originally feared by Jurgen Habermas (1962), even if the market has become a feature that influences the way contemporary media operates and communication policy is formulated. Pluralist conceptions of the public sphere or spheres have emerged with new approaches to information management. Digital platforms—such as Soundcloud and YouTube—host millions of audio and visual historical records, from cultures and languages on the verge of extinction to socio-economic documentation and policies. Citizens who formerly were separated by time and space can engage in real time. When they tune in to their radios, they are faced with the difficult choice of deciding which channel they will listen to. From the local community stations based in towns and cities, to the commercial broadcasters, the international channels such as the BBC or ABC, one has to tune out some of one's favourite broadcasters. So-called 'big data' or vast quantities of information are increasingly available but the question is, are development policy makers and practitioners listening? Are they becoming more empathetic to subaltern reflections? Who is actually listening to these multiple (or this *heteroglossia* of) voices?

Prologue

I recall a time when I worked in a western country. I was telephoned by my son's primary school. It was not urgent, but very important, the school secretary had said. I spent a day or two without going there. At home I asked my son if there was something that had happened in school. He said everything was okay, and I decided I was too busy to go to the school; after all, I told myself, teachers in schools have nothing really serious to tell parents. A couple of days passed and the school administrator called again. He wanted me to see the class teacher as soon as I could. It wasn't urgent, but it was very important. Can you tell me on the phone? Naaah, I think you better come here. Am I behind with my payments for school lunch? No you don't have any outstanding balance actually. Has my son been fighting or is he in any trouble? No. Perhaps a learning problem? Or fighting perhaps? Please just come. So eventually I visited the school.

We were ushered into the headmaster's office. Okay, so let me begin from the beginning. The "we" here refers to three parents of children including myself. Two black parents and one white. Well, the white one might actually have self-described as black because she looked underprivileged like the majority of the black people who lived in the school area of the town. In the western world, the postal code is often a form of racial, ethnic and class identity.

Why are we here?

Well it's a difficult subject but we must discuss it. Come on just say it! Well, it happens that the class teacher here is concerned with the unpleasant body odour produced by your children and we would like to request that you make sure that your children are taking a bath every morning. You can imagine the explosion from all of us who felt our children were being picked on for being black. Then there was shouting and misunderstanding. And we left the school in anger. In my heart of hearts, I suspected racism. I have experienced lots of it and I "just knew" this was it. As I left the schoolyard, the "white" parent was asking loudly, "it's just a *fooking* primary school, it's not as if our children are studying at Cambridge."

Over the next days, my routine did not change. I woke up my son; he would go to have a shower; I would prepare his breakfast and then after he had dressed and eaten I would walk him to school.

Then one morning after my son went to school—I had woken up late on this day and I went to have a shower—as I walked to the bedroom I noticed for the first time my wet footprints escorting me until my feet were dry. Next morning, I was making my son some breakfast when he finished his shower and was walking to his bedroom. Something inside me clicked. I saw him walking to put on his uniform without any wet footprints behind him. I got the little devil! Just before we left the house to go to school I told him to take off his uniform so he would take a "second" shower under my supervision. We fought over that decision until he took a "second" shower. Over the next couple of days I personally supervised the showers and I was pleased when the class teacher came to me to tell me how pleased she was that my son smelled great, and some of the kids who had complained were playing with him. So what is listening, in Freire's terms?

Listening to evidence

I was faced with the facts presented to me: your son is producing certain unpleasant smells, you need to ensure he is bathing in the morning. I chose to ignore them rather than to investigate until some days later. After I had said some things and suspected evil thoughts, I was confronted by evidence. In any development intervention, planning is crucial but it is the evidence we must allow to speak to us. It is not uncommon, for example, to find numerous donor-funded interventions claiming traditions and culture as the key causes of certain poor individual and social behaviour. As such, interventions are designed to transform or end these oppressive traditions. This is the case in numerous HIV prevention interventions. What is interesting is that numerous studies are demonstrating that it is educated people living in urban spaces, with large disposable incomes who are contracting the virus in large numbers. These are the very people who least practice their traditions, and if they do, such as during funerals, they rarely engage in practices that would transmit the virus. Similarly, think about new evidence pointing to the fact that it is married couples or people in stable relationships who are contracting the virus, much more than any other demographic group. But we seem to ignore the evidence, refusing to listen to it, instead choosing to listen to our stereotypes and orientalist fantasies and we allocate huge sums of resources to fight oppressive traditions, which it is claimed are responsible for the spread of the virus. What scientific evidence is there before us? Are we listening to it?

This problem has some of its roots in some university degree programmes. There are thousands of degree programmes in the social sciences that offer students an opportunity to read many books without really understanding them and, as a consequence, without having the opportunity to critically engage with the socio-political and economic reality. By the end of these programmes, students will have completed their exams, assignments and research projects. Throughout these programmes, students survive from one essay to the next, one exam to another, and they rarely have time to reflect on what it is that they are learning. Training to listen is not part of many such degree programmes. Contrast this with my time growing up in the peasant farms of white-owned tea and tobacco estates. In the evenings, we the children would sit around the village fires, listening to our uncles and aunts telling us stories of animal adventures, the trickster hare always surviving trouble that he initiated in the first place and getting away with devilish misdemeanours, while the villain hyena, always the one being outsmarted, gets punished for crimes and grave errors that the hare actually committed. What amazes me today is how silent we were when these stories were being told, joining in the chorus of "*Tili Tonse*" (we are together) to remind the narrator we were following them. We listened because we wanted to tell these interesting stories in school and to other kids. And we also listened because we knew that if we didn't we would have no stories to tell others. In essence, our identities were formed through appreciating listening as an art form and as a virtue. Even though the seeds of critical consciousness were laid here, it was a different and an unexpected institution that finally opened up my mind to critical consciousness: western education.

Yes, there are spaces even within these education institutions that offer students an opportunity to critically engage with empirical reality and thus acquire consciousness. The notion of western education does not necessarily refer to universities based in the west. Rather, it is the curriculum that is of concern here in that its orientation is ideologically western. My time with Chris Kamlongera (1988) at the University of Malawi or Keyan Tomaselli (2006) at the University of Natal provided me with a critical opportunity to engage with the social world. As such, acquiring this subaltern perspective has been a long journey. Even though I grew up in and under extreme poverty, I thought my world was normal. The critical perspectives about the poverty at home began to take root in high school and, later on, during my undergraduate and graduate degree programmes. In this book, I argue that it is not easy to acquire critical and subaltern consciousness, and being born in poverty is not a guarantee that one will attain subaltern perspectives. The role of western education—from reading Edward Palmer Thompson, William Shakespeare, Charles Dickens, Tennessee Williams, Langston Hughes, Lorraine Hansberry, Arthur Miller, Samuel Beckett, Raymond Williams or Eric Hobsbawm and others—has been critical in helping me understand the exploitation that we were living under. I have felt during this journey of working with and alongside communities that most white westerners have developed subaltern perspectives perhaps because of their critical western education, but also because of their patience and passion for community development.

Listening to ourselves

Freire writes about listening as a form of tolerance, describing this as a primary duty of development practitioners. There is a tendency among experts to assume that they have the divine voice. They are in conferences; they will be the first to speak; and they will also be the last to ensure their views are adopted as resolutions for action. Even when questions are raised about the local context and the need to take into consideration external and local factors, these experts (both external and internal) will bring overly complex explanations of how they have dealt with similar situations in other countries and contexts. Theories and models that do not really make sense will be introduced and thrust down people's throats so that they can work with these new strategies.

I have self-reflexively described this omnipresent and omnipotent expert who knows everything; who comes into a local context and attempts to rearrange reality in ways that suit his or her epistemology—and from that biased pedestal, begins to introduce interventions that will often end in failure (Manyozo 2010) and I have offered additional examples in this book. Unable to accept that their top-down vertical approach and style of policy making cause the failure, the expert will blame local people and move on to another donor-funded consultancy where they exert more programmatic strategies on unsuspecting local community members and local experts. Why is it that these external and internal experts refuse to listen to others?

There are many explanations. Principal among them is that their expert knowledge is narrow, reductionist and not adaptable to complex local situations. As a result, such experts thrive on incoherence, they provide partial knowledge because their job security lies in few people knowing what they know and worse, they are just incompetent. They hide in vertically organized institutions where local experts are not allowed to question their divine wisdom. Doing this over and over without being found out, they think inside boxes even if their motto is "thinking outside the box," and are dependent on formulae and the strict logic of their models and theories. It is either this model or nothing else, they say. They will claim: I know there are other models—when actually they do not—but this is the one that has been proven to work. But it's not working here! Sorry, they say, you'll have to start all over because there is obviously something you didn't do right.

Listening to others implies that we get out of our comfort zone of dominant development theories and prescriptive models, and humbly subject ourselves to intellectual scrutiny by others, to gauge whether our knowledge can withstand the test of new contexts. This involves a process of knowledge validation and it is the ethical and political duty that Freire refers to. We must humble ourselves and enter into dialogue with others about our methods and practices, and be able to admit when we are wrong and seek the correction and advice of others, often those with limited educational qualifications or a different class status. Sometimes, this might be a student with whom we engage and this is the reason that Freire (1970, 1996a, 1996b) emphasizes the need for democratic methods of teaching in which the educator does not impose his or her world view on the student, but enters into a dialogical relationship that may end up correcting the teacher.

Listening as a form of speaking

In the introduction to *Letters to Cristina*, Freire (1996a) describes reading as an element of writing. He observes that when he is writing he starts by reading what he wrote the day before, so that he can reconnect with his ideas and be able to build on them. The same process applies to speaking in that, when we speak, we have to be our own listeners before everyone else, because at a certain point we will need to question ourselves and be able to correct our thoughts when challenged or faced with alternatives. Within the development context, listening to ourselves can help us to be consistent in the way we present our arguments and it can help us to celebrate intellectual exchanges with those who are listening to us.

Listening to ourselves allows us to take a position. As we speak, we are taking a stand by formulating certain arguments. Listening to ourselves as we take that stand is an act of symbolic and cultural rebellion or struggle, enabling us to enter into a symbolic military pact and express our solidarity with our ideas. Listening to ourselves allows us to take a moral stand, committing ourselves to what we live for and stand by, even if it means some people disagree with us. Listening to ourselves offers us the opportunity to be the first critics if our ideas prove to be problematic. We then offer ourselves the privileged opportunity to be the first to correct or strengthen our arguments.

Listening therefore allows us to demonstrate our belief in a position. As observed by the pioneer of liberation theology—Gutiérrez—genuine listening manifests itself as a form of speaking for and on behalf of the oppressed. But this is only possible if an educator establishes a meaningful friendship with those he or she is wishing to educate, providing a genuine commitment to the cause of liberation, which is a demonstration of love between educator and educatee (Gutiérrez 1988).

So what is listening?

My discussion seeks to demonstrate that listening is both an act of faith and a symbolic struggle. It is an act of faith in the people we work with. As Freire (1996a,

1996b) observes, listening does not simply imply keeping quiet when someone is speaking. It is a politically conscious decision to enter into communion with other people. Listening allows us to, in Freire's (1996b, interview) words, "discover the rich possibility of doing things and learning things with different people." What this implies is that our faith in humanity moves us to be tolerant of other ideas, perspectives and ways of looking at the world, even if we strongly disagree with them. Listening is not naivety, it is a celebration of recognition that other human beings are rational, intelligent and competent to contribute to the dialogues and discourses that we engage in. As such, considering the position of others is an act of faith in that it presents others with an opportunity to question our ideas and in the process we have the opportunity to correct errors and weaknesses in our arguments.

At the same time, listening is a symbolic struggle in that it allows us to consolidate our arguments and reaffirm our solidarity with the ideas we stand for. Through listening, we open ourselves to the possibility of appreciating differences we may have with others who hold different views. If a misogynistic, racist, undemocratic or sexist person is speaking, we have the moral, political and ethical duty to listen to them, and use their arguments to strengthen ours. As a symbolic act of war, listening to others offers us the opportunity to be empathic and imagine for a moment how they must be feeling, and, as a result of this process, to formulate a certain course of action. As Thompson (1963) observes in *The Making of the English Working Class*, listening becomes a form of doing history from below in which, even in moments of the strongest disagreement with others, we transport ourselves to look at the world from their perspective. This allows us to go to war against their prejudices, against their 'facts' and the way they present them. In the process, we place ourselves in a position to stand in solidarity with our ideals but, at the same time, to formulate arguments in ways that might better appeal to the people we listen to.

To listen, therefore, is an act of sincerity, a celebration of our faith in humanity, a triumph of our firm solidarity with the ideals of democracy, equality and social justice. It allows us to become students of society and participants in a critical pedagogy, the pedagogy of listening. Listening offers participatory development practice, a methodological pathway and an avenue towards theoretical enlightenment that no other praxis does—thereby laying the foundation stone for development using local resources, community spirit, knowledge and strength.

Developing skills and tools in listening

It is important to distinguish between skills and tools. Skills are those personal attributes that comprise knowledge of phenomena and the expertise required for implementing such knowledge. These are attributes that a person has which make them an expert, enabling them to assume authority in talking about and taking a specific course of action. If, for instance, I claim to have skills in dancing *kizomba*, it means—if I am not bullshitting—that I know what *kizomba* is and I can use those skills to dance *kizomba*. Tools, in contrast, are instruments that a person with certain skills uses to implement a certain course of action. So if I want to teach people how to dance *kizomba*, I need the requisite tools in order to impart that specialist knowledge. I could use workshops, individual coaching exercises, training exercises or participatory studio practices. All these are the technical and logistical means that I could possibly employ to impart the skills of dancing *kizomba*.

One of my experiences of living in London involved Thursday evening meetings of the Brockley Assembly. Such assemblies are an integral part of decentralizing and devolving power from the Westminster Parliament and, in principle, they enable local communities to contribute towards decisions that shape their communities. I remember the heated and fruitful discussions we had over how we would spend the London Mayor's Fund, allocated by the Mayor's office to help each local assembly implement infrastructure and social projects and programmes to create stronger and safer communities.

In Brockley, projects and programmes encompassed facilities and activities for specific population groups such as the elderly, children or young people, and to tackle anti-social behaviour, improve safety, keep streets clean, or create green and open spaces. The process of encouraging residents' contributions included a traditional style of commissioning, to generate interventions based on the Assembly's action plan, which would then evolve into proposals. Eventually, local groups would bid to deliver these projects. Presentations were made to the assembly and, finally, voting was then undertaken by the residents.

For a host of governments and other institutions, there is an institutionalized mechanism for ensuring that citizens' voices are articulated and listened to. In the case of local assemblies, community engagement policies and strategies have been put in place to provide prescriptive guidance on the generation and utilization of citizen voices in policy making. What is important is that within these instrumental avenues of engagement, citizens are governed by the rules of speech and dialogue set up by the controlling organizations. Nevertheless, despite the criticisms that such approaches either placate citizens, manipulate them or co-opt them into rubber-stamping certain policy decisions, what is important is that citizens acquire a sense of community belonging, ensuring they make a social investment in strengthening their community, and building up their social capital as well. The objective of these approaches is not necessarily empowerment, but then empowerment is not a stage that one can measure. Rather, it is a gradual process, which is fraught with contestations arising out of unequal power relations.

In this case, listening and the communicative process go beyond the reception, interpretation and comprehension of messages. It is about celebrating the role of others in contributing to the formulation and articulation of a specific position. Within the context of institutional engagement, mechanisms are put in place to ensure that citizens feel they have been engaged. This feeling of being listened to is crucial, and engagement tools such as questionnaires, voting, discussion forums, community cafés, appreciative inquiries, or phone-in radio programmes, allow citizens to develop a *feeling of being listened to*, even if there are no indicators of how their contributions have shaped a final policy or intervention. One might argue that an approved project proposal is an indicator of such listening if its merits have been debated at a local council meeting and if most of the members have argued for it, since this shows that residents have been listened to—even those who had opposed said initiative.

In many of these debates, people who argue for a specific project or programme will feel excited at first because their argument may initially win the day; but then discussion moderators have the responsibility to listen to those who are outvoted, outwitted or outdebated. Thus, an approved project will end up being modified in response to questions and concerns raised by those who initially lost the argument. In this way, even the people who feel they have not won the argument may feel their concerns have been taken on board. This form of listening is not necessarily about taking individual voices into consideration, but rather about building a spirit of community-ness, of community investment, in which members or residents feel they have established an emotional accord with the community. Using this accord, they can activate other forms of social transaction in the community.

Because the meeting is a place where consultation takes place and is also a space where members meet each other, the feeling of having been there when a decision was taken can contribute to a *sense* or *feeling of being listened to*, as often the people who speak are now emotionally and physically known to each other. Within such approaches to engagement, listening is both a process of sharing a space with other community members and acknowledging the presence of all those involved when a decision is being made. It is necessarily not about a direct cause and effect relationship between voice and policy.

What is important is that when this kind of listening is for policy purposes, the onus of demonstrating that citizens are being listened to does not lie with the residents themselves. It resides with the policy makers who organize the venue, snacks, determine the seating patterns, the nature of the discussion, the moderators, the format of voting, the emphasis on certain arguments, the selection of rapporteurs, and who summarize the main arguments as well as prepare other logistical arrangements that go into shaping the quality of a discussion. At the end of the session, the policy makers compile the report and exercise control over how an engagement session will be recorded. In this case, even if the dialogue that shapes an engagement session is participatory, the communicative act of listening itself is seemingly linear and vertical but it is not necessarily top-down—that is, it is structured within institutional engagement approaches but then, contradictorily, allows for critical, horizontal debates and engagement.

In contrast, if we were to have a horizontal and radical communicative form of listening that aims to allow marginalized groups to contest the unequal flow of power within a particular socio-cultural context, the result may be different. Such dialogues are meant to achieve a variety of objectives—to develop a programme of actions, to engage in reciprocal education, and to influence how members remember and understand certain events. In most cases of alternative, community, or underground art and media, the production of communicative actions is rooted in horizontal listening and in a careful reading and appreciation of fellow contributions. Music genres like hip hop or grime, for instance, involve acknowledging what the underground is experimenting with and then later revising and improving until it is ready for the mainstream market. Listening in its 'horizontal' format therefore, is in the shape of a rhizome following Deleuze (Deleuze and Guattari 1987), in which the listeners build on each other's creativity. Thus, voice becomes a product of listening.

Listening therefore involves much more that speaking to each other, but speaking alongside each other. As Freire highlights, this kind of listening is empathic and aims to build on the identity, emotions and strengths of the other person. It is a kind of listening that respects the rules of dialogical engagement, but it also traverses boundaries and speaks across and against the dominant rhizomes or narratives of development. While such speech, and the act of listening, can demonstrate an awareness of dominant voices, they nevertheless have the capacity to undermine them, and therefore subaltern listening is itself an act of violence, an act of war, because its essence is shaped by an epistemological rejection of unequal power relations within which dominant speech is curated. Thompson (1963, 782) introduces and explains the concept of *diffusion of literacy*, in relation to the educational practices of the working classes, such as the efforts of the London Correspondence Society to educate themselves in pre-industrial England. The slightly literate workers would educate the illiterate ones, thereby enabling an increasing number of them to read literature that would open their minds and enable them to challenge oppression and even call for political reforms.

As is the case in instrumental forms of listening, horizontal and alternative forms of listening may occur within formal and informal spaces. Outside or on the periphery of modernity, listening occurs largely through interpersonal forms of communication, including indigenous knowledge communication systems, but traditional media such as radio have made contributions. Cassette recorders, photography, cinema, music or underground media—leaflets, radio, and painting—have been critical in documenting and recording subaltern voices. With the exponential growth of ICTs and social media platforms, horizontal forms of speaking and listening are undermining time, space and matter in creative ways.

Developing the skills in listening

When I grew up in the tea and tobacco plantations of Malawi in the 1980s and 1990s, I had the honour of knowing and interacting with the elderly members of my clan. My great-grandmother, Abiti Bisani—who passed away in 2010—and my grandmother, Mayikulu would assemble all of us young ones after dinner, usually hard corn flour porridge and vegetable stew; at other times, dinner would constitute roasted cassava or sweet potatoes. We would sit around the small fires while roasting maize or groundnuts. We would listen to many tales about the local history, the dawn of colonialism, the slave trade and so many fables in which animals spoke and behaved like human beings. As previously mentioned, we would listen to these stories until deep into the night, and sometimes when the grandmothers saw that we were tired, we would be told to go to sleep, which we did, with the promise and comfort that the stories would be continued another night.

Sometimes days and weeks would pass by before a story's narration would be completed. Nevertheless we knew the point at which the narration had been paused and we would remind the storyteller, if necessary, where to begin. There were cases when the grandmothers were tired and would ask one of the uncles to finish the stories, which they often did. The grandmothers were excellent at telling the stories because of the creativity within their narration, the intonation and their mastery of poetic expression, idioms and proverbs. Even today, over many moons and rivers and hills later, I can still *feel* my late great-grandmother's smell of chewed tobacco, her jokes, her beautiful dark and yellow teeth, the poetry that accompanied her narration, and the lovely sarcasm that added colour to her descriptions. I still relive the semiotic sense of *firstness*, the sense of being there. These stories had their own smells too, or to put it more succinctly, their own "structure of feeling" to borrow Raymond Williams's notion in *The Long Revolution* (1961).

This totality of experiencing storytelling developed and consolidated our listening skills. We wanted to listen and this is a critical precondition for any sincere experience of listening. There has to be a deliberateness, a prior willingness, and a wholehearted acceptance of the need to listen with the aim to listen. We wanted to listen because we wanted to tell the stories to other kids in school, but also more importantly to have them in our hearts in an existential sort of way. The knowledge of these stories was a social commodity that we valued and carried with us everywhere we travelled. Every time I smell chewed tobacco, or fire, smoke, or roast potato, or roast cassava, I am taken back to those nights, those fires, and I once again relive the experience of storytelling. Over the years I have retold these stories, and in retelling them, I have added my own poetic elements, intonation and narrative structure, but nevertheless I have drawn on my memories of what I listened to many years ago. It is evident that oral communication is not a linear process, since it morphs as it passes through people and generations.

Within indigenous knowledge communication systems, for example, there are many skills employed in listening. Children are sent to deliver verbal messages to distant places and we would deliver the messages as originally intended. It might be a message about an illness, a request for food support, an impending engagement, a funeral, in fact, all manner of messages. Sometimes the messages are complicated and delivering them requires that they be presented in the way the sender intended, as emphasized in the Shannon-Weaver model. In fact the receiver of the message could also ask for clarifications and they would get the same from the messenger, because they understood the context within which the message was delivered. Nevertheless, unlike the Shannon-Weaver model, this traditional communication model provides for a kind of listening that is not only about understanding content, but also the context. Being sent to deliver messages is a tool that communities on the periphery of modernity employ to develop listening skills. So, too, storytelling at night—it is both a skill and a tool even though that is not the reason stories are told. The skill is storytelling or delivering oral messages.

Alongside night storytelling as an important skill that is developed over a long period of time, is the skill of listening to cases at a traditional court mediated by the village chief. These are cases that involve disagreements between residents in a village. Often the plaintiff, the defendant, their witnesses and families are invited to the village chief's place. Mediating the conflict is the chief and a group of councillors or advisers who in many cases are elderly men and women. What is interesting is that the plaintiff and defendant might take more than an hour each explaining their side of their story and the mediators do not write anything. They can sometimes use small sticks or fingers to draw in the earth, sometimes drawing lines. And from here they are able to repeat what each of them has said, asking probing questions. And when judgement is handed down, it is always fair. This is not to deny that there are cases where justice is disputed and a higher traditional authority is sought to resolve the conflict. As such, cultures lying outside or on the periphery of modernity have developed these listening skills because of the need to resolve conflicts and manage governance issues and, hence, the traditional court becomes that tool for developing this skill in listening. The next section seeks to show, however, that, within the southern or development contexts, the best intentions to listen are often challenged by restricted financial resources and limited time frames within which projects are constructed.

"How many lives can radio plays save?" The investment case

My development work between 2012 and 2016 was very fulfilling because it exposed me to new, fascinating and creative approaches that are taking place in development practice. Three challenges stood out for me. The first is that the field continues to be informed by, and over-reliant on, western and modernist conceptualizations of development. Which is not a problem in itself, even though there are non-western theories and approaches that focus on the endogenous, ecological, spiritual and relational aspects of well-being that are not modernist, not civilizational and not economically deterministic. As emphasized in the last two chapters, even within western curricula, there are spaces that allow educators and educatees to critically engage with empirical reality. When I taught and directed the MSc in Media, Communication and Development at the London School of Economics and Political Science, I was given the freedom to include whatever author, reading and perspective I wanted. And I equally felt that I had the space and freedom to teach whatever I wanted. But perhaps this was an exception, given the concerns of the Post-Crash Economics Society (2014).

Secondly, I have become very concerned about the apparent increase in the capture of the field of communication for development (including deliberative development) by major international development organizations and the development industry, with their prevailing and dominant institutionalized ways of thinking and practice—a feature that Escobar (1995) describes as developmentalization. This is a result of calls for more interactions between scholarship and practice (Ramiro Beltran 1993/2004). In 1997, at a conference organized by the Rockefeller Foundation held at Bellagio in Italy, a small group of 22 professionals was brought together "to explore the vast possibilities of new communications for social change" (Rockefeller Foundation 1997, 5). This conference would contribute to shaping the communication for development practice and training; but also, significantly, it laid the groundwork for the first and only World Congress on Communication for Development, which the FAO would organize and host in Rome in 2006. These events worked to ensure the institutionalization of C4D within international development organizations. This is something to be commended. Yet it should be emphasized as well that numerous groups and grassroots organizations are beginning to experiment with the cooperative models of deliberative development, the aim being to self-finance their own interventions. In many cases, the institutionalization of the field or the feudalization of the field by international development organizations seems to be compromising the liberation ethos that should ideally drive it (Makuwira 2014).

Thirdly, deliberative development in practice today is experiencing the constant contestation between learning and evidence. The emphasis on the values of practice such as empathy, listening and empowerment of marginalized groups, or what Gutiérrez (1988) defines as the "preferential option for the poor" or conscientization, seem to be footnoted or ignored in the pursuit of evidence. I focus on this last point. With dwindling donor resources, it has become imperative that development project and programme planning emphasize and prioritize interventions that are cost-effective, but, at the same time, yield long-term results (UK Government 2013; UNAIDS 2012). Conversations with and alongside donors often focus on *where* is the evidence or *how* can we generate the evidence.

After teaching C4D at the LSE for slightly over four years, I returned to development practice, as a C4D specialist, first with the Global Fund and World Bank-supported National AIDS Commission in Malawi, and later on with UNICEF. In between, I had the opportunity to consult for various development organizations. I must confess that I was slightly unprepared for the complexities that are currently shaping C4D practice on the ground. My job description included tasks such as designing and implementing social mobilization interventions, managing stakeholder relationships, monitoring and evaluation and other basic things about C4D. Yet, it was actually a conversation I had with an England-based consultant, Bruce MacKay, who had been hired by DFID to carry out background research on investment thinking or business case in HIV prevention, that shook my intellectual comfort zones. The conversations with this consultant revolved around economic appraisals, financial and commercial management and cost–benefit analyses, especially in relation to how many lives an intervention could save with a specific amount of financial resources. Since I started working in C4D in 2000, I was being challenged to think like a businessperson—to think specifically about invested resources and intended outcomes. So what is "investment thinking"?

Investment thinking is also sometimes known as the business case. In practice, investment case consideration allows policy makers and development planners to define effective interventions in terms of their unit costs and expected benefits, for example in terms of deaths or infections averted (UK Government 2013; UNAIDS 2012). Many factors contribute to the integration of investment thinking into public health policy planning and implementation. Principal among these factors is—as highlighted in passing—the dwindling of available resources and hence the need to be smart. Applying the business case or investment approach provides an opportunity for the maximization of the benefits of interventions. It also supports the rational resource allocation based on the country's or religion's evidence base and context by prioritizing the most cost-effective programme activities (UK Government 2013). For HIV prevention, biomedical interventions are easier to cost compared to non-biomedical interventions. For example, the unit cost of HIV testing and counselling is US$10 per person; for anti-retroviral treatment it is US$515 per person per annum, while VMMC costs US$65 per person. From these unit costs, scientists are able to use goals or spectrum models (UNAIDS 2012) to forecast how many lives could be saved, how many deaths averted, and so forth. The realization from these conversations with MacKay was that my earlier training over the years had fallen short and, thus, I needed to reboot my thinking and practice. Yet it has to be acknowledged that this investment thinking is also problematic: it seemingly commodifies social change, as if it is a product that can be pre-planned, predetermined and delivered in quantifiable units and in a given period of time. These are tensions that scholars and practitioners are currently grappling with.

The challenges presented by estimating unit costs in this way are twofold. Firstly, all the indicators are biomedical. This is because it is easier to establish unit costs for such interventions. The challenge lies in the ability to establish a minimum cost for non-biomedical and social and behavioural change interventions. One might be tempted to ask: what is a minimum cost of a social and behaviour change communication package that would take a person from point A in the village to a counselling and testing centre at the local clinic? Is it one community-theatre performance, or would it have to be one radio play, combined with a community mobilization meeting, supplemented by a series of village meetings? And how would we be sure that after listening to or witnessing a specific communication intervention, a person, or persons, will take up the required health behaviour?

The second problematic factor is the difficulty, if not impossibility, of forging a link between interventions and the infections or deaths averted, or what we might cost-effectively and empirically define as the intended impact (Mansell 1982). Perhaps there would be evidence of achievements at the output or outcome levels, where a policy could be produced and disseminated, or high demand of people going to a centre where they are testing for HIV, or a village clinic where increased numbers of women are delivering their babies. But beyond that, measuring impact becomes problematic. Hence, one can test negative today and two days later contract the virus despite an intense mobilization activity that took one to the testing centre. This means a minimum package of behavioural interventions is hard to arrive at since they will continue to be required long after the biomedical intervention has been administered. Nevertheless, the process of developing health, agriculture or development communications needs to frame interventions holistically. That is, each intervention should have three dimensions—the scientific/biomedical, the structural, and the social communication aspects. This implies that there is a negotiation between planners and policy makers on the one hand, who are interested in generating results in forms of outputs, outcomes and specific impact and, on the other hand, community groups and grassroots organizations who are interested in the participatoriness and inclusiveness of the development process as a learning experience. In each development process, the evidence-informed aspects should always be in constant negotiation with the learning processes.

From speaking to listening

Writing in the *Times Literary Supplement* in 1966, E.P. Thompson outlined the notion of people's history as a form of historical reconstruction that requires historians and researchers to appreciate events from the perspective of local people. Thompson would test his theoretical and methodological observations through researching and writing his book, *The Making of the English Working Class*, which would cement the notion of history from below as a major scholarly tradition. He noted in the Preface to this timeless classic:

> I am seeking to rescue the poor stockinger, the Luddite cropper, the obsolete hand-loom weaver, the 'utopian' artisan, and even the deluded follower of Joanna Southcott, from the enormous condescension of posterity. Their crafts and traditions may have been dying. Their hostility to the new industrialism may have been backward-looking. Their communitarian ideals may have been fantasies. Their insurrectionary conspiracies may have been foolhardy. But they lived through these times of acute social disturbance, and we did not. Their aspirations were valid in terms of their own experience; and, if they were casualties of history, they remain, condemned in their own lives, as casualties.
>
> *(Thompson 1963, 12)*

In emphasizing the quest to 'rescue,' Thompson was not being dismissive of the agency of the marginalized and oppressed peoples in constructing their own history. Similarly in "Can the subaltern speak?" Spivak (1988) confirms the ability of these marginalized groups to master the art of politicizing speech. What Thompson was calling for was a scholarly pedagogy in which historical writing takes on ethnographic and moral responsibilities; ethnographic in that the studying of history of the common people involves building long and trusted relationships with these marginalized groups.

The moral ethos is illuminated by the pioneer of liberation theology, Father Gustavo Gutiérrez (1988), who, in *A Theology of Liberation*, introduces the notion of a "preferential option for the poor." He proffers an intellectual analysis of society based on Hegel and Marx in which he calls for a critical analysis of society that demonstrates "commitment to God and to human beings" (Gutiérrez 1988, 24). The human beings referred to here are largely marginalized and dehumanized groups of people.

What Thompson and Gutiérrez seem to be calling for is a reinvigorated and aspirational kind of historical writing that is not apolitical in the face of the violence and cannibalism of predatory forms of capitalism and globalization—we can no longer remain neutral in the name of scientific objectivity. To write history, for example, to design and implement development interventions, implies that we take the side of the poor, the marginalized, the classless, and that we understand their viewpoint, which then offers an opportunity to construct and imagine revised policy narratives. To write history in this case means that we are going to war against the structural inequalities that perpetuate what Aimé Césaire (1955) defines as the *thingification* of marginalized groups. In this case, history from below as a praxis becomes an epistemological antidote to Baldwin's 'view from here'.

When Thompson calls for the "rescuing" of oppressed groups, he does not only imply that we have to write their histories, and articulate their feelings and needs; we must undertake the sacred duty of historical writing with empathy, "understanding, compassion, careful study for the purposes of co-existence and enlargement of horizons," as also pointed out by Said (1978) in the revised Preface to *Orientalism*. This poses a challenge for formal and informal training programmes in communication for development and social change: how can we produce student graduates and professionals who have the tools and skills for living and engaging with marginalized groups? There are many ways but to start with, let us create intellectual spaces that allow students and professionals to be challenged by alternative discourses and paradigms.

The fields of development studies and communication for development are based on a preponderance of modernist theories of social change, development and communication. But there are other ways of theorizing, of thinking about, of explaining, of deconstructing the world that have emerged within and outside the dominant paradigm. These knowledge systems are largely oral, because even if there is the penetration of technology, the spoken word—in the form of proverbs, song, dance and spirituality—remains a powerful convention for the generation, exchange and consumption of social meaning and reference phaneroscopes and frameworks.

Marginalization, or the feeling of it, is tearing the world apart. Some are choosing to pose naked and post pictures on the Internet; others, as in the #BlackLivesMatter movement are employing contestation advocacy to expose and stop structural violence against minorities. In some cases people decide to set themselves on fire, as did Mohammed Bouaziz in 2010, sparking the Tunisian, and later the Arab Spring, which in some instances is transforming into a nightmare. As Spivak observes, the subaltern are speaking—but who is listening?

In development teaching and research there should be a deliberate attempt by scholars and institutions to destabilize and interrupt the pedagogy of the dominant paradigm of development, also known as the spectacle of development. The pedagogy of the dominant development paradigm is more often a pedagogy of disempowerment that makes oppressed peoples believe that things must be done for them. It is a pedagogy that has become a form of social control in itself, as was well articulated by Carter Woodson (1933, 84–85):

> If you can control a man's thinking you do not have to worry about his action. When you determine what a man shall think you do not have to concern yourself about what he will do. If you make a man feel he is inferior, you do not have to compel him to accept an inferior status, for he will seek it himself. If you make a man think that he is justly an outcast, you do not have to order him to the back door. He will go out without being told; and if there is no back door, his very nature will demand one.

This pedagogy comprises not just university education of this transnationalized expert or the native elite. It encompasses the training workshops, conferences, induction briefings, and all forms and manner of training development experts. The emphasis is on inculcating the idea that development can be done in a specific period of time, with demonstrable results, and then allowing local people to take over the initiative. The new pedagogy should recover the experiences and aspirations of oppressed peoples, which Thompson (1963, 12) considers "valid in terms of their own experience," and thus, deserve to be studied and embraced as a critical perspective for ensuring that students and professionals learn deep listening skills.

In development theory and practice, the question of listening looms large because it is the hinge upon which rests my whole concept of participatory or deliberative development. As much as speech is crucial in articulating the concerns and aspiration of groups who are often the target of policy interventions, the essence of development practice lies in listening. It is no use when voices and speech acts are constructed and then lost in the bureaucracy and conundrums of policy making.

In the Woi-wurrung language spoken by the Wurundjeri Tribe of the Kulin Nations in Australia, there is a concept of *Wumen Bagung Ngang-gak ba Boorndap*, which translates as "Come, Gather, Listen and Respect." In the Woi-wurrung, listening is not just about hearing others, it is about seeing them and finding them as people. When we tell someone, "I hear you," we are also saying, *I see you*, and thus are acknowledging and respecting their humanity and their spirituality. Likewise, among the Chewa people of sub-Saharan Africa, the concept of *kucheza* literally translates as "to chat, to engage." There is, however, a serious component of familiarity and respect for the other in that engagement—emphasizing that the process must be enjoyed by the participants who must *see* each other. Thus it is ethically and politically imperative that we *listen to* and *see* other voices as advised by Said, Gutiérrez and Thompson.

My discussion has built upon Gutiérrez's and Freire's observations about listening, with the aim of showing that there are two kinds of listening. First there is the policy type of listening in which institutions, organizations and governments organize and control methods of producing voices and then the mechanisms for listening as part of policy formulation and implementation. Even if it does not offer any scientific link between speech acts and resultant policies, such listening offers citizens an opportunity to acquire the *feeling of being listened to, or being heard.* This is not the same as placation and co-optation, as indeed, there are sincere interests from organizations and institutions to hear the opinions of marginalized groups.

Then we also have horizontal forms of listening that emerge in subaltern polities, within and outside modernity. Within modernity, horizontal forms of listening are made possible by the availability of audiovisual mechanisms for documentation purposes, which allow for bottom-up processes of production and dissemination of information and ideas. This is the case in popular music, as suggested by the development of certain music genres from underground into mainstream art. Outside modernity, indigenous knowledge communication systems are pathways that allow for the development of listening skills and tools.

Listening encompasses many things. Yet within development contexts, it requires that practitioners develop certain people skills and understand the tools that they can work with. Freire talks about being empathic and the moral and political duty to be tolerant. As highlighted in my auto-ethnographic accounts, listening requires that we listen to evidence, we listen to ourselves, and appreciate that listening is a form of speech act. Listening, for Gutiérrez and Freire, and for some development scholars and practitioners working within and outside the margins of dominant development paradigms, entails that we humble ourselves so that we enter into a sincere dialogue with people with low levels of social capital, with low levels of power, those more unequal, and those different from us, so that we may understand the world from their perspective and by doing so readjust our prior biases, stereotypes and positions.

As indicated in the first chapter, this book is an interrogation of the theory and practice of communicating and doing development with and alongside the community. My narrative and perspectives are born of a rediscovery of my voice that for a long time was captured by and smothered under dominant discourses and epistemologies of development theory and practice. I tell these stories with a sense of responsibility and do so with care, with the aim of offering empathic criticism and an understanding of the marginalization that I lived through. Recalling and relating these experiences was a struggle. I was trained in educational institutions that subscribed to orthodox values and epistemologies. I learned to think and to imagine as a *non-myself*. Writing this book involved a long, winding and problematic journey as well as moments of rapture for me. I revisited the plantations, the ancestral graveyards, the initiation ceremonies, the shebeen liquor houses and the village swimming spots where I had learned the proverbs and idioms that now help me to reconnect with critical perspectives that I could not recognize before. Like the symbolic exploration in Conrad's *The Heart of Darkness*, this book has thus involved an epistemological expedition in which I have attempted to tell the stories with the critical mind of a westerner, but also of an insider who is in the process of rediscovering and reconstituting a dismembered subjectivity. This is the spiritual essence that characterizes the stories and experiences recounted in this book. Therefore, the 'development' which is talked about in this book is itself a space "where dream and its incarnation of an aesthetic ideal meet, the place of a revolution" (Djebar 1992, 133). I have examined the tradition of the practice of development spectacles—the conceptions, values, attitudes and the consciousness—that governs the design and implementation of development interventions by people and institutions. More specifically, throughout the book, I have employed communication for development as a critical perspective in deconstructing the culture of development in practice.

Concluding thoughts

Chapter 1 opened with an observation by Assia Djebar (1992) regarding the arrival of Eugene Delacroix in Algeria. This was critical for the ensuing analysis. The famous painting by Delacroix, *Women of Algiers in their Apartment* can be considered the beginning of organized forms of orientalism in the south (Said 1978). As a form of the view from here, this painting constructed an orientalist, flat, static and problematic representation of the women Delacroix encountered in an Algiers harem that had nothing to do with history (Djebar 1992). Delacroix would keep changing the angling and colouring in the original painting. In effect, this famous painting actually launched the spectacle of development in practice, in which concern was not with how the others felt or saw reality, but rather with the way the external agents imagined and conceived of what would become dehistoricized and fictionalized events. Djebar's (1992) spectacle could be linked to Mansell's (1982) dominant paradigm and what this book has done is to explain how this paradigm works in terms of its principal characters and networks. A greater part of this book has been an attempt to redeem the experiences and the voices of the four women in the painting. It is the epistemological reason this book was written.

Communicating Development with Communities examines the critical communicative spaces that can allow for the method-driven and theory-informed praxis of negotiated or deliberative development that puts listening and experimentation at the centre of its practice. The successful design and execution of such interventions depends very much on understanding these spaces, namely, (a) the language of the oppression, (b) the voice of the subaltern, (c) living with the people, (d) encountering development, and (e) the pedagogy of listening. Yet to unpack these communicative spaces one needs to undertake a critical audit of development in practice and that is what this book—especially Chapter 1—has done.

As outlined earlier, this book comprises two parts. The first part is a deconstructionist project that has attempted to undermine the spectacle of development in theory and practice, and the institutions that govern its systems and language of oppression. It comprises two chapters, both of which have shown the network of actors and discourses that make it challenging, but not impossible, to design, experiment and implement realistic development interventions alongside communities. Despite its deconstructionist endeavour in the first part, the book is not calling for a revolutionary approach towards abandoning the previous efforts in deliberative development. It is problematic that certain strands of post-colonial and Marxist perspectives seem to suggest that until real revolution happens, there is no hope for experimentation with sustainable, realistic and meaningful development. That is not the case. Notwithstanding the prevalence of oppressive practices and individuals, there are spaces of liberatory practices that offer creative opportunities for well-meaning funding organizations, development practitioners, community workers and policy makers who genuinely care about real transformation on the ground. This book argues that there are available opportunities, even if the political economy of development is not conducive, that offer a platform for the construction and experimentation with deliberative development at the community level.

The first chapter in the book explored the spectacle and bullshit of development. As conceptualized in this book and in Chapter 1 specifically, such bullshit is similar to what Mansell (1982) conceived as the dominant paradigm of development that never passed away, itself a methodological pathway that allows the oppressors in development contexts to achieve specific organizational objectives—be they ideological, political or socio-economic—which, considered together, constitute Escobar's notion of developmentalization. For Mansell, the dominant paradigm referred to modernization, its ideologies, practices and the traditions and practices that governed and continue to govern the way interventions are conceived and implemented. The dominant paradigm, as represented in the scholarship of Lerner (1958), Rostow (1960), Schramm (1964) and others with similar modernist perspectives, encompassed the whole regime of doing and speaking development theories taught in universities, the cultures of policy making, and methodological approaches in evaluation. The dominant paradigm was, and remains, a system of thought. In the exploration of these development spectacles, three forms emerged: the missionary position, the cooperative development, and the community-driven perspective. Whereas the discussion rejected the transformative ability of these approaches for their inherent oppression, the analysis showed that possibilities of rescuing and recovery are underway in some parts of the south and the north. Yet it was pointed out that there is not necessarily a category of oppressors but practitioners, policy makers, scholars and even community members who employ the language (and practices) of oppression in order to achieve certain personal or institutional objectives. It was shown, especially in the analysis of the missionary position, that the attitudes and practices of marginalized communities are equally contributing to development bullshit.

The second chapter examined the notion of the language of oppression, which was extrapolated as not just referring to discursive practices by some western and international organizations that exhibit the characteristics laid out in this book. Rather, they also comprise endogenous and local organizations that display horizontal violence and similar attributes. The chapter elucidated the attributes of the language of oppression and then examined the historical process of becoming an oppressor at the local level. A major argument emerging from this chapter is that the oppressor is no longer foreign, white nor westerner. The oppressor is actually neither here nor there. It should also be emphasized here that not all experts are oppressors and, as with Escobar and this book, reference is made to the category of experts whose thinking, behaviour and practices exhibit the attributes of the language of oppression identified in this book. Within the system and network of doing development, we all have the capability of becoming oppressors. In fact, to implement deliberative development, planners and policy makers must study, understand, unmask and uproot the processes and networks that produce oppressors and oppression.

The second part of the book is a response to the first part and explored some of the empirical and fictionalized initiatives that were conceived and experimented within what Mansell (1982) criticized as dominant development systems. It raised the question: having examined and unmasked all these institutional, methodological and theoretical challenges of thinking about and experimenting with development spectacles, is there any hope for realistic practices and approaches in community development? This part is a discursive project of reconstruction and recovery in itself and highlights four critical factors that are very crucial which, considered together, comprise the pedagogy of listening that Freire propounds.

Firstly, it demonstrates the contradictions and difficulties of working with communities to design and implement development. Even though as a black person I have emotional and social capital in Southern Africa, there were moments I behaved like and was treated as an outsider in some of the places I worked. This shows that the politics of class and identities are very complex and go beyond skin colour and education. Visiting Kalahari in the early 2000s on Professor Keyan Tomaselli's *Semiotics of the Encounter* Project, I had assumed that as a black person I was going to be well received within the marginalized ≠Khoman San communities who have been subjugated by years of colonial violence and again under apartheid. I was shocked when it was pointed out to me that I was white and it was clear that to get any cooperation in the research I had to work with and through my white professor, who is well respected in these communities. What this and other experiences in this book show is that concepts such as outsider and insider, external and internal or westerner and southerner are fluid categories that say nothing about how we relate to local people. This book points out that what matters is how radical and liberatory educators reject Baldwin's (1986) view from here, and instead acquire the subaltern perspective, because it is this viewpoint and their understanding of subaltern condition that shapes their relationship to and with local communities and becomes implicated in the politics that govern a community's ability to speak and experiment with deliberative development.

Secondly, the role of education in providing the learning spaces that enable students to critically engage with social reality has to be acknowledged. Here I am referring to both formal and informal education. Informal refers to the experiences of living through marginalization, either through birth or through research. I have observed in the previous chapters that my acquisition of this subaltern perspective has been a long journey, starting with my growing up in extreme poverty. The poverty seemed normal until we realized that the same tea and tobacco estates that were spread out over huge swathes of land that surrounded our tiny villages also housed other well-to-do classes and families. This book argues that it is not easy to acquire a critical consciousness and that being born in poverty is not a guarantee that one will attain subaltern perspectives. What is significant is that development is a process that involves financial, physical and social assets at certain points, and thus, participants have to be accountable to themselves and their partners.

It was through western education, from reading Henrik Ibsen, Walt Whitman, Maya Angelou, Konstantin Stanislavsky, E.P. Thompson, Shakespeare's *Julius Caesar*, or *European History* by Eric Hobsbawm that I would begin to understand the exploitation that my folks were living under. As such, it is not just about the books placed in the curriculum, it is the style of teaching. *Julius Caesar* and *Oliver Twist* opened up a critical spirit in me more than any other books I knew. They would lead me to Thompson's *The Making of the English Working Class*, and from there I could comfortably read Freire, Gutiérrez and Marx. In fact, it would be studying with Keyan and Ruth Tomaselli at the University of Natal that would connect me with radical and critical theories of liberation, largely born of the Tomasellis' own opposition to apartheid. This is the contradiction of the processes that underlie the formation of critical consciousness: that the same western education, content and curriculum being criticized by the Post-Crash Economics Society (2014) for being too westernized, linear and deterministic in its outlook, if supported by a radical educator, allows for a transformative pedagogical approach that conscientizes students as much as any dehumanizing conditions one might live through. I have felt during this journey of working with and alongside communities that most white westerners have developed very radical and revolutionary subaltern perspectives perhaps because of their critical western education, but also because of their patience and passion for community development, even if they have found themselves working within these spectacles of development.

Thirdly, the book explains that liberatory educators who are westerners, outsiders, and who are not from oppressed groups, can offer critical opportunities that enable local people to speak and unspeak realistic development interventions so long as they acquire the subaltern perspective. It should be highlighted that this book employs Spivak's (1988) definition of subaltern as a position and not necessarily an identity. In this case, a westerner or an outsider does not have to become an oppressed person in order to appreciate alternative development discourses. But they can acquire subaltern perspectives that allow them to speak and unspeak dominant development syntax with and alongside oppressed classes. This is in contrast to some positions in the post-colonial literature that assume that because one is western in identity or perspective there is no way that one can contribute to the design and implementation of interventions alongside oppressed groups. This book contends that development is not necessarily a black and white process, one that pits outsiders against insiders, oppressors against oppressed, northerners against southerners. These are fluid labels and concepts. In my experience, northerners or outsiders who have acquired subaltern perspectives can demonstrate a great understanding of local politics and how this shapes deliberative development.

The fourth observation is that in development theory and practice two contending elements are constantly antagonistic to each other. On the one hand, there is the need to generate evidence and use that as a platform for programming—this is known as investment thinking. On the other hand, there is the demand for more participatory, action-oriented and more democratic forms of learning and doing development. This is a crisis, not in theory, but in and of practice. It has pitted mostly external institutions (that are interested in achieving impact and its evidence in the forms of outputs, outcomes and impact) against endogenous institutions and expectations that are more clearly fascinated with the learning processes and which are more concerned with the process of becoming and ensuring that all involved acquire subaltern perspectives.

In this book, all these positions come together in the pedagogy of listening. It is through listening that all participants are invited to attend, in the words of Janie Mae Crawford in *Their Eyes Were Watching God*, the big "association of life" or the "big convention of living." This association of life, the convention of living, is what this book describes as the pedagogy of listening, a pedagogy that allows outsiders and insiders, northerners and southerners—and all other stakeholders to come together, acquire a subaltern perspective, and through that be able to speak, to rapture, to destabilize development itself. The aim is to experiment and implement development interventions that go beyond achieving economic indicators, but embrace indicators of what Escobar defines as *buen vivir* discourses.

The six chapters in this book have examined the culture or the tradition of communicating and speaking development with and alongside communities. As pointed out in the first chapter, it is significant that the book's title is *Communicating Development with Communities*, since this is intended to signpost a critical concept which implies a number of reflexive actions and behaviours that amount to a praxis. This *speaking* combines elements of listening, using evidence, learning and experimentation. Another critical aspect of speaking development revolves around the notion of becoming as it emerges in the works of Gutiérrez, Freire and Thompson. For Thompson (1963) class is an active process of becoming, and not necessarily a pre-formed social category. As used in this book, it refers to historical groups that are engaged with daily struggles to define their place in the world. These historical groups could be oppressed, oppressors or somewhere in between, since there are moments when one is neither oppressed nor an oppressor. It must be emphasized that there are spaces of negotiation, spaces where oppressed or oppressing groups deviate from the norms and expectations and are able to experiment with interventions that speak to local needs. It should also be emphasized that it is not always the case that local people know what is best for them. And it is the role of those who Freire describes as the catalyzing educator to challenge oppressed groups to rethink their understanding of the world.

In conclusion, I critique and reject the forms of development spectacle in theory and practice. Nevertheless, I acknowledge that there is a growing body of scholarship relating to community engagement, participatory communication and deliberative development that assumes that policy makers and stakeholders can achieve the necessary conditions that may allow for a sincere effort to devise and implement development interventions; interventions that reject a view from here, and instead refuse to invoke an orientalist perspective and which do allow the subaltern voice to be heard. These necessary conditions are centred in the art and science of listening vertically and horizontally. This is the kind of listening that enables a critical communion in which relevant stakeholders can celebrate together as they strive to improve people's lives, create stronger communities and ensure sustainable use of the environment. A critical pedagogy of listening has at its centre a reconsideration and celebration of what Escobar (1995) understands as relational and indigenous ontologies. This is a pedagogy of empathy, of understanding, and one that recognizes that the east does not necessarily want to become the west. In this pedagogy, the radical educator's passion lies in working with subaltern groups in developing, contesting and implementing deliberative development within communicative spaces that allow for the process of becoming for individuals and groups that exist at the periphery of the periphery.

Afterthoughts: Listening to the colour of people's words

"Our land has a big story. Sometimes we tell a little bit at a time. Come and hear our stories, see our land. A little bit might stay in your hearts. If you want more, you come back," observes Jacob Nayinggul of the Manilakarr Clan, Chair of the Board Management of Kakadu National Park, Australia.[1]

I have always been fascinated by the experiences and the memories of growing up in a small village, where it used to be a miracle to read English, to speak to white people, let alone go to university and attain a "white man's education," as my mother coloured her definition of higher education. It was from my mother, grandmother, and of course my favourite person in the world, my great-grandmother, Abiti Bisani, that I learnt about the colour of words. To twist Blanche DuBois's words in Tennessee Williams's (2009) *A Streetcar Named Desire*, "I have always depended on the kindness of these women." The stories and lessons I learnt from these three wise women were masterpieces in discursive painting.

Our clan has always had this way with words. As we grew up, we would learn to pay critical attention to their colour because it was in the words that we children were made to discover the world, to learn its secrets, to construct its gender, to discover its possibilities. The fascinating thing about the words and their colours was that whatever we learned from the parents, from the clan elders and from the community, was consistent with what we discovered as we grew up. The traditional circumcision rite, which involved staying at the river bank for a month during a very cold season, allowed our group of boys to become inducted into the more sacred and secret stories that were preserved as a privilege of those who entered adulthood. These stories had their colour; they had their smell.

I remember the beauty of our unhealed penises, as we sat around the warm fires in the dead of night, how beautiful yet painfully surreal it seemed, eating roasted cassava, and listening to the elders who gave us all this wonderful wisdom about life, about *Napolo* (the serpent snake) who made a pact with the womb of the woman to create and destroy life. I can still feel the trance-like sensation in my soul, as I swallowed in all this rich wisdom, when we really believed the *Azimu* (the spirits of the dead) accompanied us on the journeys through life—from the womb of the woman through the serpent snake and then finally, back into the womb again, the womb of the earth.

What we learned in the colours of the words was that both the woman and the earth give but also swallow life—it was upon the insistence of the *Nankugwi* (the wise traditional counsellor) that out of recognition of this fact we were sternly advised not to have sex with a menstruating woman, not to beat up women, not to walk behind a woman's back without asking her permission, let alone jump over women's legs. Things would make sense but at the same time seem to confuse.

The colour of this wisdom was not just in the actual words. The colour was also in the smells we could recall when the words were spoken. The colour was tied to our respect for the traditions, to the environment, and to the centrality of the woman in giving and sanctifying life. It wasn't just about understanding the meaning of the words, it was about respecting the words. Almost venerating them.

Having travelled the world, I am beginning to understand, as did the three wise women, that language has little to do with the accent, nor with the artistic aspect of it, the arrangement of the words, the nouns or the qualifiers.

It is about the science of its frame, its dreams, its smells, the ability to construct not just a picture on the wall, but even the frame that has to carry that picture. The colour of words encompasses the respect that is accorded to the intentions and the spirits of the words.

One day, just before I finished primary school, my mum called me from the playfield to put a little salt in the dried kidney bean stew she was cooking. This was something she used to do at certain times of the month. Thinking she was delaying my participation in the games, I retorted, "why can't you do this yourself anyway?" I remember her saying nothing but stretching out her hand to pour the salt in my hand, then slapped me hard and said "ask your father." She proceeded to give me the salt, which I poured into the boiling pot. Off I went into the distance, holding back tears, thinking she was the most terrible and horrible mother ever.

It was this incident that would see me being sent for initiation; and it would be a rite of passage that would teach me the spirituality surrounding menstruation, and why menstruating women do not put salt in a cooking stew. Then as today, my mother's slap and rebuke continue to smell of dried kidney beans no matter how long and far away I may have travelled from home.

I carry the memory of that slap with me. Such was its colour, that it exhibited both love and anger. As a communicative action, that slap and perhaps several others I cannot remember, had elements of colour to them. Every time I remember the colour of the slap, I remember the smell of kidney beans stew, my favourite dish. The colour of the slap contained other acts of love that I could remember. For example, when I was in class one, I recall my mother carrying me through a flooding river after the bridge had been washed away, so that I could go to school.

What I learnt from these three generations of women is that each word we speak, each of the syllables articulated has a smell, a spirit, a ghost that accompanies them. Maya Angelou talks about the power of words, that they become a thing, growing like plants and eventually becoming part of our identities and being.

Words, when spoken, become articles and conventions of social contract between those who speak them and those who hear them. These words are colours in themselves and when we pass on messages, they are not just words we are communicating; we are transporting material pieces of paintings comprising the living and dead spirits that are invoked in constructing the sentences, the paragraphs, the smells and the emotions that accompany such discourses.

In dominant social science thinking and practice, words are increasingly being reduced to imaginary interpretants that can be made sense of within a given context. As students of society, development and social-change practice entails that we work towards discovering the rich essence of the colours of people's words. Not because we want to meet certain obligations with regard to achieving participation. Rather, to demonstrate our respect for other people, and other ways of knowing.

There is an ancient tradition in the south, when certain deceased members of traditional royal lineages are buried at night. On this last journey, the burial ceremony takes place under lamps and torches. The aim being to remind the departed spirit of the road that leads back to the village should it decide to visit once in a while.

Such is the power of the colour of words. Like the guiding lamp to the spirits of the dead, the colour of the words takes us places—guiding us through the complex meanings, proverbs and figures of speech. Some places could be uncomfortable to explore. But when one has the relevant instruments of signification, one rides—as if on a horse, on the colour of the words, and is transported to where these words originate from. As spirits and ghosts of the people that spoke and inherited them, the colour of words allows us to enter into spiritual communion with the storytellers.

Among the various Aboriginal nations of the first peoples of Australia, telling stories is closely tied to people's belief in the land, in the sea, the sky; and all this comes together in the sacred process of dreaming. Through dreaming, telling stories allows Aboriginal nations, clans and communities to express their solidarity with the past, future and present. Dreamtime is a testimony to the generations to come, that the land is the mother of not just life, but the foundation of dreaming, of being and the essence of it.

In our community interventions, let us take time to dream with local people, as we learn and appreciate the beauty of the colour of words. Only then will we be able to enter into communion with local people, and thus enable us to engage in what the Marxist historian, Thompson (1963, 782) defines as the horizontal "diffusion of literacy." And instead of extractive and exploitative interactions we will build long, sustainable and trusted relationships with people and the land, which Jacob Nayinggul, quoted above, emphasizes, has lots of stories.

In conclusion two titanic shifts within the last decades have had a huge impact on the way we think about speaking as a form of engagement. The global financial crisis of 2008 took a lot of universities and experts by surprise. One explanation has been that such academics, experts or students have been taught the same dominant thinking in classic and western economics without any recourse to alternative social science perspectives. On the other hand, Brexit and Trump's ascendancy to the US presidency have clearly shown how distant mainstream politics has misunderstood and marginalized the 'silent majority' left behind by capitalism, globalization and trickle-down economics. These and other realities remind students of society the world over of the need for a new, empathetic, communicative and respectful way of engaging with empirical reality and people. This kind of engagement is being curated and defined as *speaking*, and is encapsulated in what this book defines as the pedagogy of listening. Communicating development with communities is thus an act of becoming in itself, that allows for a deliberate contestation of power and hegemony between and among various interests within the deliberative development process.

Note

1 Nayinggul, Jacob. non-dated. "Kakadu—The place." Accessed April 3 2017. www.parksaustralia.gov.au/kakadu/people-and-place.html.

References

Baldwin, James. 1986. "National Press Club Speech," 12 October 1986. Accessed March 20 2017. www.youtube.com/watch?v=CTjY4rZFY5c.

Césaire, Aimé. 1955/1972. *Discourse on Colonialism*. Translated by Joan Pinkham. London: Monthly Review Press.

Chambers, Robert. 1980. *Rural Poverty Unperceived: Problems and Remedies*. Staff Working Paper Number SWP 400. Washington, DC: The World Bank. Accessed September 30 2016. http://documents.worldbank.org/curated/en/909311468766763144/Rural-poverty-unperceived-problems-and-remedies.

Chambers, Robert. 1981. "Poor visibility: How policy makers overlook the poor." New Internationalist website. Issue 96. Accessed January 20 2016. http://newint.org/features/1981/02/01/poor-visibility.

Chambers, Robert. 2005. *Ideas for Development*. London and Sterling: Earthscan.

Deleuze, Gilles and Félix Guattari. 1987. *A Thousand Plateaus: Capitalism and Schizophrenia*. Translated by Brian Massumi. London and Minneapolis: University of Minnesota. Accessed January 20 2016. http://projectlamar.com/media/A-Thousand-Plateaus.pdf.

Djebar, Assia. 1992. *Women of Algiers in their Apartment*. Translated by Marjolijn de Jager. Charlottesville and London: University of Virginia Press.

Escobar, Arturo. 1995/2012. *Encountering Development: The Making and Unmaking of the Third World*. Princeton: Princeton University Press.

Freire, Paulo. 1970. *Pedagogy of the Oppressed*. London: Penguin.

Freire, Paulo. 1996a. *Letters to Cristina*. New York: Continuum.

Freire, Paulo. 1996b. *An Incredible Conversation*. YouTube Channel. Accessed January 20 2016. /www.youtube.com/watch?v=aFWjnkFypFA.

Gutiérrez, Gustavo. 1988. *A Theology of Liberation: History, Politics, and Salvation*. Translated by Caridad Inda and John Eagleson. Maryknoll, New York: Orbis Books.

Habermas, Jurgen. 1962. *The Structural Transformation of the Public Sphere: An Inquiry into a Category of Bourgeois Society*. Cambridge: Polity Press.

Kamlongera, Christopher. 1988. *Theatre for Development in Africa*. Bonn and Zomba: University of Malawi Fine and Performing Arts Department and German Foundation for International Development.

Lerner, Daniel. 1958. *The Passing of Traditional Society: Modernizing the Middle East*. New York and London: Free Press and Collier-Macmillan.

Makuwira, Jonathan. 2014. *Non-Governmental Development Organizations and the Poverty Reduction Agenda: The Moral Crusaders*. London and New York: Routledge.

Mansell, Robin. 1982. "The 'new dominant paradigm' in communication: Transformation versus adaptation." *Canadian Journal of Communication*, 8(3): 42–60. Accessed September 20 2016. www.cjc-online.ca/index.php/journal/article/view/278/184.

Manyozo, Linje. 2010. "The day development dies." *Development in Practice*, 20(2): 265–269.

Post-Crash Economics Society. 2014. "Economics, education and unlearning: Economics education at the University of Manchester." Accessed January 20 2016. www.post-crasheconomics.com/download/778.

Ramiro Beltran, Louis. 1993/2004. "Communication for development in Latin America: A forty year appraisal." Accessed October 8 2016. www.southbound.com.my/communication/cul-ch.htm.

Rockefeller Foundation. 1997. "Bellagio Conference Report – Communications and social change: Forging strategies for the 21st Century." Accessed October 8 2016. http://web.asc.upenn.edu/gerbner/archive.aspx?sectionID=114&packageID=560.

Rostow, Walt. 1960. *The Stages of Economic Growth: A Non-Communist Manifesto*. Cambridge: Cambridge University Press.

Said, Edward. 1978. *Orientalism*. New York: Random House.

Schramm, Wilbur. 1964. *Mass Media and National Development: The Role of Information in the Developing Countries*. Stanford, CA: Stanford University Press.

Spivak, Gayatri. 1988. "Can the subaltern speak?" In Nelson Cary and Lawrence Grossberg (eds), *Marxism and the Interpretation of Culture* (pp. 271–313). Chicago, IL: University of Illinois.

Thompson, Edward Palmer. 1963. *The Making of the English Working Class*. London: Vintage Books.

Tomaselli, Keyan (ed.). 2006. *Writing in the San/d: Auto-ethnography among Indigenous South Africans*. Lanham, New York, Toronto and Plymouth: Altamira Press.

UK Government. 2013. "DFID Malawi HIV prevention programme: Business case." Lilongwe and London: DFID and UK AID. Unpublished policy document.

UNAIDS. 2012. "Investing for results - Results for people: A people-centred investment tool towards ending AIDS." Geneva: Joint UN Programme for HIV and AIDS. Accessed September 30 2016. www.unaids.org/sites/default/files/sub_landing/files/JC2359_investing-for-results_en.pdf.

Williams, Raymond. 1961. *The Long Revolution*. London: Chatto and Windus.

Williams, Tennessee. 2009. *A Streetcar Named Desire*. London: Penguin Books.

Woodson, Carter. 1933/2006. *The Mis-Education of the Negro*. Drewryville: Khalifah Publishers.

INDEX

For Product Safety Concerns and Information please contact our EU representative GPSR@taylorandfrancis.com
Taylor & Francis Verlag GmbH, Kaufingerstraße 24, 80331 München, Germany

www.ingramcontent.com/pod-product-compliance
Lightning Source LLC
LaVergne TN
LVHW021129300926
849160LV00010B/932

9781138746046